Neil LaBute: Stage and Cinema

Neil LaBute is one of the most exciting new talents in theatre and film to have emerged in the 1990s. Influenced and inspired by such writers as David Mamet, Edward Bond and Harold Pinter, he is equally at home writing for the screen and the stage, and the list of films he has written and directed includes *The Wicker Man* (2006), *Possession* (2002) and *in the company of men* (1998). As a playwright, screenwriter, director, and author of short stories, he has staked out a distinctive, and disturbing, territory. In this first full-length study on LaBute, Christopher Bigsby examines his darkly funny work which explores the cruelties, self-concern and manipulative powers of individuals who inhabit a seemingly uncommunal world. Individual chapters are dedicated to particular works, and the book also includes an interview with LaBute, providing a fascinating insight into the life of this influential and often controversial figure.

CHRISTOPHER BIGSBY is Professor of American Studies at the University of East Anglia and has published more than thirty books covering American theatre, popular culture and British drama, including *Modern American Drama* (Cambridge, 1992), *Arthur Miller: A Critical Study* (Cambridge, 2005), *Remembering and Imagining the Holocaust: The Chain of Memory* (Cambridge, 2006) and *The Cambridge Companion to August Wilson* (2007). He is co-editor, with Don Wilmeth, of *The Cambridge History of American Theatre*, which received the Barnard Hewitt Award for Outstanding Research from the American Society for Theatre Research. He is also an award-winning novelist, has written plays for radio and television and is a regular radio and television broadcaster.

CAMBRIDGE STUDIES IN MODERN THEATRE

Series editor
David Bradly, *Royal Holloway, University of London*

Advisory board
Martin Banham, *University of Leeds*
Jacky Bratton, *Royal Holloway, University of London*
Tracy Davis, *Northwestern University*
Sir Richard Eyre
Michael Robinson, *University of East Anglia*
Sheila Stowell, *University of Birmingham*

Volumes for Cambridge Studies in Modern Theatre explore the political, social and cultural functions of theatre while also paying careful attention to detailed performance analysis. The focus of the series is on political approaches to the modern theatre with attention also being paid to theatres of earlier periods and their influence on contemporary drama. Topics in the series are chosen to investigate this relationship and include both playwrights (their aims and intentions set against the effects of their work) and process (with emphasis on rehearsal and production methods, the political structure within theatre companies and their choice of audiences or performance venues). Further topics will include devised theatre, agitprop, community theatre, para-theatre and performance art. In all cases the series will be alive to the special cultural and political factors operating in the theatres examined.

Books published
Maria DiCenzo, *The Politics of Alternative Theatre in Britain, 1968–1990: the Case of 7:84 (Scotland)*
Jo Riley, *Chinese Theatre and the Actor in Performance*
Jonathan Kalb, *The Theatre of Heiner Müller*
Richard Boon and Jane Plastow, eds., *Theatre Matters: Performance and Culture on the World Stage*
Claude Schumacher, ed., *Staging the Holocaust: the Shoah in Drama and Performance*
Philip Roberts, *The Royal Court Theatre and the Modern Stage*

Nicholas Grene, *The Politics of Irish Drama: Plays in Context from Boucicault to Friel*

Anatoly Smeliansky, *The Russian Theatre after Stalin*

Clive Barker and Maggie B. Gale, eds., *British Theatre between the Wars, 1918–1939*

Michael Patterson, *Strategies of Political Theatre: Post-War British Playwrights*

Elaine Aston, *Feminist Views on the English Stage: Women Playwrights, 1990–2000*

Gabriele Griffin, *Contemporary Black and Asian Women Playwrights in Britain*

Loren Kruger, *Post-Imperial Brecht: Politics and Performance, East and South*

David Barnett, *Rainer Werner Fassbinder and the German Theatre*

Mary Luckhurst, *Dramaturgy: A Revolution in Theatre*

Scott Boltwood, *Brian Friel, Ireland, and The North*

Neil LaBute

Stage and Cinema

by
Christopher Bigsby

CAMBRIDGE
UNIVERSITY PRESS

CAMBRIDGE UNIVERSITY PRESS

Cambridge, New York, Melbourne, Madrid, Cape Town, Singapore, São Paulo, Delhi

Cambridge University Press
The Edinburgh Building, Cambridge CB2 8RU, UK

Published in the United States of America by Cambridge University Press,
New York

www.cambridge.org
Information on this title: www.cambridge.org/9780521882545

First published 2007

Printed in the United Kingdom at the University Press, Cambridge

A catalogue record for this publication is available from the British Library

ISBN 978-0-521-88254-5 hardback

Contents

vii

1 Introduction

I've absolutely no qualms in saying that I'm a lucky son of a
bitch to get where I am ... The village idiot made a movie
and it did well.
                                                    Neil LaBute[1]

All life ... comes back to the question of our speech, the medium
through which we communicate with each other; for all life
comes back to the question of our relations with each other.
                                                    Henry James[2]

There was a time when the playwright who turned to film was
seen as betraying the purity of his craft, exchanging a dangerous present-
tense art for the banality of mechanically recorded images and being
immoderately rewarded for doing so. For Clifford Odets, Harold
Clurman remarked, Hollywood was sin. For Arthur Miller, one of those
offered what he thought of as a Faustian pact by the significantly named
Colonel Joy, talent spotter for Twentieth Century Fox (who was, Miller
observed, shipping writers to the West Coast in cattle cars), it was a
temptation to be resisted in the name of his aesthetic and political
allegiances. In his own case he was not altogether wrong. When he
eventually went to Hollywood, clutching a radical film script, it was
rejected even as he was offered his pick of aspiring young actresses, one
of whom, as it turned out, went by the name of Marilyn Monroe.

For a later generation, however, the move carried no such overtones, though the Pulitzer Prize-winning novelist and short-story
writer Richard Ford has observed that, 'All the writers I have seen

who have gone to Hollywood who are real writers either came back and went back to their work or became gobbled up and became something else.'[3] Having himself written a screenplay and avoided being gobbled up, he plainly saw the risk as exchanging one loyalty for another. Sam Shepard and David Mamet felt no such qualms, moving with ease and assurance between theatre and film, maintaining a double loyalty, even though it took them a few years to find their way towards the cinema. For a young writer who emerged in the late 1990s, that double loyalty was there virtually from the beginning.

Neil LaBute, of French, English and Irish heritage, son of a truck driver who had wanted to be an airline pilot, was born in Detroit on 19 March 1963, the second of two boys. His mother, ten years younger than her husband, worked as a hospital receptionist. He was raised in Liberty Lake, Spokane, in Washington state. The small family home was surrounded by woods. Much against his will, he worked on a farm owned by his father. Though he is understandably resistant to biographical readings of his work, his early years nonetheless seem to have left their mark and he acknowledges that one function of writing is to reshape experience the better to understand it. In a preface to *The Distance From Here* he confesses that basic elements of the play can be traced back to his own schooldays. 'I think,' he said, 'that is often why writers write and painters paint and musicians play their instruments. It's not just because they have a gift, but also to create something even slightly more beautiful or coherent or illuminating than the frenzied, scrambled memories of their own pasts.'[4] He is, he has explained, 'fascinated with psychology. That is all I deal with as a writer, the psychology of people. I will plunder myself and my upbringing, no doubt, for as long as I write.'[5]

Shepard's and Mamet's trouble with their father and stepfather respectively offered an early lesson in the dysfunctional nature of relationships and of the suddenness with which moods could change. LaBute's childhood seems to have been scarcely different. Asked what stayed with him from that time, he replied, 'The wreckage!' Childhood, he observed, 'is not something I remember a great deal of, and I think that's indicative of a childhood that was fraught with a fair amount of tension. It was an idyllic setting, in the mountains and so forth. But

2

my father was a kind of tough, interesting character ... "a son of a bitch." He was challenging – the way Hitler was challenging. So, you never really knew what you were waking up to.'[6] He recalled tense car journeys with his parents, he in the back seat, they, arguing with one another, in the front, and invokes the memory of this in his preface to *autobahn*. As a truck driver his father was away from home for periods of time, his return not necessarily welcome. 'I can remember when he came home, a great sense of anticipation, because of not knowing what mood he'd come back in.' His father's anger, he confessed, taught him 'how much damage could be done with language ... I can remember working with my father on a car. He'd gone inside. The only thing that really sets me off is inanimate objects, because there's no reckoning with them. I let out a tirade that would have made someone proud. I didn't realize he'd come back into the garage. He looked at me, and I got the sense of "So this is part of the legacy I've left behind."'[7]

He has confessed that 'There's a great deal of my father in a lot of the characters that people find somewhat unseemly ... As a kid you get a sense of betrayal that you can't put specifics to – a sense of women down the line is what one can make a leap to ... There must be something there that I don't necessarily want the answer to, because it helps fuel the writing.'

Scarcely a coded account, his introduction to *The Distance From Here*, which acknowledges the absent fathers in the play and the shattered families, suggests an early life that offered lessons that would only be fully learned with time. At school, meanwhile, he already evidenced an interest in theatre and film, while at home with his mother he watched foreign films on the local PBS affiliate: 'It was a survey course of the greatest hits of world cinema. I saw *La Strada* early on, *The Seven Samurai*. *The 400 Blows* was a favorite. I'm as happy watching *La Dolce Vita* as any movie I've ever seen.'[8] As a teenager, he was passionate about Woody Allen's *Annie Hall* and it would not be too fanciful to hear echoes of that in his work. Adam, in *the shape of things*, has something of a Woody Allen character about him, intellectually acute but emotionally adrift, physically unappealing and socially inept. LaBute, too, falls back on humour and though the cruelties of human relationships in Allen's work are presented less caustically, betrayal is equally a defining aspect of those relationships. Allen would prove a major influence not simply in terms of subject matter but also with respect to his approach to film making, but theatre also appealed, especially when he saw a production of *King Lear* at his older brother's college. At school, he acted in a number of plays, including *Arsenic and Old Lace* and *You're a Good Man, Charlie Brown*.

LaBute was class president at Central Valley High School. On leaving, he worked in a movie theatre to raise money. Though he was not a Mormon, at the suggestion of a student counsellor, who was a Mormon, he now applied to Brigham Young University in Utah and secured a 'minority scholarship', reserved for non-Mormons. Once at the university, however, in 1981, he converted, joining the Church of Jesus Christ of Latter-Day Saints. He remained a member, albeit somewhat tenuously, until 2004. At BYU, he continued to act and began writing brief monologues for fellow students who were taking part in an acting competition. As he explained to John Lahr, 'I had a quick ability to write short, kind of pungent sketches and monologues ... I had the hardest time writing anything of length, because I hated the idea of stopping. I loved to sit down and finish something. I was always writing short pieces. It was the opposite of writer's block.'[9]

In 1985 he graduated and married Lisa Gore, a devout Mormon, born in South Africa, who would become a psychotherapist and bear him two children as well as having to deal with the fact that her husband was writing plays of which she should disapprove. They now moved east: 'after graduating from byu I moved to new york to pursue a career in writing – playwriting was certainly of interest but I was also keen on doing some sketch comedy, like "Saturday night live" or that type of thing. After only a year in nyc, I went after a masters degree in Kansas.'[10] It was here he met Paul Rudd who would subsequently appear in his plays. He was in Kansas from 1986 to 1989, at which point he enrolled in a two-year MFA course in Dramatic Writing at New York University, which qualification would later enable him to teach college-level courses in Indiana. He spent the spring semester of 1991 in London at the Royal Court Theatre, an experience which he later claimed to be influential to his development as a writer. Then, in 1991, he returned to BYU to work on a Ph.D. in theatre theory and criticism, a degree which, to his later regret, he never finished.

Why did he become a Mormon? He had been a church-goer as he grew up but his conversion was, he explained, in part a product of being in Salt Lake City. They were, he said, 'everywhere. They were an influence that at the time was very welcome to me as opposed to the way I was brought up.' (SBS) The plays he now began to write and direct, however, not only evidenced a fierce dedication but showed an almost total disregard for how church authorities or audiences would respond. 'I'm only interested,' he would later remark, 'in my work concluding in a way that is true to the characters and the tale, without any concern for the audience.'[11]

As his friend, Aaron Eckart, later to appear in a number of his plays and films, remarked, 'In school, he wouldn't explain his work. He doesn't feel the need to give any justification for his work ... He was loved and hated, revered and reviled.'[12] As he explained, 'there is a blanket of security over that School. Nothing really gets into it. You feel secure because it's a very clean campus. Everybody's safe, but on the other hand you don't get to explore your dark side. But when Neil came into town everybody said, "well, we have a dark side here."' (SBS)

The hostility came in large part from the kind of plays he began to write, plays which explored the human potential for cruelty and violence, even if that was at first viewed obliquely. As he later remarked, he saw his function as 'looking to cause trouble on the stage ... isn't that the job description? To turn heads? To deliver something new?' It was not, he insisted, 'as if I want to be provocative for the sake of provoking. I at least try to make something that is going to look beyond the momentary shock.' He had, he confessed, always 'been a bit of a cold fish ... I'm someone who has said, "Oh, here's a person in pain. Let's bring the microscope down closer."' Causing trouble, though, was not what the authorities at BYU favoured. Nor was his interest in 'cruelty and maliciousness' shared by the Church of Latter-Day Saints which became increasingly concerned with the direction of his work.

As Professor Eric Samuelson, Chair of the Film and Media department at BYU, remarked, 'some of the faculty and the staff were taken aback by the strength of his opinions and perhaps the disinclination to modify those opinions.' Tim Slover, professor of theatre, recalled that the committee responsible for choosing the season's plays did not select *in the company of men*, written in his playwrighting class, because one of the members of that committee saw it as 'savagely misogynist'. John Lahr reports that in order to prevent the staging of his play *Lepers*, later to morph into *Your Friends & Neighbors*, and which he had been rehearsing for months, the administration locked up the theatre. There is, Samuelson confirmed of BYU, 'certainly some material that we cannot do on stage. There's certain language that we just don't hear.' Slover confirmed that 'The faculty hated it ... They couldn't deny Neil's talent but they didn't want to see it. They didn't want to hear about it.' Aaron Eckart recalled that, 'the other students were violent about it to the point where we would be in our classes and they would be just yelling at Neil. And he and I would just laugh.' (SBS)

There was, he suggested, 'a mindset of a certain kind at BYU that they don't want to expose themselves to that kind of material.' It was simply not a central proposition of the faith that 'We humans are a fairly barbarous bunch ... We abuse people through words. We shred each other with what we say,'[13] even if that is what LaBute had derived from the work of Mamet, Pinter and Bond. Significantly, among the works he staged at BYU was Mamet's *Sexual Perversity in Chicago*, virtually a manual for a young playwright interested in male–female relations, language as aggression, shifting patterns of power. LaBute was, he claimed, 'a wide-eyed realist', it was simply that his realism took the form of staging the contradictions in human nature. As Aaron Eckart remarked, in an interview with Mary Dickson in the *Salt Lake City Weekly* (on 21 September 1998), 'If we really look at each other closely and I listen to what we say to each other in tense moments, we can be really cruel ... If we put the camera on ourselves, our friends and neighbors, we come up with some scary stuff.' In the same interview, LaBute observed of those in the Mormon church who disapproved of him, 'They look at me and think, "What kind of Mormon is he?" Many think I need more practice ... I have a healthy view on what one can do with art. They're looking for good examples for their audiences. The idea that you can show something bad and the end result can be good is hard for them to accept.' As to his approach to staging drama, Eckart, who he first met in an ethics class at BYU, explained of LaBute that 'his plays would be rehearsed for lengthy periods of time and then be performed only once, usually only once, usually in the morning.'[14]

'I can take any empty space,' Peter Brook remarked in 1968, 'and call it a bare stage. A man walks across this empty space whilst someone else is watching him, and this is all that is needed for an art of theatre.'[15] For LaBute, a non-formal location for drama was at first less a case of a theoretical proposition than necessity. As he himself recalled, 'I would look for a play that fit spaces that I found. In college I couldn't get time in a theatre so I would go to the natural history museum and there was a stairwell where I'd stage something in that space and put the audience on the stairs. I staged Pinter's *One for the Road*, a political parable, down there. Not that he ever got paid, but the idea was pure. But it was that kind of hunger – nothing was going to stop me from doing what I wanted to do.'[16] As he explained,

> I love the simple confines of a theatre – a black box, a proscenium, a found space. Even in my film work I prefer to move people within the frame rather than to move the frame itself. As a student, I used to hunt down new spaces to work in, trying to adapt shows to the places I would find ... Bond's *Passion* in the open air of a city park; my own work in a local bar with people sitting around, drinking and interacting with the actors. Movies require a technology, a screen, a bucket of popcorn. Theatre only needs someone to stand up and say: 'Listen to this.'[17]

The theatre, he explained, was about 'what if?' At the end of *The Empty Space*, Peter Brook had made the same observation: 'In everyday life, "if" is a fiction, in the theatre "if" is an experiment. In everyday life "if" is an evasion, in the theatre "if" is the truth.'[18] Whatever else it would be, LaBute's drama would never be about evasion.

In order to support himself LaBute worked in psychiatric hospitals and taught, all the while continuing to write and place his plays. He took up a post at St Francis College in Fort Wayne and it was here, drafting in local citizens to help, that he made the film of *Your Friends & Neighbors* which transformed his life.

LaBute is unsettling. He disturbs in the same way as Harold Pinter, describing a familiar world but one in which motives are often obscured, relationships seldom what they appear. His characters frequently lack something more than the tact required for social living. They lack a concern for the consequences of their actions, treat life as a game in which their own needs take precedence. Sometimes, as in *The Distance From Here*, a kind of blank incomprehension leads to a spasm of violence. More often, he catalogues the small betrayals, casual deceits, instinctive cruelties which characterise daily experience. As LaBute has explained, in a preface to *Fat Pig*, 'I love to make life unpredictable for a lot of my fictional characters as they face terrible mishaps, calamities, and upheavals.'[19] John Lahr quotes Wallace Shawn, for whom LaBute has confessed admiration, as remarking that 'The difference between a perfectly decent person and a monster is just a few thoughts.'[20] If some of LaBute's characters never seem to have become acquainted with decency, others, particularly those in *Fat Pig*, precisely exemplify that sense of the thin line between civility and betrayal, genuine feeling and calculation, concern for others and concern for the self. For LaBute, it is the step from the one to the other that compels attention, and not because of the distance between his characters and those who see or read his plays but because of their moral proximity.

In his preface to *This Is How It Goes* he explains his admiration for Pinter's work and in doing so identifies something of his own concerns. What he was drawn to in Pinter was 'his fearless examination of men and women while searching for answers, hoping for change, raging for equality – but never ducking for cover. Who', he enquired, 'can ask for more? What I really admire about Pinter's work – and strive for in my own – is that the point of it is not merely to upset people, but that what's being addressed is worth getting upset over.' He had also, he confessed, learned something about structure from his work and the need to maintain interest rather than succumbing to a desire to please.[21]

The 'hoping for change' and the 'raging for equality' may seem surprising. In the case of Pinter, the need for change is implied by the very bleakness of the world of *The Birthday Party* or *Mountain Language*. The rage for equality is rather more difficult to find within the plays, whatever we know of his politics. This would seem to be equally true of LaBute. He does stare into the dark to testify to the light but there is little sign in his work of a yearning for equality. What is most striking about his work is the coldness of his eye. He is an anthropologist exploring human behaviour with a detachment that can seem chilling. Dean Mendell has drawn attention to Émile Zola's comment on *Thérèse Raquin*: 'I simply carried out on two living bodies, the same examinations that surgeons perform on corpses.' Asked what painting most corresponded to his own vision, LaBute identified the work of Caspar David Friedrich. He did so, he explained, 'because so many of his figures are turned away from the viewer and there's a certain distance I put between my characters and my audience, the audience and myself. Things are kept at bay.'[22] At first glance this might seem an odd remark from a writer whose reputation is for sometimes brutally direct works in which the subconscious seems to bubble to the surface, repressed instincts are allowed free rein. But in fact there is a degree of detachment to his style as we are seemingly invited to witness, with something approaching a scientific objectivity, a series of exemplary actions (or the narration of those actions). Beyond that, at times indirection seems a key to his aesthetic as well as to the strategies and tactics of his characters, though a number of them are inclined to lay out the details of their moral failings, even if they obdurately refuse to acknowledge them as such.

In 1992, the year he abandoned his Ph.D., LaBute made a brief appearance Off Off Broadway as writer, director and actor in *Filthy Talk for Troubled Times: Scenes of Intolerance*. The title was hardly misleading. He was about the business of provocation. John Lahr has recalled the impact of one speech, in a series of overlapping monologues. In the context of a diatribe about AIDS a character remarks, 'I say, put them all in a fucking pot and boil them . . . just as a precaution.'

9

At this, a member of the audience shouted out 'Kill the playwright.' LaBute confessed to a certain trepidation but the man stayed and his response underscored LaBute's conviction that theatre 'is a contact sport'.[23] The play was not published and in 2007 he was still working on it for a possible future production, having stolen a line or so for his later plays.

It was to be a further five years, however (during which he taught at a college and wrote for regional theatres) before LaBute first registered on the national consciousness, when he won the Filmmaker's Trophy at the 1997 Sundance Film Festival with *in the company of men*, financed in part by money that two communication major friends had won as a result of a car-accident insurance policy. Audiences were simultaneously shocked by and admiring of a film which dealt with the emotional destruction of a young deaf woman by two businessmen, Chad and Howard. The portrait it drew of the relationship between men and women as America moved towards the millennium was bleak. If the business of America was business, then America seemed in crisis. One nation indivisible was exposed as divided along lines of gender and race, a young black man being as casually humiliated as a vulnerable young woman. It made for uncomfortable viewing. Its protagonist, with movie-star good looks, charm and wit, was wholly amoral. Language was no more than a tool of the confidence trickster. Yet the film was wholly compelling. Audiences found themselves in the uncomfortable situation of watching an act of calculated cruelty and thereby in some sense becoming complicit. As LaBute has confessed, 'I love the idea of pulling people in and then turning on them. For instance, seducing them into thinking that the character of Chad is amusing and even charming, only to leave them shocked when they discover later just how much of a viper he really is.'[24]

Careers have seldom started so explosively or been sustained with quite such energy. Careers have seldom been quite so controversial. Though his work covered a wide range of subjects and styles, at its heart was a seemingly pitiless exploration of human pathology that left many uncomfortable. He appeared to be a combination of Edward Bond and David Mamet (indeed he dedicated one of his plays to the latter and praised the former for his engagement with an innate human cruelty).

Neil LaBute has been accused of misogyny, misanthropy and obscenity. *Sight and Sound* magazine scarcely knew what to make of him, describing him as phoney and opportunistic. Audiences are as likely to be disturbed by his work as entertained. There is no doubt, though, that he was the most powerful and original playwright and screenwriter to emerge in turn-of-the-century America, and by some way the funniest, even if his humour was born out of and generated discomfort.

Arthur Miller observed of his own work that betrayal lay at its heart, the small change of daily betrayals and the larger social, moral and political betrayals of a century of failed hopes and tainted ideals. LaBute is prone to disavow this larger ambition but it is hard not to see his work as a comment on a culture whose rhetoric of shared endeavour and family values seems increasingly detached from a reality of estrangement. As he has said, 'I often write about betrayal. It is just such a fascinating topic. Especially with intimate groups of people. To feel that anguish of having been betrayed.'[25]

He is prone to say that too much has been made of the dysfunctionality of his own family, believing them not to be atypical. Miller certainly suggested that such generational contention, between father and son, was almost definitional of the American writer. Certainly Eugene O'Neill, Sam Shepard and David Mamet have written about the tensions they experienced and seen in them evidence for a more general collapse of connectiveness. Men and women, in their work, meanwhile, seem to meet across an all-but-unbridgeable divide. Such tensions are hardly limited to the United States but this is a culture whose myths have always had to do not merely with family but also with male relationships, friendships that have stood in place of other intimacies. It is the loss of such intimacies that provides a subject, for Shepard and Mamet in particular, as it is the loss of values that once gave substance to national myths but which now survive only in the broken language and half-remembered pieties they utter without fully understanding. LaBute's work scarcely offers a more generous vision.

In his work, friendships seem to exist in order to be negated. Men and women come together out of a need that is real enough but which they can barely articulate or express. Identity defers to performance. People meet in familiar environments – an office, an apartment, a shopping mall – but remain isolated, dedicated to their own feelings and ambitions, disregarding of others, sharpening their blunted sensibilities by self-consciously breaching not merely conventions but moral principles. Yet, at the same time, his are ironic, witty plays, morality tales which, as he has said, are either handbooks for behaviour or admonitory stories depending on the audience's own predilections.

Because they are morality tales he has a tendency to avoid being over-specific about locations and even characters' names, which are sometimes omitted or offered as echoes of mythic figures. His plays, he has said, 'exist in a geographic vacuum'.[26] More surprisingly, he added that they also exist in a 'moral vacuum'. What he seems to mean by that is not only that his characters are frequently happy to suspend an ethical sense but that they inhabit a world in which there seems no moral imperative. Few refer outside themselves to any agreed values. What they often do is embrace a code of their own devising, convincing themselves of the authenticity of their actions and attitudes. They seem oblivious to collateral human damage even as they respect the rigour of their own position, whether it be Evelyn in *the shape of things* or Charlie in *Nurse Betty*, the latter part not written by LaBute (he was its director) but recognised by him for its affinity to his own work.

While his reference to a moral vacuum may describe the world he creates in his plays and films, it plainly also describes the world he sees beyond the stage and screen. His subject is the human comedy, the attempt to justify ourselves to ourselves no matter how unjustifiable our actions, the triumph of selfishness over selflessness. His, it appears, is a culture in which moral issues seem increasingly to defer to other necessities.

The fact that he was a convert to Mormonism – a quintessentially American religion – was initially the source of confusion and concern to some critics. After all, his were plays that hardly shone with a redemptive light. For some reason Mamet's Jewish faith seemed to cause rather less perturbation, though there had been a time when

Philip Roth brought down the lightning of Jewish wrath for his own sexual explicitness. LaBute, after all, has never matched Mamet's *American Buffalo*, where Teach uses the word 'fuckin'' five times on his first appearance, but his language does tend to be scatological while his work is sexually direct.

His own Church was unsettled but unwilling to cast him into the outer darkness. There are other Mormon playwrights and, indeed, film directors and actors (perhaps surprisingly there is a web site which helpfully lists Latter-Day Saints writers and directors together with the grosses of their films), including his fellow student Aaron Eckhart, who was subsequently to appear in virtually all his films, but they are not prolific, certainly not prolific enough for the Church to sacrifice one merely because his language and subjects are not likely to be the daily reading of those raised on the Bible and, in more recent years, the Book of Mormon. The more surprising thing was the interest critics showed in his religion, perhaps because Mormonism itself has not been without its moral flaws, from its historic flirtation with polygamy (which became the subject of a television soap opera in 2006) to its dubious role in Las Vegas, where despite its own injunctions against gambling it became a major player and where a hugely impressive temple looks out over a city dedicated to what it should regard as sin.

It is true that at first, and not too surprisingly, he chose to make his characters Mormons but he was happy to negotiate on this, rewriting and retitling his first stage success. As a result of this Salt Lake City stand-off, his characters are no longer identified as Mormons. Nonetheless, he was determined to stake out his freedom of action as a writer, sometimes, he admits, with a commitment so fierce as to make him disregard other concerns. Indeed, in *the shape of things* he seems to satirise his own position, acknowledging the price that such commitments can exact.

In so far as he was responding to the American society in which he had been raised, however, it is clear that all was not well. President after President might assure citizens of their natural goodness and explain that theirs is a society which acts as a city on a hill, a beacon for the world, but he saw something else. He was not an Arthur Miller, making public speeches and firing off articles to the Op Ed page of the *New York Times*, nor was he inclined to mirror Sam Shepard in writing gnomic but fierce dramas which responded to a paranoid politics. Nonetheless, his characters are prone, at times, to acts of extreme violence or, more often, to a breathtaking callousness and self-concern. They are often coldly calculating. Relationships are fraught, particularly those between the sexes. As he remarked, 'I think men and women have a difficult time dealing with each other and often take the low road.'[27]

Looking back on his still brief career in 2004, he remarked that he had been predominantly concerned with 'power or cruelty or maliciousness'.[28] Yet he also claimed that his stance was one of scepticism rather than cynicism. Indeed, he defended his portrayal of human fallibility as a necessary corrective to an unquestioning acceptance of private and public pieties which could be no more than another name for a dangerous indifference. As he remarked, 'If we don't evaluate and re-evaluate ourselves, we fall into patterns and believe that what we're doing is right. You fall into movements where no one questions the company line. That's how fascism began. We have to constantly look at the ways we deal with each other.'[29] The leap from disregard to fascism may appear excessive, but what he seems to be calling for is a certain moral alertness that requires individuals and states to acknowledge their own capacity to betray the very principles they seem to embody. LaBute is not a political writer in a narrow sense. He is political in the sense that he looks in private lives for those radical imperfections equally observable in public life.

His most powerful influence was plainly Mamet and he once confessed to being a virtual stalker of his fellow writer. The connection lies in part in the language. His work is not, for the most part, as peppered with expletives as Mamet's, though *in the company of men* has its fair share as does *The Distance From Here*. But his characters do, on occasion, speak the same fractured prose, with its repetitions and incomplete sentences. As a character observes in *in the company of men*, 'Somebody rejects me, you know, a woman, it just drives me, ahh! It just seems like everything, I mean … work, these women.'[30] The connection lies, too, in both writers' fascination with characters for whom communication implies vulnerability, who deliberately hold each other at arm's length. Most of his works are marked to indicate overlapping dialogue. This is less because his characters cannot wait for someone to complete a thought or even a sentence before responding than because they believe that what they wish to think and say has primacy. They speak out of a self which demands space, attention, centrality.

There is often a hermeticism to the settings his characters inhabit which forces them together, the better for him to explore the dynamics of relationships, the wary circlings of the human animal, simultaneously vulnerable and aggressive, always looking for advantage because always motivated by self-interest. Both Mamet and LaBute (and, indeed, Pinter) have a fascination with power as if relationships were essentially unequal, that inequality fuelling personal and public actions.

Both writers have a fascination with the amoral actions of individuals who come together only in temporary alliances which always threaten to dissolve, men and women never quite connecting because structured by different needs and perceptions. Both are drawn to moral confidence tricksters who deceive others and themselves with equal facility. Take each writer's characters together and what emerges is a portrait of a society of solitary individuals responding to what they take to be their needs, elevating their predatory or simply self-serving instincts to the level of moral principle. And both writers present this portrait through comedy. In Mamet's work this is liable to emerge from the mismatch between action and language, as characters deploy a vocabulary at odds with their situation. In LaBute's work it is often self-consciously deployed by characters for whom it is a defence against insecurities, or a means of distancing themselves from the implications of their actions. On occasion, humour is a weapon of choice.

Evelyn, in *the shape of things*, is not remote from Carol in Mamet's *Oleanna*. Both conspire to gain control over a man and justify their actions by reference to a self-serving language. In both plays the men's loss of control is signalled by a sudden lurch into obscenity. In *Oleanna*, John, the professor whose life has effectively been destroyed by

Carol (as she precipitates his public exposure), a man whose concern for the precisions of language had been a function of his career, shouts out, 'I wouldn't touch you with a ten-foot pole. You little *cunt.*'[31] In *the shape of things*, Adam, a student of literature, similarly held up to public ridicule, responds by saying, 'up yours, you heartless cunt.'[32] At first glance, where Mamet had set out to stage a work in which sympathies shifted in the course of a play, in which he consciously re-balanced the power system between the two central characters in the second act, LaBute seems to create a more one-sided drama, though even here sympathies move uncertainly. Both men create a portrait of a deeply un-communal country in which what is shared is liable to be no more than fragmented memories of long-gone television shows, books and films of minority interest, myths that have survived only in distorted form, words that no longer mean what they once did, indeed words whose meaning has been reversed or hollowed out.

Mamet and LaBute both write about those whose personal lives are defined by ambition or simple egotism. Theirs are characters for whom friends, lovers, colleagues are less companions to whom loyalty is owed than means to advantage, those who may be betrayed without compunction when it serves their purpose. They are frequently game players for whom the game offers a frisson lacking from the quotidian, as cruelty may add relish to what otherwise might seem the banality of their existence. Yet in some ways both writers stand as moralists, offering warnings about the collapse of that very sense of shared values on which their theatre depends for its existence.

There is another parallel. Like Mamet, LaBute has had a double career, in the theatre and the cinema. At college, he was fiercely committed to theatre, sometimes, he admitted, to a fault. He acted, directed and staged his plays wherever he could in a virtual guerrilla theatre. When he moved to film it was almost by accident and when he did so he carried across a theatre aesthetic. Language and character remained central. So they do, of course, for most writers, but in his case his approach to film making was designed to preserve what seemed to him the special virtues of theatre. At the beginning of his film career he thus tended to shoot in sequence with actors who were already off book, either because they were transposing a stage play to film or because this enabled him to work through a series of long shots. Often he utilised the wide screen in such a way as to allow the audience to observe the simultaneous reaction of characters or positioned them towards the edge of the frame, just as in theatre characters are not simply placed at centre stage.

He has an eye for the geometry of character and set alike, is alive to colour as a key to mood. In his first film, indeed, the bleakness of the moral world was to be echoed by bleaching colour out entirely. Initially, he eschewed music, and was suspicious of computer-generated effects and of an active camera which he suspected was often a cover for the inadequacy of writing. He shot in days or weeks rather than months and was happy with the discipline of small budgets.

Arthur Miller's suspicions of the cinema came in part from the fact that it marginalised the writer and handed power to the director and actor. LaBute had no such fears, not least because he combined two of those functions and because he believed that the distinction between theatre and film was overstated. In writing about the importance of theatre to cinema, David Hare has offered a sceptical view of what have become familiar theories of film making.

> The first gift a playwright has is to write for actors. The better the playwright, the better the roles. This is as true of film as it is of theatre ... There is a ... cliché, tirelessly repeated in film classes the world over: film, they say, is a visual medium. Oh yes? Is that why, in the past 20 years, the shot has become so much more important than the sequence? The lighting more than important than what is being lit? The action more important than the acting? The special effects more important than the story? Is that why everything at the Odeon now seems to drag? And is that why, in the United States, everyone in search of entertainment prefers to watch television ... How many times have we heard the tired injunction, 'Show, don't tell?' Of all the specious screenwriting rules peddled by gurus fleecing the young, this is the most annoying of the lot, because it's plain to anyone who's ever bothered to watch a play or a film carefully that the best writers invariably achieve their effects by mixing showing and telling.

Hare wrote in the context of a consideration of the work of Harold Pinter whose virtue seemed to him to lie in his reticence, in scripts whose dialogue was of central importance. 'In *The Pumpkin Eater*', he observed, 'we never see Maggie Smith making love to Peter Finch. We don't need to. Finch tells us about it, more powerfully than any shot of flailing limbs could ever achieve. And even more powerful, because at second hand, in Anne Bancroft's eyes we see a glare of pain and betrayal which tells us more about what went on than any mere showing could hope to show.'[33]

There would be some flailing limbs in *Your Friends & Neighbors*, not least because in that film sex is a prevailing subject and metaphor, but language, the language of visual representation as well as of self-referring monologues and intransitive dialogues, has remained of crucial importance to LaBute. In works in which performance is a central trope (as characters play out their own contrived scenarios, consciously shape their appearance or behaviour as if they were actors perfecting their craft) he draws on theatrical techniques – on stage or on film – because they are consonant with the world he chooses to dramatise. Meanwhile, in *Possession*, his adaptation of Antonia Byatt's novel, he rhapsodises about love, even as he acknowledges the anguish as well as the ecstasy it engenders.

It would be a mistake to believe that LaBute can be defined by what he has done. He remains a writer who takes pleasure in shifting his direction of travel. As he explained, 'I don't see my career as this steady building to a point, it's just a path that wanders for me to do anything I'm interested in doing.'[34] Asked how he knew whether a particular project would turn into a play or film, he replied, 'I just write and then if people go to a grocery store it's a movie.'[35]

One minor quirk of his published plays is, somewhat oddly (especially to copy-editors), that a number are printed in lower case, as are their titles. Asked why, he replied,

> beyond the inevitable e. e. cummings connection – whose work I admire and adore – it's a simple matter of being able to type faster, to write more and in a way that allows the work to flow out of myself more completely, without stopping for the 'shift'

each time it's expected. I still punctuate – punctuation is the gift and weapon of the writer – but I skip the niceties of capitalization and try never to do what's been bred in me/or whatever's the standard requirement.[36]

The email was timed at 7.02 a.m. He was in Hollywood working on post-production for *The Wicker Man*. Asked why he was checking his email so early, he replied, 'it's true – that's part of the official biography. "able to operate on little or no sleep. busy paying for his sins."'

Aside from the fact that use of the shift key involves no more than a microsecond, there is no apparent reason why lower case should be retained in the published version, beyond the sense of that flow to which he refers. But for a writer who was to shock and surprise, refusing to conform even to the expectations which he himself seemed to provoke (his choice of Antonia Byatt's *Possession* was a shock to many precisely because it seemed so at odds with what he had done before), the final words of his reply have the sound of a personal manifesto. He does, indeed, resist what has been bred in him and what seem like the standard requirements.

2   *bash*: *latterday plays*

> We made it down to New York
> With everything intact
> But as for getting back –
> It was Boo who made the joke,
> They don't give you any hope
> But they'll give you plenty of rope

Aimee Mann, 'I've Had It'

Neil LaBute wrote *a gaggle of saints* (an echo of Euripides' *Bacchae*) at Brigham Young University. It was a deceptively simple play in which two characters – John and Sue – recall the events of a distant evening. They each speak from their own perspective. They are discovered, sitting apart, dressed in what we are told is to be the popular evening fashion of the moment. Sometimes this appears to be a mutual tale, mutually told; at other moments they seem to exist in quite separate worlds oblivious to one another's stories. When Sue remarks that her sister had been at the party which they had both attended, he remarks, 'we ran into sue's sister, did she mention that?'[1] They are together and apart and that in itself is the story of their lives. They see the world differently. In part that is a gendered difference, or seemingly so – a brutally direct male world running in parallel to but scarcely intersecting with a sentimental female one, rather as in David Mamet's *The Woods*, in which the conflicting needs of a man and a woman hints at a more fundamental dissonance. In part, it is a difference of perspective. We see what we see and constitute our worlds accordingly.

20

The two characters address an invisible third party, recalling events which now lie behind them – but plainly not wholly so, or why revisit them. They describe a trip to New York's Plaza Hotel with a group of fellow students from Boston College. It had been John and Sue's anniversary. They had, we learn, been dating for six years, since their time in high school. The story they tell is at first less than compelling as they describe the details of the clothes they wore and the car in which they travelled. Both are evidently members of the Mormon Church. His father had been a bishop. They had both attended a seminary and he had been on a mission.

Into this banal narrative LaBute slowly infiltrates hints of something more sinister. When John pins a corsage on Sue's dress he pricks his finger and a drop of blood falls on his white shirt. In 'a weird way', she confesses, 'it excited me, the blood.' (42) Later, when John recalls their first encounter he remembers too that he had beaten her former boyfriend in front of her: 'just turned on him and flipped him over onto the ground and started pounding on his head ... and sue's just standing there ... waiting.' Later, they kiss. Male violence, it seems, is not entirely without its attraction.

The two narratives then edge towards the point of the story, though Sue remains seemingly oblivious to a key part of it. Plainly for her the meaning of the trip to New York differs radically from that which drives John to elaborate what turns out to be an account of extreme violence. Strolling through Central Park before the party they come on two gay men emerging from the bushes, smiling. It is that smile which stays with John so that later, when he and some of the other male students return to the Park and encounter them again, the girls being asleep back in the hotel, he is resentful and angry. The two men kiss, which seems to John an offence against his religious principles: 'i know the scriptures, know 'em pretty well, and this is wrong.' (58)

He follows one of the men into a dilapidated toilet block, already planning an assault. The others remain outside, awaiting his signal. What follows is an ambiguous account as John seemingly provokes a sexual approach by the man which is to be his justification for an attack. The encounter, however, is described in such lubricious terms as to expose something about this morally indignant, self-righteous Church member which he himself cannot confront as he finds himself embraced by a man who reminds him of his own father: 'he moves in, his lips playing across my cheek. Let his tongue run along my teeth and a hand, a free hand, tracing down my fly ... I just smile at him, smile and even lick his chin for a second.' (60) Then the man is fiercely beaten, a beating described in a clinical prose: 'so many of us hitting, tearing at him, it's hard to get off a clean punch but i know i connect a few more times. i feel his head, the back of it softening as we go, but i just find a new spot and move on ... this man is not moving, may never move again ... tim leans into it one more time, takes a little run at it, smashing his foot against the bridge of the man's nose and I see it give way. Just pick up and move to the other side of his face.' (61) Finally, and shockingly, Tim pours consecrated oil on their victim and offers up a blessing as if this were, indeed, a sanctified act. Tim prays as the others giggle, tears running down their cheeks before they go 'running back toward the plaza in the dark and whooping it up like Indians'. (62)

In order to explain the mist of blood on his shirt, the shirt which had previously been marked only by a single drop of blood from the pin on the corsage, John asks Tim to punch him in the face. They then invite the girls to breakfast, explaining the blood away as the result of an accident. At breakfast, John presents Sue with a ring taken from the man they had left for dead and who may, indeed, be dead, wishing her a happy anniversary. On their way back from New York on the train they witness a violent dispute between a man and a woman, Sue taking pride in John's agreeing not to intervene as if it were evidence of his control over his emotions. Her memory of the trip is thus of what seems to her a romantic moment. John, it appears, is a man who has laid aside his violence in favour of love. His memory, however, is of the beating of what he perceives as a pervert who offends against God's law and not incidentally his own equanimity.

Originally subtitled 'a remembrance of hatred and longing', it is, indeed, a memory play, if we mean by that that the action is recalled. Remembrance, however, implies something else and that something else is what provides one of the more curious moments in the play, and one which the Mormon Church was liable to find disturbing, if not simply objectionable: an act of violence seemingly becomes a perverse sacrament, while its subsequent recall itself has the feel of a ceremonial moment. Hatred and longing, however, scarcely seem the right words in that the reported violence at the heart of the piece hardly seems generated by anything as positive or unambiguous as hatred while 'longing' implies a level of commitment which is precisely what is withheld. LaBute's are not characters who would seem to repay psychological analysis, any more than are Harold Pinter's or Edward Bond's, even if it is tempting to see them in Freudian terms as expressions of the return of the repressed.

In one sense they are alienated products of a society that manufactures and consumes its own images of the desirable – and here, and in *iphegenia in orem*, with which it would be joined in its New York premiere, the reference point for his characters tends to be the films and television programmes they watch. Here they find the paradigms for their behaviour. It is in that sense that his characters seem close to stereotype in so far as they resist notions of their autonomy, preferring to present themselves as playing out necessity, trapped in scenarios not of their own making. They are curiously detached from their own feelings, observers of their own actions. LaBute, indeed, seems to set up a world of surface equanimity, though he does so in order to expose the anarchy beneath.

His characters are capable of moments of sudden violence, spasms of anger, calculated cruelties, even as they seek to rationalise such by reference to what seem to them familiar tropes – ambition, moral affront, a sense of injustice. In *a gaggle of saints* they are also specifically the product of a set of beliefs which propose a Manichean world of good and evil as if the victory of the former over the latter were simply part of the decorum of experience, the logic of existence, even if naivety masquerades as innocence. Of the two characters, one resists the implications of the violence she embraces by proxy, her brittle brightness not so much a defence against cruelty as in alliance with it. Though she would never admit as much, she is excited by the implications of violence, even as she convinces herself that she is abstracted from it. The other character, though an instigator of that violence, has the ability to deny his agency. As an American Defense Secretary would later explain when asked about deaths for which he might be felt to have held some responsibility, 'Stuff happens.' A stone is thrown into a still pond and then the ripples settle.

But only seemingly so. His characters' need to recount, here and in others of his plays, to return to what had seemed to be finished business, is precisely what is unsettling about LaBute's work. If there is less to his characters than meets the eye, there is also more. There is less in that they value what is least essential, dwell on trivia, distract themselves with irrelevancies. There is more in that they plainly bear a wound which they are desperate to cauterise even as they assure themselves and others that they remain entire and intact. The plays exist because these characters are not content with their seeming contentment. They are aware at some level that they have offended against the very principles they believe themselves to embrace. Thus the central character reassures himself that beating up homosexuals is justified on the grounds that 'I know the scriptures, know 'em pretty well, and this is wrong,' (58) yet returns to this moment, conscious that there is an issue to be addressed even if he is unclear what it may be. LaBute explained the origin of the play in a 1998 interview:

> I got the idea from the beauty of a flock of geese . . . When you see them from afar in a field, they look great, but if you go out in the field, it's covered with shit. The geese are looking at that shit saying, 'where did that come from?' There is a lot of absurdity sometimes, not just in Mormonism but often in other religions that want to pretend that no bad happens in their church, rather than taking care of what bad does happen. I think there has to be that willingness to say, 'Hey, here's our mess. Now what can we do with it?' They're just people.[2]

bash: a remembrance of hatred and longing, LaBute's first published play (in fact a triptych of plays: iphigenia in orem, a gaggle of saints, medea redux), appeared in the December 1995 issue of Sunstone magazine. Four years later it was produced in New York as bash: latterday plays. As its subtitle implies, one connecting thread, in plays in which characters testified to disturbing acts of violence, lay in the fact that the characters were either Mormons or related to Mormons. This led to complaints from the Church. 'I was led into this meeting with ten or fifteen men in suits and was reprimanded. I was "disfellowshipped",' a fate shared, two years earlier, by five writers whose work covered Mormon history and theology. Disfellowship strips the individual of the right to attend temple, serve a Church calling, give talks, take the sacrament or offer public prayers. It was, he confessed, 'a difficult thing to do'. (SBS) Nonetheless, in response, he did undertake to remove the Mormon references and to refrain from using Mormon characters, though these do seem intrinsic to the work. Why had he originally chosen to make the connection with Mormonism? It was, he explained, because,

> I felt I could give the thing some resonance, and give it some truth, by filling it with language that was specific to the rituals of the church, the dynamics of the church. That seemed the best route to go, at the time. I wanted to juxtapose people who, ironically, the world would look at and say, 'We think of them as good people, in a broad way, we think of them as good, church-going folk.' The point was not that they were also blood-thirsty killers, but that going to church, and having a testimony – or being around those who do – is not insurance against having choices appear in your life that cause you to go the wrong way, to falter or even to fall. It seemed like an honest and interesting juxtaposition to me, but one that ultimately, I think, the church saw as damaging.[3]

His agreement to remove the Mormon references, along with the plays' subtitle – *latterday plays* – was the more surprising but clearly evidence of the nature and depth of his commitment. Equally surprising, however, is the Church's assumption that the plays would bring it into disrepute while its decision to police the work of a creative writer would not. The plays are, indeed, violent, not in terms of dramatic action but with respect to the events the protagonists relate. Rather as in Greek drama – and LaBute has made the connection himself – that violence is reported rather than displayed. What is at stake is the nature, the impact and the meaning of that violence. LaBute's strategy is to approach it by indirection. That is no less the strategy of his characters, for whom these events are central but which they are hesitant to address directly, threatening as they are to their sense of themselves. In the case of two of the plays – *iphigenia in orem* and *medea redux* – which concern infanticide, the Greek resonances are particularly clear. Indeed, in the latter they are specifically spelled out as a woman who we subsequently discover is accused of killing her child recalls being introduced to the Greek concept of *adakia* (properly *ataxia*), which envisages a world out of balance.

The protagonist in *iphigenia in orem*, like those in *The Iceman Cometh*, *Death of a Salesman* and *Glengarry, Glen Ross*, is a salesman, albeit one who claims temporarily to have risen above travelling. As with those other plays, this is a story of values sacrificed to ambition, of necessities deferring to human desire. It takes place in a hotel room, as the character identified only as Young Man addresses an unseen figure. It is no more a conversation than is that in Eugene O'Neill's *Hughie*. Indeed it is rather less so in that in the latter a desk clerk is a physical presence even if little is required of him beyond a wandering attention. For O'Neill's hotel guest and LaBute's Young Man alike, speaking is a way of filling a menacing silence. Language is less a way of revealing truth than of holding it at arm's length. The assurance implied in narrative structure is undermined by the fact of the narrative as words are spilled into the void. These are so many Scheherazades. As the Young Man remarks, 'it's almost time for the last call.' (29)

All three plays which constitute *bash* begin and end with the same stage direction: 'silence, darkness', the concluding silence and darkness differing from the first (though this would become his characteristic stage direction). These are narratives, seemingly complete in themselves. In fact, it is their incompletions, their ironies that disturb. When the Young Man in *iphigenia in orem* insists in his final words that 'i'll be ... fine, i will (AFTER A MOMENT) goodnight,' (29) the ellipses, the assertion, the pause, all deny the truth of the conventional farewell. He will plainly not be fine. The night will not be good. In *a gaggle of saints*, a young woman interprets her partner's literal whistling in the dark as 'the sound of angels calling us home', (68) when in fact this comes at the end of a day in which, unbeknown to her, he had launched a violent and possibly murderous assault on a gay man. The concluding ellipses and darkness signify something more than the end of the action. In *medea redux* a woman who has killed her own child smokes a cigarette seemingly revelling in the defeat of a man she believed herself to love.

The plays are confessionals but what is confessed is something more than personal culpability. In each case innocence and violence co-exist. The characters exist on a spectrum. They have a potential for good or evil. As LaBute has said, 'whether I'm in an organized religion or not, the moral structure that was instilled in me early has always been interested in those larger questions of good and bad, of sin and morality. I often grapple with them, and they often get swept aside today.'[4]

iphegenia in orem (an echo of Euripides' *Iphigeneia in Aulis*, in which Agamemnon is prepared to sacrifice his daughter to secure fair winds for his expedition to Troy) begins with a Young Man, its only character, insisting that, 'i'll tell it once, one time because it deserves to be told, and then never again.' (11) There is no reason to believe this to be true. The self-accusation which eventually constitutes the narrative is told to a man assumed to be drunk enough to forget it by the following day. Like Coleridge's Ancient Mariner, he accosts a stranger less out of a desire to communicate than because of a need to hear himself speak what is unbelievable until it is spoken aloud. What is not clear is whether speaking it will be sufficient to ensure expiation. The banality of his situation – a salesman in an hotel room, a married man who has put pain behind him to live happily with his wife – plainly conceals a guilt that has yet to shape itself into an accusation.

There is a second character in the play, albeit one we never see, one for whom, in a sense, we have to act as proxy. When the protagonist says of the man who is to listen to his story that 'when I spotted you, alone like you were and going through that bottle, I figured you'd be a great listener,' (12) he plainly means the opposite. The guarantee would seem to be that he will not listen, that he is wrapped up in his own privacies and even desperations. Beyond that, we eventually discover that the listener is in some sense a mirror image of the man who speaks, plainly a lonely traveller killing his loneliness, sensitive about the nature of his job ('you're in what, sales? Yeah, I thought so. You look like ... well, no, I mean it in a complimentary ... you just look like you could sell things, if you wanted to ...'(13)) The implication is that there is something in the man that betrays his occupation and that he regards that occupation as something less than desirable. The further implication is that he is not in fact successful, that he could sell things if he wished to do so but apparently betrays the fact that he does not. The protagonist, too, at first anxious to boast of his success, is slowly revealed to be a failure in more senses than simply his career.

The story he sets out to tell seems at first little more than an extended anecdote about office politics, its tensions and ironies, but this quickly gives way to another story, the one that had sent him looking for someone he could safely tell. The story is of his daughter who had died at the age of five months. It is, he explains, something that 'just happened'. (14) The baby had 'smothered herself' under her covers, tangled in the blankets. The accident is thereby a mischance or even the fault of the unfortunate child, though this is not, apparently, as others saw it. He thus speaks resentfully of the police who suggest that he might have prevented the death had he checked instead of staying in another room, implying thereby that he was 'not a good father'. (16) Only the sympathy of his wife made him feel 'at peace'. (17) Otherwise, the police activity made him 'feel queasy', though he also puts this down to 'the heat of the room'. Nonetheless, he describes the presence of 'this almost unbearable thing' which unfolded in front of him and his wife, that not being the death of his child but the intimidating atmosphere of the investigation. The investigation was unbearable; the death of his child, it seems, was not.

When the police officer had subsequently telephoned to reassure him that the death had been ruled a result of 'natural causes' he had put the phone down because 'he'd put us through enough that day ... a day no parent should ever have to face.' (18) The story, it appears, is to be one of the tragic death of a child for which blame attaches to no one but whose effects are exacerbated by the unfeeling response of a bureaucracy. It is also, though, it seems, to be the story of a life engendered in the presence of death since he and his wife mark the passing of their baby by conceiving another on that same night. And if the ability to continue in the face of death is not without a certain guilt, as if continuance implied a degree of forgetfulness, then 'you thank your heavenly father for giving you the strength to stand up to his trials and figure there must be a plan behind it all, a reason for so much pain and you just . . . go on.' (20) So, on the night of their child's death they make love, accepting the death, it seems, as an expression of God's will, as is their hurried copulation. The protagonist thus stands absolved of all responsibility. He is, he implies, little more than an agent of fate, destiny, a divine plan.

There is a scene in David Mamet's *Glengarry, Glen Ross* in which a salesman accosts a stranger in a restaurant and engages him in what seems to be a philosophical conversation about human nature, only to flourish a real-estate plan and attempt to close a deal. LaBute's salesman does no less, except that what he is selling, like O'Neill's Hickey in *The Iceman Cometh*, is self-justification masquerading as revelation. And revelation follows.

His company, he explains, had been in trouble. People were losing their jobs, mostly, he notes approvingly, 'women with their m.b.a.s and affirmative action nonsense'. Of the remaining middle-management positions in his office, four were at risk, though he notes that three of them 'should have gone a long time ago'. (21) The final spot seems to lie between the narrator who, like Miller's Willy Loman, is, he notes, 'well liked', and a woman who takes public issue with what she takes to be his chauvinism, this gaining her, as he insists, an unfair advantage over him.

Then, he explains, he had received a telephone call from an old college friend who worked in the Chicago home office telling him that he would be among those to be fired. In a state of shock, he now explains, he had discovered his baby daughter with her head under the blanket. His response is what precipitates his need to accost this stranger in an anonymous hotel. For instead of rescuing the child, 'i realized that's what this was, an opportunity, and I wasn't going to waste it.' (25) The opportunity, it turns out, was to kill his daughter on the assumption that even the most unfeeling company would not fire an employee who had just lost a child. Accordingly, he pushes her further under the covers before going back into the now ironically named 'family room' (24) and lying down on the equally ironically named 'love seat'.

As he explains to the hidden listener, however, 'it didn't have to be like that. if deb had just hurried a bit, if she hadn't stopped to look through *people* magazine or her mother hadn't gone next door to fill a prescription.' It was, therefore, 'fate that took her ... it probably would've happened anyway, and it did happen, and so you go on ... you just go on.' (26)

At first it seems as though the ploy has been successful. He is retained while his female rival is fired and, in contrast to his passion-less account of his daughter's death, he now animates as he described what he plainly regards as a victory. Only later, and in passing, does he learn that the call he had received from his friend, and which had precipitated his actions, had been a practical joke. In fact, he was never to be fired. In a company that seems to have a record of misogyny, the woman had always been the vulnerable one. His response, though, is less shock than admiration for a friend who had a history of playing such jokes: 'he'd gotten me, alright. he got me good, just like the old days.' (28)

He is not, though, a triumphant survivor. The career for which he has sacrificed his child seems to have gone into reverse. This man who had assured his listener that as middle management he no longer went on the road, is back on the road with time on his hands, time to contemplate what he has done and who he is, unable to tell anyone but a fellow salesman with an evident fondness for the bottle, a man who, he trusts, will care little and remember less. His one redemption, it seems, is that he has not been able to accept his own rationalisations, that he has not moved on, that he feels obliged to tell the story to himself as if there might be a moral to it.

The testimony over, he sends the listener on his way with no more than a conventional question about his family, a platitude, however, that has now accreted a powerful irony which sends him back into silence as he sits alone in the dark: 'you have any kids? no?

well, when you do, you be good to them, okay? there's nothing like 'em in the world . . . believe me.' (28)

In *medea redux* a woman is seen alone in what seems an interrogation room. She addresses an unseen listener. She has a story to tell but wishes to 'sort of ease into it'. (73) She, like many of LaBute's characters, indeed like LaBute himself as playwright, prefers to work by indirection, that indirection being an essential element of the play's aesthetic. Given the setting, some offence, it seems, has been committed but against whom is not clear.

From the beginning, it is apparent that this is to be a confession (to what crime is not yet evident). It is, it quickly seems, to be a confession of her lack of agency: 'things get worked through . . . or work themselves through. we probably don't have all that much to do with it. we like to think we do, though, right? . . . you wanna know what i feel, i think we're just spinning around out here, completely out 'a whack and no way of ever getting it right again, i mean back on track or whatever.' There is, she recalls, a Greek word which describes this sense of lost control: 'he taught it to me.' (74) The 'he' is a teacher who had taught her that 'mortals are to blame' but that this is a part of the human condition.

It quickly emerges that the man who had taught her this lesson had taught her other things as well. In the accompanying two plays the protagonists choose to tell their own stories in obedience to feelings of guilt, incompletion, bewilderment. The woman in *medea redux*, never named, is required to tell hers by those who have arrested her and hence has a vested interest in denying culpability even as she tries to offer a rational account of her actions.

The secret she is now required to share is that, at the age of thirteen, in junior high school, she had an affair with a teacher (this would be echoed in LaBute's later play, *autobahn*). As in Paula Vogel's *How I Learned to Drive*, he seduces her by his seeming concern and, also as in Vogel's play, exploitative as the relationship is, there is seemingly a mutuality to it, even if each perceives it as meaning something different. When he kisses her it is, she explains, 'how it must have been when they first invented it, like back in the days of myth [. . .] when, you know, men were heroes and you could get kissed like that and you'd wait a lifetime for him to return [. . .] and you could still taste him on your lips, years later, because back then kisses meant something,' (80–1) except, of course, they mean something different to him than they do to her. Not for nothing does he present her with a book of Greek stories, offering her a romanticised context for his actions. At the same time this foreshadows later events, for while he insists that Euripides was the most "humanistic" of the Greek writers, most at war with a disordered world, Euripides was also the author of *Medea*, a story of betrayal and death now effectively to be re-enacted.

The teacher was not, she insists, 'a molester', though he plainly was, nor was it 'my own fault', (81) though she equally plainly has some culpability even as she denies it. Instead, she offers an idyllic, romanticised version of their relationship which, she insists, amounted to little more than kisses and hugs, except that, at the age of fourteen (on Shakespeare's birthday, as it happens), she discovers that she is pregnant.

When her teacher/lover learns this he resigns and leaves town without telling her that, as she comes to feel, 'the cosmos was laughing down at me.' (83) She was a victim of fate, it appears, rather than of him. At the age of sixteen, however, she decides to re-establish contact with him, not to upbraid him or enter his life but simply to have a continuing if remote relationship. She never betrays him. Indeed she continues to love him, can still feel his kiss on her lips. Neither she nor her lover is named. She refers to herself as her son's mother and to him as her son's father. She does not even to lay claim to speaking his name.

When the child is fourteen, the woman leaves Utah, where she has been staying with Mormon relatives, and drives to meet her errant lover in Arizona, though he is now married, if without children – his wife being incapable of bearing a child. She reads in his face a love for his child but also a pleasure at having kept his secret, suffering no penalty. In his own eyes, as it seems to her, 'he'd beaten fate . . . and gotten away with it.' (88)

The son is called Billie, for Billie Holiday, the favourite singer of her teacher/lover. When she kills him by dropping a tape recorder into his bath and electrocuting him, in one sense it is an act of revenge as she destroys the one person she assumes her former lover to have cared about, even though there has, in truth, been little evidence for that. In another sense, it is a balancing out of the fates. Whatever else it was, though, it was not a spontaneous gesture: 'i planned it [...] maybe longer than you thought, lots longer.' (89) Now she is consoled by the thought that her one-time lover will be distraught, that he will pay a price for the disorder he engendered. It is as though she sees herself as an agent of some cosmic mechanism. A crime against nature neutralises an anterior crime. She feels part of a broader drama than that which she enacts through a melodrama of seduction, desertion and revenge. Medea, too, had killed her children as an act of revenge against the man who abandoned her, but also as a means of restoring a lost order.

LaBute's protagonist narrates the details of the murder with perfect equanimity and detachment, deploying a passive construction. She does not throw the recorder into the bath, the recorder 'hit the water'. She is an observer of her own actions. At the end she is left, with the two people whom she seems to have loved most – her lover and her son – both dead, though there is nothing in the text that suggests a powerful love for her child. Her triumph is illusory. What is gained is lost. Was her action willed? She says it was. Or was its logic set in motion by the arbitrariness that brings together those who can generate nothing but their own defeat? That the woman at the heart of this story seems to show no sense of the catastrophe she has brought down on her own head, along with that of the man she insists she loves but feels obliged to punish, is a sign of the tragic irony she inhabits.

She speaks of a lover and a child but does so dispassionately as if they were indeed nothing more than figures in a drama, secure, finally, against all feeling until, at last, she lovingly contemplates the despair of the man she punishes by depriving him of what he has anyway chosen to abandon. In the end the play is not about balancing the scales of justice. Justice is a sub-plot, not the plot of tragedy. There is, in fact, a desolation at its heart. LaBute's character rather too self-consciously invokes her sense of a disordered universe in which humanity in general, as opposed to individually, has been complicit. It is an idea that would seem to relieve her of responsibility for her actions as it similarly relieved the man who had first implanted the idea in her.

At the heart of tragedy, and at the heart of LaBute's play, is the idea of disproportion. Whatever her lover's offence and whatever her sense of a radical injustice, the death of a child is more than a balancing mechanism. It is a reminder of perversity, a misalignment of motives and desires. Yet, that she acted as she did, even in such a way as to destroy her own fulfilment, is a sign of an unaccountable strength of the kind that did indeed allow Medea to commit an ultimate act, thereby revealing a God-like potential to act without fear of consequence. Even while seeing herself as the volitionless product of a damaged and disordered humanity she has the power to seize her own fate and make it her own. That does not drain her act of an ultimate irony but it does compact within that irony the autonomy she would seemingly deny.

LaBute's protagonist, cigarette in fingers, sitting in a soulless interrogation room under the glare of a harsh light and with a tape recorder running, is nonetheless at one with Medea, a woman who regarded the murder of her own children as a gesture against something more than one man. In LaBute's play, she is stripped of almost everything. The story she weaves is all she can wrap around herself. It is her meaning. In concluding it she has drained herself of energy and purpose, unless this is a story which, myth-like, will be repeated. She expects to hear nothing back just as she imagines the man who wronged her and whom she has, she hopes, now damaged irrevocably, will receive no reply to the question she believes he will shout at the sky, 'why?' There can, she knows, be no reply.

medea redux is not a cautionary tale: do not sleep with your teacher. It is not an admonition nor yet a gothic tale. It is not a story about paedophilia. It is in part a story about power, and how it shifts, and Paula Vogel would chart a similar shift in her portrait of a young girl seduced by an older man. But it is also, surely, a story about desire, which has nothing to do with rationality or social etiquettes and everything to do with anarchy. Desire is evidence of contingency, of the frightening proximity of passion and violence. The question is: how does human agency operate given the equivocal and fluctuating balance between what is willed and what is merely arbitrary?

In Alan Bennett's *The History Boys* a teacher is sexually drawn to his pupils but this is only one side to a man whose resistance to the norm in other respects is his particular strength. For Bennett, his sexuality renders him vulnerable in a repressive system but in his resistance he offers his pupils a lesson not neutralised by his evident sexual need. There is a trade involved. He is never presented as a threat. He is a rebel teaching the virtue of rebellion. He is a non-conformist in a conformist culture. Neil LaBute's teacher is cut from different cloth, though he, too, seems engaged with his pupils, alert to their interests. His breach of faith, however, is more radical than that of Bennett's protagonist. He is unwilling to accept the consequences of his actions. Bennett's character is driven out. LaBute's walks away. And so, too, does his killer, as if her act were whole and complete in itself, stopping the clock so that all that can follow is a recapitulation of what has already occurred.

John Simon, in *New York Magazine*, greeted the plays with a not untypical diatribe. 'Loathsome', he suggested, 'is the word for Neil LaBute.' He detected a 'gloating tone' and a 'smirk on the author's face'. His characters were 'stupid twits whose speech is numbingly banal, awash in verbal detritus'. He was guilty of 'some totally improbably highfalutin poeticism or some staggering enormity delivered with utter blandness'.[5] More surprisingly, he put himself forward as a defender of Mormons against a writer who seemed, to him, to have dedicated himself to traducing them. LaBute had plainly touched a nerve and Simon would not be the only critic to have difficulty in orienting to a writer whose characters do not invite empathy and whose plays explore the darker aspects of the human psyche.

3   *in the company of men*

... the coldness of a losing gamester lessens the pleasure of the winner. I'd no more play with a man that slighted his ill fortune, than I'd make love to a woman who undervalued her reputation.

William Congreve[1]

I want the excitement of watching her betray everything that's most important to her. Surely you understand that. I thought betrayal was your favourite word.
No, no, cruelty: I always think that has a nobler ring to it.

Christopher Hampton[2]

So baby beware
I'm just pretending to care
Like I'm not even there

Aimee Mann, 'Lost in Space'

Unsurprisingly given its suspect Mormon characters, *a gaggle of saints* was never staged at Brigham Young, though it was given a reading at the nearby University of Utah in a class taught by the play-wright David Kramer. At his suggestion, LaBute attended the Sundance Institute's Theatre Laboratory where he workshopped a play called *Lepers* which it was suggested should be adapted as a film. That film was *in the company of men*, which in 1997 won the Filmmaker's Trophy at the Sundance Film Festival and subsequently the New York Film Critics' Circle Award for best first feature. As Aaron Eckhart observed, 'We were in the library with 400 people at Sundance seeing it for the first time ... and Matt [Malloy], who plays Howard turned to [us] and he said, "Whoa." And we started to view the audience. And as soon as we got up there was a roar of talk.' It came as a surprise. As LaBute observed, they had had no inkling of its possible success as they worked together, 'not showing it to everybody so you have no idea how they'll react to it'.[3]

It is tempting to feel that the title *in the company of men* derives from William Wycherley's *The Country Wife*, equally a point of reference for *the shape of things* and *Your Friends & Neighbors*. In Wycherley's play, in which seduction is presented as a form of sport, a character is described as someone who can pass as what he is not in 'the company of men of sense . . . a company of reasonable men'. In *The Country Wife* human values defer to the game. Women are playthings and men contrive to deceive them, along with such other men as they regard as their inferiors. In a 'short-sighted world',[4] true and false are not distinguishable. True feelings exist to be mocked. In LaBute's play the company of men is both a literal company, serving its own obscure purposes, and a group of men for whom women are natural prey and who owe loyalty to no one, least of all to one another.

Perhaps, too, LaBute is alluding to an essay by David Mamet in *Some Freaks* also called 'In the Company of Men', in which he explores some of the differences between men and women who 'do *not* want the same things'.[5] Men, he notes, 'get together to do business', 'to bitch', or to bond. The essay is essentially a defence of male camaraderie but its stress on emotional differences is familiar enough from his plays and a link with LaBute's.

The premise of *in the company of men*, Neil LaBute has explained, 'came all at once, and I wrote it in a burst of energy'. This is not to say that he did not surprise himself. Like his own first audience, he liked to be shocked by unplanned plot twists. In fact he regarded one of the film's strengths as lying in the fact that 'you go in thinking the film's about one thing, and leave thinking it's about something else.'[6] Like Mamet's *House of Games*, *The Spanish Prisoner* or *Heist*, it gains its effect precisely from an act of legerdemain by its principal character. There is a game being played but the rules are not quite what they appear. It is, LaBute has said, a cautionary tale but a different kind of caution is necessary in approaching a work which is itself a kind of three-card trick.

This, indeed, is the most Mamet-like of his works. Like *American Buffalo* and *Glengarry, Glen Ross*, it offers a mordant portrait of the American business world and beyond that of a society in which relationships are attenuated, no more than self-interested alliances easily broken. LaBute had worked for a computer company and, while in graduate school, travelled on a train watching men who appeared trapped in a routine, dissatisfied with life. In Mamet's two plays women are absent and the cause of resentment. In *in the company of men* misogyny, along with the search for personal advantage, seems the only glue that holds this particular company of men together. Certainly we never learn what product the company produces or what services it offers. It is a machine that seems to serve its own processes. What matters most is hierarchy and power. As in *Glengarry, Glen Ross*, ultimate power lies elsewhere. In Mamet's play, decisions are made 'downtown'; in LaBute's they are made in another state, in another time zone.

Like Mamet, LaBute is fascinated by a language that is sometimes a blunt weapon, sometimes a fine-spun web and sometimes little more than a form of phatic communion or an hermetic and self-annihilating utterance, as when one of the three central characters in *in the company of men*, speaking on the telephone, says, 'No. No, no. That's not it at all. No, it's not. No, that is not the point I'm making. No it isn't. Don't tell me it is, I'm here, I'm talking to you right now and I'm telling you no, so it's not. No. No ... look, we're not getting anywhere, because it's not, and I can't keep saying that because I'm not, and see, I'm working and this is a company line and we're going in circles here.'[7] Ironically, this conversation, which we take at first to be a business call, is with his mother. There seems no clear distinction between the public and the private world, both, apparently, defined by the same corrosive self-concern, vulnerabilities, desires.

The same man, in trying to ask a woman on a date, explains that 'I just think everything's a business ... Whatever you go into – your typing there, my opportunity ... Every walk 'a life is an industry, from child care on up and we need to, ahh, take advantage of the situation.' (25) As LaBute has said, 'In the corporate world, people tend to adopt a siege mentality. Today's business philosophies are comprised of just a few catch phrases – "take control," "watch your back," "go for it" . . . After a sixteen-hour day, it's hard to shift gears and become a person again, to realize things like "love is not a commodity" and "it's okay to lose." '[8] In business, it is never okay to lose, nor is losing validated in a society which offers a dream of success. And since winning and success are defined in terms of power, dominance, position, the possession of commodities, when this bleeds into private life people are commodified, satisfaction is demanded, a process once satirised in Edward Albee's *The American Dream*.

LaBute, however, for all the surface similarities to Mamet, has his own clear voice, his own fascinations. The two writers share a dark view of aspects of human nature but the cruelties LaBute chooses to expose and explore cut deeper. Mamet's characters betray, deceive, manipulate, serve their own interests, oblivious to or disregarding of the needs of others. They are not, for the most part, calculatedly cruel. They do not play with the lives of others for the sheer pleasure of doing so, as a demonstration of their power, their capacity to do what they wish (though *Edmond* and *A Boston Marriage* are perhaps exceptions). They do so for gain. LaBute's characters behave as they do to give a charge to empty lives, to reclaim the power they fear they have lost, a significance they suspect has drained away. Sometimes the damage they wreak is inadvertent. More often it is the source of a perverse pleasure. The misogyny in *in the company of men*, though real enough, is, it turns out, a tactic. It is an expression of power but it is also a card to be played in a game only tangentially related to gender politics. As LaBute has said, 'I think America in particular has a love of gamesmanship and a need to win.' (SBS)

When he started writing, he had a single line in his mind: 'Let's hurt somebody.' (14) It was, in effect, the line that generated the character who speaks it, one of two men in their twenties who behave like children pulling the wings off flies because they can (indeed, the directions sometimes refer to the characters as 'boys'). The result is a work almost entirely devoid of physical violence but in which emotional and psychological damage is done to a vulnerable individual. The lack of violence aside, it has echoes, perhaps, of *American Psycho* in its unblinking portrait of an amoral character exploring the limits of possibility. If that has been called an 'aversive' novel there are aspects of *in the company of men* that make equally painful viewing. Watching it is liable to inspire an admixture of horror and fascination that is likely to leave audiences compromised as the most attractive and socially assured of the characters creates his own scenario in which the witnessing of the pain of others is offered as the source of a curious fascination. The film is not without its humour, but, like the attractiveness of the central character, Chad, this is part of the game that LaBute plays with his audience. As he has remarked, 'The film does have a lot of laughs. Then the situation turns vicious.'

in the company of men is a low-budget film with a highly professional look in which LaBute makes a virtue of his limited resources. With an eventual running time of ninety-three minutes, it was filmed in eleven days at a cost of $23,000 (the coffee budget for a Hollywood film), rising to $250,000 after post-production (less, one suspects, than the coffee budget of *Lord of the Rings*) and shot in Fort Wayne, Indiana, then his home town. LaBute reportedly mowed a neighbour's lawn to help raise funds. The cast survived on bologna sandwiches. There was no budget for location shooting, no video play-back; there were no dailies and most of the film was shot in The Lincoln Tower, an art deco precursor to the Empire State Building. There were virtually no specially built sets, though certain of the building's rooms were adapted for the seventeen different locations. When a scene on board an aircraft was required he was offered free use of one, towed to the side of the airport, provided that it took no more than forty-five minutes to shoot. This was not to be a film of multiple takes. Of necessity, everything was carefully planned.

There was no time for the kind of rehearsals he was used to in theatre but the actors had already learned their lines and in some senses LaBute treated the film in theatrical terms. It was shot in sequence and in extended takes. 'There are no complicated camera moves in the film,' he explained. 'I prefer visuals driven by the story. I like actors and I like long takes. I like the idea of just sitting back and watching, almost voyeuristically, what's going on between the characters.'[9] 'I think I have three travelling shots in my movie, and I almost

ended up cutting them out ... In retrospect, I wish I had done it without any movement.' When the actors 'got together', he explained, 'it
was intense just building their characters. They knew they were going
to be allowed to live on screen in chunks rather than these little
moments that have to be edited together. So they didn't have to
worry where their hands were in the last shot. It's just about overlapping lines and being very real.'[10]

As he noted, 'Words are action to this movie ... It's all through
dialogue ... You can ... do it through what you say. And it's so much
cheaper. Words are free. That's what you find as an independent film
maker. This isn't going to cost me a damn thing other than film
running through the camera,' though since mistakes in a long take
can be costly it put a premium on preparation. What mattered was the
story: 'I'm definitely not going to say how you should feel. Nor am I
going to do a deal of editing in terms of pointing you toward what I
think is significant ... To me it's all about servicing the story and not
trying to find places to put the camera to enhance the scene. The scene
should be good on its own.'[11]

The original screenplay, he explained, had a five-act structure,
with intertitles which used painting titles from Fragonard – *The
Invocation of Love, The Stolen Kiss, The Pursuit, The Lover Crown* –
and was to have been in black and white (only lack of time in securing
a black-and-white print from the original colour version in time for the
Sundance festival prevented this). It was to have used classical music.
In the end, it was pared down. The intertitles simply counted off the
weeks of the action – First Week, Second Week – while for classical
music he substituted music inspired by an Elvis Costello piece which
he described as a 'furious chant of drums and piano ... Lord of the Flies
meets Wall Street.' 'I wanted the music to be like in *Last Tango in
Paris*,' he explained, 'with angry saxophones' to reflect the fact that
this was to be a film set in a business world in which 'just underneath
those white shirts they're in the jungle'.[12]

LaBute has explained that he was attracted 'to the notion of
premeditated agony inflicted on someone'. (Introduction, ix) Those
who set out to inflict this agony are two businessmen, Chad and
Howard, apparently resentful of their stalled ambitions and as

bemused by the behaviour of women as Mamet's Bernie and Dannie had been in *Sexual Perversity in Chicago*. Something has plainly changed in terms of the relationship between the sexes but neither man is clear quite what it is. 'The '90s. Can't even afford to blink ... I miss too much,' (4) observes Chad. The film opens as Howard confesses to having been hit by a woman simply for asking her the time. 'What the fuck are you laughing at?' asks Chad, as he hears two women laughing.

His model for *in the company of men* was, LaBute remarked, Restoration Comedy, a world effectively evacuated of moral concern, indeed one in which moral concern is mocked. Beyond that, but carrying on the spirit of Restoration Comedy, one play, in particular, offered a paradigm – *Les Liaisons Dangereuses* (Christopher Hampton's adaptation of Pierre-Ambroise-François Choderlos de Laclos's novel – in which a couple deliberately set out to engineer the seduction of an innocent girl for no better reason than the pleasure of the game).

'The script', LaBute has said of his own play, 'is centered around wealthy, blasé characters who do unspeakable things just because they feel like it. It's a simple story: boy meets girl, boy crushes girl, boys giggle.' (Introduction. ix) The seemingly off-hand nature of his description mirrors the mood of the play but it is also a wilful simplification, part of that manipulation of the audience which is a defining characteristic of much of his work. The fact is that it is not only the 'girl' who is crushed, while the two men are themselves caught up in a wider game, aware, as they are, of the arbitrariness of their own situation as two none-too-successful businessmen, sentenced to a temporary assignment in a marginal city, who thrive or do not at the behest of those above them who remain anonymous.

There is, indeed, more than one game being played. In LaBute's Darwinian world everyone thrives at the expense of others and there are no exceptions. If what is at stake is power then this takes many forms. Chad, described by LaBute as having the 'mouth of Belmondo and the eyes of Caligula', may appear to survive intact, the last predator in the aquarium, but there is nothing in his situation that suggests that he is immune. He seemingly exists only to compete, to deceive, to play what he takes to be the game of life, as if he alone is free of contingency. There is no hint of transcendence in his life, no suggestion that anything exists for him beyond the game. Like Caligula, indeed, he exists in a world without moral parameters. There is, seemingly, no one he will not betray, as he draws his energy from the gap between how he appears and what he believes himself to be, except that there is no evidence that he exists outside the terms of his own contract with experience. His last name, Piercewell, turns out to be disturbingly accurate as well as itself reminiscent of Restoration Comedy.

He appears supremely relaxed and in control but there is anger, hatred and venom – LaBute's words – in him which explains his need to control and humiliate everyone he deals with. A compulsive cigarette smoker, who is never apologetic about being such, he discharges his tension in elaborate schemes to manipulate others quite as if those schemes, rather than his job, were the source of his real satisfaction. But there is an absence at the heart of the film, a scene which LaBute wrote in the first draft in which Chad makes reference to an abusive relationship with his mother: 'I wanted to allude to that, but not tell you. Chad now identifies totally with the abuser. No one wants to be abused; it's a much safer place to have the attributes of the abuser, so here's a person who must dominate every situation.' He dropped the scene. What remains is the more menacing for lacking a rational explanation. As he explained, 'Chad is a fascinating case to me. What makes him tick? I don't show what I suspect, because I want the audience to finish off the profile themselves.'[13] The greater absence, then, is not the missing scene so much as the vacuum at the heart of the principal character. He may be evil, and the word is LaBute's, but the more disturbing fact is the moral, psychological void at his centre. LaBute uses the word 'cipher', which is dangerous in so far as it is difficult for an actor to invest a cipher with conviction or for an audience to identify with aspects of his personality. But it does suggest the degree to which he appears to lack an inner life, an actor who never lays aside his role.

And beyond these characters is a society in which everything seems temporary, marginal, un-rooted. The action takes place in an airport lounge, on an aircraft, in a courtesy van, a bar, a corridor, a motorised walkway, temporary offices lit by fluorescents, a men's room, a café, a hotel bar, a park, on a roof. In Gertrude Stein's words, there is no there there. People are on the move, commuting, en route to meetings, snatching a sandwich. The various decors underscore a fundamental anonymity: 'endless rows of maroon benches', 'A narrow hallway of formed plastic and multicoloured cloth seats', 'strip of well-lit carpet and doors. Gray and mauve dripping everywhere', 'a tangle of shelves, desks, and work areas ... A makeshift windowless war room', 'A cardboard cutout of the last one', 'Faux marble everywhere', 'Midwestern chic ... Lots of plants', 'medium-sized skyline out the window', 'Massive windowless structure', 'An expanse of concrete', 'quaint Western eatery ... a smattering of small tables betrays its pseudo-atmosphere', 'Expanse of concrete and blacktop', 'An unfinished living room. Plastic sheets over most of the furniture.'

The noise likewise is anonymous and aggressive: 'The roar of morning. Endless desks and computer keys being punched. The sound is deafening,' 'Like cattle at the slaughterhouse – lots of milling, mooing, and tension. The clacking of keyboards,' 'buzzing with bright lights', 'Glasses slam down onto the table,' 'PARTYGOERS pass by with some regularity, blowing horns ... A COWORKER moves along the passageway, kicking a balloon savagely past,' 'the sound of the party rages on nearby,' 'snaps open the blinds, light spilling in as the razor-sharp CLAP! Of the metal shades rings out.' The film ends as Howard pursues Christine, the young deaf woman who works for the company, and screams at her, 'his voice soaring to the heavens ... Listen! Listen!! Listen!!! Listen!!!!' (89) until the sound disappears and he continues to shout impotently and, from the point of view of Christine and the audience, silently. The music, LaBute instructs, now roars in.

Nor are these the only directions which slowly construct the alienated and alienating world of *in the company of men*. There are other notes that indicate LaBute's take on the various characters. Thus, Christine 'seems removed from the rest of the office frolic and frenzy', her silence lifting her out of the contaminating brashness and raucousness of her surroundings. Chad, who spends much of his time looking in mirrors, literally reflecting on himself, is described as

44

staring out of a window, increasingly aware that something is wrong. Towards the end, Howard 'sags into a corner ... then purges. The vomit flows and flows.' These are all something more than directions for action and actors. They are the narrative voice of the author. They are interpretative gestures.

Though the film is set in the 1990s, in fact LaBute was anxious not to root it too securely in time in so far as the business world which lies at its heart had, it seemed to him, remained unchanged since the Second World War. He wanted the film to have what he called an antiseptic and timeless feel, since the 'business world has looked relatively the same since the fifties ... so I tried stylistically to be very timeless. The men wear nondescript shirts and ties. I didn't use a lot of outdoor shots.' (Introduction, xii) Business itself, it seemed to him, had the power to drain energy out of people, to bleach out distinction. 'It sucks the life out of you,' he insisted, 'the individuality out of people.'[14]

The film opens in an airport smoking lounge, 'All soft neon and reflective surfaces'. (3) People are passing through. A commuter aircraft taking off provides 'a momentary spectacle for anyone sober enough to care. Few do.' (3) The film has all the advantages of its small budget. We seldom see more than a small part of a setting, a bench in the airport lobby, part of a men's room, a fragment of a corridor as largely anonymous people line up for an unseen Xerox machine. Each scene is metonymic. The compressed and fragmented spaces say something about the possibilities of these people who are no more than a small part of the system they serve without understanding. In a situation in which everyone is implicitly a rival, no one trusts or values anyone else. Conversations are charged with hostility towards those who might be the source of threat. Motives are ascribed, scenarios invented. The only slogan in which they are liable to put their faith is 'watch your back', (7) though, notably, it is usually Chad who creates the suspicion, seeds the doubts. Cynicism is the only validated emotion. Attention must be deflected for fear that blame might be attracted. And in a world in which everyone is required to show loyalty to the commodity the company sells, personal loyalties are likely to be commodified.

45

When someone retires at work no one seems to know his name, certainly not Howard who is supposedly in charge. No one appears to have a private life, except Chad, and his private life, it transpires, is evidently not a life but simply another part of his game playing. As in Mamet's *Glengarry, Glen Ross* they are selling something but where in that play the product was real estate, in *in the company of men* we never know what it is and the characters never seem to care. They are simply part of a machine, an organisation that will reward them or not, seemingly according to arbitrary principles. As LaBute has said, 'That sort of nameless, faceless corporate environment seemed to me the ideal setting for Chad and Howard to pull off their scam.' (Introduction, xi) Beyond the window are other office buildings, as if this story could be replicated in the world beyond.

When Howard is on the telephone employees enter and leave his room with no acknowledgement. Like John in *Oleanna*, he conducts a private conversation, blanking out those around him. With the exception of the conversations between Chad and Howard, and between them and their victim, Christine, communications are fragmentary. They, alone, are granted fluency, itself an expression of their power. When LaBute was asked why he chose to make Christine deaf he explained that, 'Words are weapons for Chad and Howard. For that reason, it was more interesting for Christine to have a difficulty with the power of speech. By being deaf, she's not just preyed upon as a woman.' (Introduction, x)

In one sense it is Christine's deafness that explains not merely her vulnerability but her humanity, the two being intimately related. Though she is herself a temporary typist (in an office that is itself temporary), the fact that she hears nothing of the denatured language, the backbiting and lies is precisely why she responds to those she deals with on a human level. Despite her deafness, she chooses to wear earphones as if she were trying to insulate herself from the world in which she finds herself.

The screenplay opens with what LaBute calls the roar of tribal music and what we see is a tribe, a group of people united by shared myths, language, behavioural strategies but by little else. There is a shared bafflement. Humiliations are accepted as a part of the system, though no more understood than the system itself. *in the company of men* may have a kind of scientific experiment at its heart – as two men test another human organism to breaking point – but in itself it is reminiscent of an anthropological study. It is morning in America, President Reagan was fond of remarking, as if the promise of America was renewed each dawn. It is morning in America at the beginning of LaBute's film but it offers little sense of promise. People are on the move but what purpose is served by this movement is far from clear.

As Howard laments, 'we're doomed ... As a race, men like us, guys who care a smidgeon about the work-place, their women. We are doomed if this is how they're gonna treat us ... Everybody! I mean, look at us – sitting in some courtesy lounge, middle of the week and time just passing us by at the whim of those bastards upstairs.' (5) Howard is twenty-eight and already baffled. Chad, a year older, insists that he feels under threat from 'these young dudes after my desk ... vultures waiting for me to tire out. Low numbers two months in a row? Huh? They're gonna feed on my insides.' (5) What is not clear at this stage is whether he is, indeed, anxious for his position or whether he is encouraging Howard's sense of paranoia. It is, perhaps, in this mood that he warns Howard against the 'new guy', painting a picture of a man he has never met: 'he's new and clever and hell of a shortstop, Fourth of July picnic ... 'til the company has a slight recession and he's bandying your name around as somebody for "the Phoenix office." And he's off collecting another woodgrain plaque ... all I'm telling you. Watch your back ...' (7) The warning appears to be a piece of friendly advice. In the context of the rest of the film, however, it seems, in retrospect, an ironic, even taunting remark since the real enemy turns out to be Chad himself, the confidence trickster who warns against deception the better to win trust.

Howard has, he explains, been abandoned by his girlfriend of six months. Some contract seems to have been breached ('feels like things are getting out 'a balance'). (8) Chad, in turn, offers his own story of abandonment. His girl, he explains, has walked out after four years and as a result, 'that really makes me wanna fuck somebody up, but good!' (10) Commitment seems to mean nothing to her and so commitment means nothing to him: 'it comes to me ... the truth (*beat*) I do not give a shit. Not about anybody. A family member. The job. None of it. Couldn't care less.' (9) Again, what seems like an off-hand response subsequently turns out to be an accurate account of his position, even if the story he has told is false. Perhaps it is no wonder that in preparing for the role Aaron Eckhart studied the anti-social behaviour of socio-paths and frequented Wall Street bars to listen to men talk about their wives and girlfriends. 'Chad is alive and well,'[15] he concluded.

Ironically, it subsequently turns out, neither man has been telling the truth. Chad's girlfriend has not walked out on him while Howard's, we subsequently learn, has been trying to get in touch with him, even as he has done his best to keep his distance. Indeed, there is a suggestion both that he had been at fault for the breach and that he is anxious to maintain it. In a telephone conversation with his mother, he insists that he does not want his girlfriend's new telephone number and denies what seems to have been the remark that led to the breakdown of their rela-tionship: 'That bitch. No, I didn't. No, I didn't say that ... I mean, I didn't mean it.' (16) Both men, appearing to share privacies, in fact spin their own stories to serve their own separate purposes.

Chad's misogyny is real enough but it is also strategic. Howard's real sense of betrayal and abandonment are the soil in which Chad now plants a seed: 'We keep on playing along with this "pick up the check, can't a girl change her mind?" crap, and we can't even tell a joke in the workplace?! ... there is gonna be hell to pay down the line, no doubt about it. We need to put our foot down.' (10) The relationship between men and women seems to have changed, in ways the two men can only regard as threatening. The quotation from Congreve at the head of this chapter comes from an edition edited by a woman in the 1950s. On the rear cover of this Penguin edition we are told that, 'Her recreations, interests, and tastes are those proper to a woman.'[16] In turn-of-the-century America, there is no longer anything proper to a woman. What once seemed fixed is now in flux.

LaBute has said that,

> I would probably place men at the bottom of the food chain. On a grander scale, I would say they are reacting to change. Feminism has got to be a part of that. What's absolutely frightening to men

like Chad and Cary (in *Your Friends & Neighbors*) is loss of control. The American businessman – the Chad figure – has been a certain way for fifty years, and so have a lot of his dinosaur thoughts. But the last thirty years have been very volatile. We went through a period of giving lip service [to feminism] and saying, 'Yes, that's fine.' There was a shorter period, around the time *in the company of men* came out, when I had the sense that people were saying, 'I really don't care what's correct. I'm tired of you telling me what I should think and I'm not going to take it. And if I can't do that overtly, I'm going to find some other way to let that feeling out.' That's how Ben Stiller in *Your Friends & Neighbors* thinks.[17]

The means of putting his foot down Chad proposes is to find a woman – 'vulnerable as hell . . . the wallflower type, whatever – or disfigured in some way . . . some woman who is pretty sure that life . . . and I mean a full, healthy sexual life, romance, stuff like that . . . is lost to her forever . . . some cornfed bitch . . . and we both hit her . . . then one day, out goes the rug and us pulling it hard . . . Trust me, she will be reaching for the sleeping pills within a week.' (11–12) He is, he explains 'just talking', a distinction equally made by Moss in *Glengarry, Glen Ross*. It is Chad who makes the proposal but Howard who acquiesces. Indeed, though Howard finds himself momentarily in charge of the project that has taken them to this mid-western town, at every moment he is the one least in command, least secure, linguistically no less than psychologically and socially. His response to what is plainly an outrageous proposal is to say, 'Whoooa . . . Well it's . . . Right, no, that sounds, ahh . . . yeah . . . No, yeah . . . it's funny. It is. 'S just . . . way out there.' (12) When he agrees to the idea he 'smiles weakly'. (13)

In his directions, LaBute paints a portrait of Howard, a vacillator, uncomfortable with himself and the world, a facilitator of evil rather than its instigator. We see him 'swabbing at the tender flesh' of his ear, having been attacked by a woman, 'hunched up' next to Chad who is himself relaxed. He looks at Chad who in turn looks straight ahead. He fiddles with the buttons of his shirt as he talks, while a blast of light from a photocopier is enough to obliterate his features. He signs documents 'with some difficulty'. He is seen holding a 'limp sandwich'. He fingers a diamond ring 'nervously'. When he drives a car he squints as he does so. When he is slapped by the young woman he is trying to seduce he 'doesn't fight back'. And when his own betrayal comes home to him, 'He stands, trying to form words, but nothing comes out. He moves to CHAD, trying to strike out at him' but does not 'find the strength for even this'. (86) He 'simply wanders off into the night' before sagging into a corner and vomiting. Chad is the leader, Howard the follower. It is by no means clear, however, that the latter is the less culpable, that his own responsibility is reduced simply because he is, we eventually learn, as much a victim as those he has been invited to despise.

Chad and Howard find their vulnerable, cornfed, 'disfigured' woman in the form of Christine, the attractive but deaf typist. She is the butt of cruel office banter of a kind which is the more shocking for its casualness ('I think she has one of those voices, you know, like .../ yeah, like a dolphin/'S like having a Sunday chat with Flipper.' (18–19) 'I am sitting across from the fucking Elephant Man! . . . Working to put the simplest sounds together . . . After about fifteen minutes, I can't watch any more saliva form, the corner of her mouth, or I'm gonna lose my taco salad.' (20) This is the world of the playground, of *Lord of the Flies*, played out in the seemingly urbane world of business. And woe betide the audience that laughs, only to be trapped in their own equivocations.

Chad's litany of abuse is interrupted, from time to time, by a series of questions from Howard which suggests that he has a different agenda: 'But she's attractive, though? . . . was she nice?' (20) At all times he seems to be dragged along reluctantly in the wake of an altogether more fluent Chad. Chad's contempt, though, is not reserved for women. Thumbing through a copy of the company newsletter, he checks off those who are featured there and while he dismisses a woman as a 'cunt', the others fare no better: 'I hate that dude . . . Craig or Greg, one 'a those . . . He sucks dick' (29); 'I despise that sales rep from Indiana, a major fucker.' (30) When the co-worker he is addressing leaves the room he says: 'I hate that prick.' (31)

Chad shows little interest in business. He specialises in inaction. Howard seems weighed down by the responsibility he has been given and oblivious to the extent to which he is subtly undermined by Chad who corrects, upstages and sabotages him. Work 'comes first', he insists, albeit in the context of an attempt to remove Chad for a few days to give himself a free run on Christine, for the fact is that, little by little, as Chad observes and encourages, Howard becomes romantically drawn towards Christine. Chad, meanwhile, systematically seduces her. Even as he plots the downfall of both Howard and Christine, he presents himself and them as merely the agents of chance. ''S a serpentine road, we travel,' he hazards, 'this life', (43) while himself performing the role of serpent.

His misogyny is partly real and partly a means of goading Howard, who is oblivious to the double game he is playing as he sets both Christine and his partner up for an emotional fall. 'Women. Nice ones, the most frigid of the race, doesn't matter in the end ... inside, they're all the same. Meat, and gristle, and hatred. Just simmering', (58) he observes to Howard who is even then secretly planning to propose to Christine. There is, indeed, more to Chad than misogyny, which is only one aspect of his power.

Perhaps the most obvious homage to Mamet in *in the company of men* comes in a scene in which Chad confronts a black employee and which echoes the extra scene which Mamet wrote for the film version of *Glengarry, Glen Ross*. In the latter, a character played by Alec Baldwin displays a pair of brass balls in a speech which is designed simultaneously to motivate and humiliate the salesmen. He challenges their manhood in a casual display of power. LaBute does something similar as Chad confronts a young male intern: 'You want a job like mine, one day, sitting back and part of a show such as this one? The ring is dangling there, you've come this far, just gotta grab for it ... but you need the big brass ones for the task.' (63) In Mamet's films the balls are literally made of brass and are produced as a visual aid. LaBute makes the humiliation more literal as the intern is required to lower his pants and underwear. In a film which to that point had seemed concerned to stage the humiliation of a woman, this is the first clear intimation that Chad's contempt is more general. It was a scene which shocked many. Asked why he wrote it LaBute explained that,

> I think by that point the business element has started to shift away and we've watched this really personalized story and we go back to the business and see this powerplay simply because he's got the ability to do it. It really shocks people . . . To me it was important to show this breadth of hatred and casual arrogance with his power . . . He has absolutely no interest in anybody other than himself. It's important to show what he ultimately does with his power with that intern.[18]

The intern had not been black in LaBute's original script. The man who eventually played that role had, fortuitously, simply been working on the film when it seemed to LaBute that casting him in the role would add a new layer of meaning, in his own words, a new 'vitriol'. Serendipidous or not, the racial humiliation sharpens Chad's sense of power. His contempt for those he judges weaker than himself is a social ethic made personal as racial prejudice is perhaps a personal ethic made social.

Chad is the arch-manipulator, the amoral experimenter in human needs. It is he who contrives not merely to cause pain but to cause others to become the agents of pain. His cruelty lies in his detachment. His passions and commitments are simulated, the brush strokes of an artist for whom the aesthetics of his artistry matter more than any human content. Indeed, his power lies in his ability to register vulnerabilities the better to exploit them, to prompt desire in order to take satisfaction rather than pleasure, pleasure suggesting altogether too positive an emotion. When Christine declares her love for him it carries the force of her needs and commitments. When he declares his love for her it is no more than a word, a snare, part of the game, though LaBute has suggested this hardly distinguishes him from others. As he has said, 'A lot of times we do trade love as a commodity . . . It's another bit of currency to use, to buy leverage, to get what we want.'[19]

Indeed, part of the force of *in the company of men* lies not so much in the alien nature of Chad's attitude as its familiarity. As

LaBute has said, 'As a writer, I'm interested in what makes people betray each other, because they are usually close-knit groups of people. They're romantically linked, they work together, and something drives them apart. I am interested in small betrayals.'[20] It is precisely the ease with which friend betrays friend, lover betrays lover which fascinates. Chad is merely the logical extension of a cruelty that is bred in the bone, a cruelty which is the more disturbing precisely because it is not unfamiliar. As he has said, 'I think people are capable of everything I've written. Would they ever do it? I don't really know and really don't care, because that's not my business. My business is to create a world that's possible ... I've created something that could easily happen ... I think everybody's capable of it.'[21] Everyone, he has insisted, 'has a little bit of Howard and Chad in them. I think there's Christine in all men as well. There's maybe a particularly male streak in the gamesmanship that Chad and Howard display, how everything becomes a contest to them. But all of us have been hurt and have hurt people, hopefully not as maliciously or intentionally as Chad and Howard do.'[22]

Howard seems to offer a contrast, not least because he is the primary target of Chad's plans. But he is scarcely innocent. His vague air of incompetence, his failure to manage either his public or private life, does not absolve him of responsibility. Indeed, little by little, other aspects of Howard's character are exposed. His earlier complaint, that he had been abandoned by his former fiancée, is subsequently exposed as a piece of self-justifying cant. As he takes his grandmother's ring to a jewellery store to be cleaned, he drifts into a reverie in which his underlying bitterness and violence are exposed. He had, he confesses, ended up 'practically ripping it off a girl's finger! Didn't want it, first time, a few weeks later I couldn't get her to give it back ... "Just want to try it on," ended up wrestling on the floor one night. Me pulling on her hand, she's screaming, neighbors at the door.' (60) And when Christine refuses his advances he becomes violent in a scene that is hardly less disturbing for his ineffectualness. He moves from supposed love to vindictiveness in a matter of seconds.

In some ways he is more culpable than Chad. Not merely does he conspire in the original plan to exact revenge on a vulnerable woman but he betrays his own feelings, as he is also happy to betray Chad. As LaBute has observed, 'In a way the viewer detests Howard more because they identify with him more, and he continues this perpetual cycle of having really bad dealings with women ... Howard seems doomed to fail, and I think everybody has felt that, gotten into a situation over their head, and instead of cutting things off, worsened the situation. I have all those traits, and so does everybody else.'[23]

Frustrated by Christine's failure to respond to him, Howard tells her, 'You are handicapped!! You think you can choose, men falling at your feet?' (72) In revenge, he reveals the conspiracy between himself and Chad and when she confronts him Chad quickly abandons all pretence to care for her and asks, 'how does it feel? I mean right now. This instant. How do you feel inside, know what you know? Tell me.' (80) She replies by hitting him. ''S that all?' he asks, 'It only hurts that much?' (80) As far as he is concerned the game is simply over. It is, anyway, only part of a larger game. She is left in tears.

She is not, however, destroyed and this is not the last we see of her. Howard follows her to her new job at a bank in a distant city, his life in chaos. But as he shouts at her she merely turns to her work. She looks, we are told, 'radiant'. As he screams 'impotently' she is self-contained, plainly with a tensile strength of her own. Howard, meanwhile, has not only lost her and his job, being demoted, he has been confronted with his own naivety and made responsible for his own cruelty. Appearing in the early hours of the morning in Chad's apartment, he learns that Chad had never been deserted by his girlfriend, Suzanne, that merely being the story he had told to ensnare his supposed friend in a scheme that was never directed primarily at the young woman supposed to be the victim. She, he suddenly realises, was merely Chad's means of betraying him.

Meanwhile, Suzanne, lying in Chad's bed, is one more of his victims. 'You know me,' he says to her, when he suggests that the voice she had heard was not Howard's but his own, 'I can sound like practically anybody.' (87) The fact is that she does not know him and if he cannot sound like anybody he can mimic sincerity with conviction. It was not she who betrayed him but he who betrays her. She plainly knows nothing of what he has been doing with Christine and makes love to him as Howard goes on his fruitless chase. This is the last we see of Chad. He stares ahead, smiling. When Howard had asked him why he did what he did his reply was, 'Because I could.' (85) There is a curious equanimity about him but also, it seems, a vacuous quality.

Howard pays for his sins; Chad, apparently, does not. Howard is broken, Chad seems whole. Christine appears to emerge stronger, except her defences are also potentially her prison. LaBute has said that, 'I have both despair and hope ... I'm a humanist with sceptical leanings. I'm a realist ... I know the capacity we have for good and bad, and it's anybody's guess which way we [will] go.'[24] It is not too clear that the capacity for good has much of a showing in *in the company of men* unless it be in the survival of those very instincts which make his characters most vulnerable, in the trust that is so readily turned against them – that and the feelings of revulsion provoked in an audience simultaneously made aware of its own moral equivocation.

Responses to *in the company of men* were curiously mixed. On the one hand it picked up a series of awards, as did Aaron Eckhart. On the other it inspired considerable hostility. Kate Sullivan, in reviewing a later work – *Nurse Betty*, which he directed but did not write – broke off to observe that 'it feels sad to insult LaBute, since – if his movies are any indication – he's a deeply lonely, self-loathing guy, and his art probably represents a heroic effort to grapple with that.'[25] John Simon, too, later suggested that LaBute was in the business of passing off psychotherapy as art: after all, how else account, here, for a play in which a man manipulates another man into trying to destroy a woman, how else account for a character who takes pleasure, and derives his identity and sense of power, from ensnaring others in a story of his own devising, unless, of course, one recalled Shakespeare's Iago?

LaBute is not seduced by his own creations, still less concerned to displace his own neuroses into art. His plays and films, for all their emphasis on human frailties, on the extremes of human behaviour, serve a moral purpose. It was the defence he offered to those who thought his Mormon beliefs at odds with his works, if it was also the defence that theatre had always mounted when attacked by those who accused it of immorality (indeed he had won an Association for Mormon Letters Award for the play version at Brigham Young

University in 1993). It was in that spirit that he projected a future for Chad which seems at odds with his amoral progress through life, a life that takes the shape it does precisely because of the advantages he possesses, advantages which he shares with his culture. As LaBute explained,

> I was very careful to cast guys who were good-looking and very fit and had a certain sense of privilege about them, because with that sense of privilege comes contempt. It isn't enough for Chad to do the things he's doing. He has to then go to his boss's office to humiliate an intern. He doesn't just have to bed Christine, he has to do it in his boss's hotel room. He's always pushing the envelope a little further. Inevitably, the odds are going to go against a person like that. I don't show it in the film, but I could see where the trail was leading: Ten years later, Chad is in prison.[26]

There is little in the film to suggest such a fate. Indeed, its power lies precisely in its refusal to offer the consolation of retribution, to grant the existence of a moral system in which Chad will seem aberrant. In a society, perhaps in an existence, in which there are no sanctions, no sense of transcendent values, he accretes power and finds in it a meaning manifested by nothing else. It is, though, a self-reflexive meaning, reflecting nothing but his own desire to observe an absurdity of his own creation. He is an actor who never steps out of his role because it is only within the factitious world he generates that he feels alive. His power over others is what convinces him that he exists free, as he supposes, of those who would shape him to their purposes, require him to perform at their behest.

4 *Your Friends & Neighbors*

Jules Feiffer's *Carnal Knowledge* (directed by Mike Nichols) is a comic but painful film that follows the lives of two men, Sandy and Jonathan, who were once room mates at Amherst. When we first encounter them they are desperate for their first sexual experience. College women are little more than targets selected for their physical attributes. Sandy, played by Art Garfunkel, appears sensitive and vulnerable; Jonathan, played by Jack Nicholson, is more manipulative, perfectly willing to betray his friend. ('I'm dating your best friend. / He won't mind. / How do you know? / I won't tell him.') Their apparent emotional commitments are no more than moves in a game. Though Sandy does not know it, they share their first woman, a Smith College student called Susan, intelligent, independently minded but to them, at first, no more than prey.

In their first encounter, at a college mixer, Sandy and Susan have a conversation which spells out a central truth of what is to be their lives:

> Everybody puts on an act.
> So even if you meet somebody you don't know who you're meeting.
> Because you are meeting the act.
> That's right. Not the person.
> I think people only like to think they're putting on an act but it's not an act.
> It's really them. If they think it's an act they feel better because they think they can always change it.
> It is an act but the act is them because they're an act.[1]

The film then moves forward in time, tracing their subsequent lives which seem at first merely extensions of their college selves. Sandy marries his Smith girlfriend, still unaware that she has betrayed him with his best friend; Jonathan continues to play the field until he, too, marries, only for the marriage to break up. In the end both men live empty lives, sex proving ever less fulfilling. Jonathan objects to his partner's passivity, Sandy to Jonathan's habit of shouting out instructions 'like close order drill'. Jonathan, indeed, who takes pride in his exploits, ends up impotent, resorting to the services of a prostitute, who obliges by performing a fantasy he has scripted and in which he requires her to be word perfect.

Carnal Knowledge offers a portrait of a suspect male camaraderie, of adolescent game playing that extends into an adult life in which the stakes are higher. Sandy and Jonathan never cease playing roles, performing lives which seem to have ever less substance. They fail to grow up because they never understand what that might entail. It is a film which explores that gap between the needs and expectations of men and women which is the product of something more than changing times, though those changes are reflected as the two men grow older and the world around them alters. It is a witty and articulate film in which language is central. It is also a bleak film in which the gulf between people never closes.

It was this film that Neil LaBute screened for the cast of his second film, *Your Friends & Neighbors*, not least for what seemed to him to be the honesty with which it approached the nature of personal interactions. Beyond that, the film they were about to shoot shared certain concerns with Feiffer's script, notably his fascination with the performative component of identity, with sex as the assumed currency between men and women, with the game playing involved in relationships, with the betrayals, cruelties, self-concerns of characters who place themselves at the centre of their personal dramas. Barry, in *Your Friends & Neighbors*, would share something with Feiffer's Sandy as Cary and Jerry would with Jonathan.

If *Carnal Knowledge* was an influence, then so, too, was Woody Allen, at least in so far as he, too, had chosen to explore fraught relationships in a similar setting. It was an influence to be acknowledged but transcended. Both Allen's and LaBute's films deal in the dark comedy and pain of betrayal, in passions at odds with psychological and social necessities. *Your Friends & Neighbors*, LaBute confesses, prompts the question:

> how do you approach a movie that is so unremittently harsh and
> expect an audience to go with you. You can't make it into a
> romantic comedy. [Woody Allen] pioneered a lot of that,
> beautiful people in beautiful places talking about contemporary
> relationships. I am probably as big a fan as there is. I love his
> work. Going into this knowing that we're not making one of
> those films, we're not trying to ape that, we're trying to find our
> own [approach], it was difficult to steer clear of that because you
> have the same kind of milieu. You have people of the same
> kind of age.[2]

In the end, though, there is no confusing LaBute's characters with Allen's. For Allen's wit, LaBute offers irony. The humour of *Your Friends & Neighbors* is not consciously deployed by the characters but a consequence of their lack of self-awareness. Though both writer-directors are fascinated by betrayal, in LaBute's case this bites deeper. There is a cruelty, a lust for power, an unrelenting exposure of casual contempt not to be found in Allen's work. In Allen's films people are bruised; in LaBute's they are lacerated, witnesses to their own humiliations. The film did, however, reflect Allen's interest in ensemble work. As Allen had remarked, 'I like those books ... where you get a little bit of somebody's story and a little bit of somebody else's and then back to the first person and back to the second ... I like that format of ensemble.'[3] *Your Friends & Neighbors* has something of that quality about it.

The budget for *Your Friends & Neighbors* was higher than for his first film, at $4.3 million, though this was still laughably small by Hollywood standards. LaBute's approach to filming scarcely differed from that which he had adopted for his first film. The shooting took just twenty-two days and involved the construction of a single set. The other scenes were shot in existing locations. The producers allowed virtually as much time for rehearsals as for shooting, a fact that seemed to LaBute to be especially important in a film essentially about relationships. 'I don't think you can meet on a set and say, "I'm playing your husband." These people are our special effects.' (Director's Commentary)

Looking back over the manuscript of the play which eventually became the final film, he noted that his original impulse had been to call it *Lepers* (the title of the play on which it had been based) 'as I felt that it dealt with a particular social disease of the nineties – our inability/unwillingness to connect and our rabid desire to serve our own interests at any cost'.[4] In the end, though, the word 'lepers' seemed to suggest box-office death. As he explained, Jason Patric, the producer, and he were subsequently drawn to George Harrison's song 'I Me Mine', suggesting, as it did, a step beyond the 'me generation' to the 'me me generation', but copyright problems made this equally implausible. In the end he settled for a title which implied precisely that uncomfortable relationship between the audience and characters who simultaneously horrified and caused a shock of recognition.

Those displayed on the screen are in one sense a cast of moral grotesques. In another, they are disturbingly familiar, exemplary fig-ures in a society in which self-interest is presented as a primary value. Financial security has relieved them of everything but the need to seek satisfaction which they do in part by acquiring the accoutre-ments of success and in part through sexual relationships. The art gallery and the health club define the outer limits of their spectrum. In the centre, though, is sexuality, as they demand the same kind of satisfaction as they would of consumer goods or the artefacts with which they surround themselves and which are a marker of their achievement.

These are all characters with a sense of insufficiency, an aware-ness that things have not worked out. Despite their seeming success – and they are all professionals supposedly moving forward with their careers – they have not lived up to some unvoiced, undefined require-ment. In a culture that has always been in pursuit of happiness, they lack precisely that. Where once this had been defined in terms of material achievement, now fulfilment must be sought elsewhere. Where once there were manuals offering to teach people how to win friends and influence people, to improve physique, attain nirvana, now, as Barry is aware, there are manuals which give advice about sex, addressing an anxiety to which today's unwelcome cascade of spam emails offering to treat supposed sexual inadequacies attest.

These are essentially bored people seeking to reboot their lives, spiritually depleted individuals who look for meaning where meaning has been evacuated. The spontaneous has become the programmatic, behaviour transformed into performance. When Mary, the only married woman in a cast of five, smiles at her husband it 'means nothing. Not to give or receive.'[5] These are characters who observe themselves being observed. Sexual encounters are rehearsed, recorded, or carry running commentaries. They are a form of display, like the art hung ostentatiously on the walls, like the interior decorations designed to be expressive of their status, like the music they play. Sex becomes a language and as such potentially the source of deceit. Behind the assurance of this late twentieth-century group of yuppies is a profound self-doubt, a barely suppressed sense of inadequacy and lack of purpose. Everything is a substitute for everything else. They seek to fill a void to which they cannot confess. Though these are husband and wife, partners, friends, these are social descriptors rather than indicators of closeness. For all the intimate sex in the film there is no intimacy. For all the declarations of loyalty, betrayal is a natural instinct. These are people for whom others are mirrors expected dutifully to reflect nothing but themselves, like so many children looking for affirmation of their accomplishments, confirmation of their existence. Stripped of their clothes, in health clubs or bed, they remain posturers who simulate closeness but hide behind their own inadequacies.

For LaBute, *Your Friends & Neighbors* is a comedy 'that has a strong set of truths'.[6] His approach, he conceded, might be 'a bit clinical, my outlook often troubled, but my hopes for us all are untarnished. This script', he insisted, 'represents life as it easily can be lived if one is not careful, so proceed with caution.' (Introduction, viii) It is, then, a cautionary tale.

With *Your Friends & Neighbors* LaBute tackled a familiar subject, though scarcely in a familiar way. As he remarked, 'You're dealing with material that's pretty tried and true – men, women, relationships, adultery. That's been dealt with so if you're going to go to that place, then you have to have something, a new way into it.' His answer was a comedy 'that can still whack you about a bit' because 'I think in the best sense comedy can still have a little sting to it.'[7] The sting in this case lies in a brutally direct engagement with a series of relationships characterised by cruelty, sexual malfunction and hypocrisy. The sting lies in its presentation of soulless sex and still more the casuistry, self-deception and dismaying self-regard which accompanies it. As he has said, 'The unspoken is often spoken in some of my stuff. In *Your Friends & Neighbors*, it made people uncomfortable to have people talk about sex that much. They're happier watching it. Give me some nudity and saxophones playing and I'll be fine but don't talk about it.'[8] Not that there is no sex to watch, it is simply self-reflexive. These are people who hardly need partners who only serve to spoil the perfection of self-regard.

This is no longer the suspect world of business, featured in *in the company of men*, in which characters inhabited a provisional world, bleached of human touches, corporately sterile. They are middle-class professionals whose homes and apartments are sleekly modern, carefully designed to display their perfect taste and social equanimity. Cary, who is a health professional, has a studio apartment, a 'modern room erupting with African art. Statues in various corners. Paintings on the wall.' A raised bedstand is 'all drenched in black bed dressings'. (3) Jerry, a college lecturer in drama, lives in an apartment that is 'handsomely decorated' with a beautiful bed. Barry and Mary live in a newly converted brownstone. It has a warmly tiled entryway while 'Ficus trees guard a massive door that holds back the street.' (20) In the living room the huge windows are covered by designer sheets: 'Martha Stewart in the making.' (9) Even Barry's office is described as a 'handsome space . . . Glass on one side.' (8) When these people go out it tends to be to a 'sleekly tiled' health club (of which Barry has corporate membership), an art gallery (a 'towering marble and wood structure' in which 'Corinthian columns abound' and which features 'overlit representations of modern life' (39)) or a book store. They are, it seems, successful products of a successful society, good friends and neighbours. Even adultery is practiced in an 'upscale hotel overlooking the lake ... Straight out of a Victorian magazine.' (47)

Barry and Mary appear happy and fulfilled, well suited to each other. The problem is that whatever held them together is seemingly beginning to dissolve. Barry is no longer sexually competent while his wife accedes all-too-easily to his best friend when he proposes an assignation. That friend, Jerry, is an actor who is having sexual problems of his own and, indeed, is soon abandoned by his partner Terri in favour of a young woman who calls herself an artist's assistant. She is to be found at an art gallery where she meets each of the others in turn as if this were the axle around which the wheel of the play and their relationships turn. She commits herself, physically and emotionally, only to find Terri distracted.

Meanwhile, another of the trio of male friends, Cary, treats women with a withering ferocity which suggests his hatred of those he lures to his apartment. When a woman retreats to his bathroom he demands to know whether she is 'borrowing toiletries in there', and insists that if she uses his towels she should 'set them on one side', (88) evidently anxious to avoid any possible contamination. There are no grace notes in his approach to women. His opening gambit to a woman he has never met is, 'I bet you're tremendous in bed,' (37) while his idea of a compliment is 'I'm always gonna think of you as a very special fuck.' (50) When Barry asks him if he is good, Cary's response is to recall an occasion (based on a real incident told to LaBute) on which he revenged himself on a woman who had had the effrontery to drop him. Using hospital stationery, he sent her a letter telling her that her name appeared on a list of previous partners who had tested positive for HIV. 'The bitch', he insists, 'deserved it' because 'she never understood me'. (70) Was he good to do this, he asks rhetorically? The question is irrelevant to him. What mattered was that it gave him 'a certain clarity'. (70) Morality is beside the point.

Friends and neighbours, it seems, are held together by nothing but their sense of incapacity and their talent for casual cruelties. When Cary meets Terri in a bookstore, he closes in on her, as LaBute indicates, 'like a shark spotting a swimmer off Miami Beach. His teeth flash a wicked smile. MacHeath and then some.' (76) When she fails to respond he dismisses her as 'a useless cunt'. (71) He is, indeed, a predator with a predator's instincts and lack of remorse. He feels fully justified in everything he does. As LaBute has remarked, he has a code. He rehearses his life, because he has a clear sense of the text to be played out. Those who disrupt his sense of right behaviour represent disorder: 'every time he talks about something, he has been crossed by someone. He is setting the world right. It was just the way a common, decent person would react. And we fairly common, decent people who are watching it say, you're a little bit off.' (Director's Commentary) That gap, of course, is crucial in that it presupposes the survival of values seemingly evacuated from Cary's world.

By contrast, the cruelties of the other characters remain unarticulated. They are more commonplace, yet they are no less cutting for being more recognisable or for being less crudely expressed. It is not difficult to feel revulsion for Cary. By contrast, the other characters seem closer to a recognisable norm, their compromises thus compromising an audience which finds it easy to judge Cary but less so to condemn those whose vanities, self-concern, spiritual vapidness seem more familiar.

The characters are called Mary, Barry, Terri, Cheri, Cary and Jerry, though those names are never uttered in the film. They sound and behave like a group of children or adolescents. Acting out their playground games, they switch loyalties, as best friends become victims, and live out fantasies which barely survive the moment. They do have jobs but these, too, seem little more than games. If there is a life out there it scarcely seems to impinge. Instead, theirs is an hermetic existence of shifting alliances, confidences shared and betrayed, experiments in living. They behave as if there were no consequences, celebrate a non-existent camaraderie.

It is not for nothing that the bearded, pretentious Jerry is in part an actor (the bearded pretentious character in *Annie Hall* is also called Jerry). He is first seen playing in Wycherley's *A Country Wife*, a play in which adultery is seen as a legitimate game for the rich and insouciant. The character he plays is 'a young man of fashion' called Horner who pretends to impotence the better to seduce women who, believing themselves safe, thereby become vulnerable. The irony is that Jerry is actually suffering from impotence in a play in which seductions prove singularly ineffectual. In Restoration Comedy, no blood flows from the wounds inflicted. Everything is a matter of manners rather than morals, with seduction regarded as a sport. *Your Friends & Neighbors* is not so remote from such a world, except that for all the sexual game playing, pain, in LaBute's world, is a reality. LaBute has remarked of Restoration Comedy that it was 'well-to-do people with time on their hands who go around hurting each other, doing things that are pretty unpleasant, just because the opportunity presents itself'. As he recalled to John Lahr, there was a gap between appearance and reality which lay not only in the plays but in the world which generated them. 'Behind that great sense of costume – the wigs and makeup – there was a sense that all was well, even while bugs were crawling in the wigs and the physical self was falling apart ... There was still the sense that it was better to look good than to feel good.'[9] In a sense, things seemed little different in the 1990s, a period not simply style-conscious but also content, on a personal, social and political level, to privilege presentation over substance.

Very little light escapes the black holes that are the lives of LaBute's characters. The phrase 'is it me?' echoes through the film but it is a rhetorical question. None of these characters believes that he or she is at fault. In a blame culture, all inadequacies are to be shifted onto others. Failed satisfactions must be traced to their origin in their failed partners. The word 'me', however, is the operative one. Their religion is solipsism. Theirs is a world wholly lacking in mutuality and transcendence. Sex is intransitive. The men are sexually dysfunctional, preferring masturbation which has the advantage of requiring no reciprocity. For Cary, women are disruptive. They contaminate the purity of his self-concern as well as the cleanliness of his apartment. They serve less to satisfy his sexual needs, still less his romantic aspirations (of which there is no evidence), than to earth his anger.

Asked what his most satisfactory sexual relationship had been, in a scene in which LaBute keeps the camera on him throughout a four-minute aria, Cary recalls the homosexual rape of a teenager, a brutal act he has managed to burnish with a sentimental glow. It was, LaBute observes, 'the most connected he ever felt to anyone'.

(Director's Commentary) 'You'd have taken the same steps,' Jerry assures his companions. 'Common decency dictated the whole thing. I just didn't expect to find somebody who ... understood me.' (59) The gap between language and referent is the basis of an irony he is incapable of perceiving, so completely does he misread those around him. Common decency, of course, is precisely what he lacks, what he is incapable of understanding. The further irony is that in a film where the word 'fuck' is ubiquitous, the word 'love' is uttered only by Cary in describing his relationship with the unnamed victim of his violence and by Terri when she immediately delimits the word: 'I love being with you.' (79)

The ultimate irony is that Cary appears to be a gynaecologist, or medical researcher, who is shown in one scene beside a cutaway model of a woman's reproductive tract as he discusses the 'tits' of a graduate of the Harvard Medical School. In his hands he holds the model of a baby in a foetal position which, after a few moments of what appears a barely suppressed anger, he drop-kicks across the room like a football. Originally, LaBute has explained, he was to have been shown shooting paperclips at the model of the woman. The serendipitous discovery of the model baby, however, served to sharpen the scene. There are no children in this world. Sex has nothing to do with reproduction. These are couples who couple and uncouple but whose relationships are fragile. It takes no more than a whimsical remark or a momentary glance to dissolve whatever is presumed to hold them together.

These scenes with Cary elicit a sense of discomfort and embarrassment in audiences, and LaBute is a specialist in provoking such feelings. The nervous laughter they elicit is a clue to his method. The parallel in terms of television was later to be found in *Curb Your Enthusiasm* and *The Office*, two shows which turned on the insensitivity of characters not only towards the feelings of others but with respect to the social niceties in which self-concern is cloaked. LaBute's Cary allows his thoughts and feelings to spill out unregulated by discretion. For him, subtext is text. And that subtext is power, albeit a power which takes sexual form.

In the world LaBute conjures up, lives have given way to lifestyles. Nor is culture a protection. Their apartments are tasteful but appropriately sterile. Art is mere décor as a gallery is a place for assignations. Books are places in which to scrawl messages to other people's wives; the theatre is an excuse for seductions. Stripped of their clothes, they are not unaccommodated men and women but inadequate performers seeking elusive satisfactions.

One of the ironies of *Your Friends & Neighbors* was that it was released at the same time as a documentary film by Nicholas Barker called *Unmade Beds* and which was, accordingly, discussed alongside it by Laura Miller in her *Salon* review. The film is based on interviews with four New Yorkers whose sexual and social lives seem in disarray. One of the four is a man in his fifties who describes himself as a screen writer, wears black shirts and dark glasses and says to any woman who visits his home: 'You're here to fuck. If you don't want to fuck, leave.' He describes his best sexual experience as sleeping with three women in two days before, as Miller explains, confessing that if he had been faithful to any one of them he would not have been alone today. For those who believe LaBute's satanic Cary to be a pure invention, *Unmade Beds* offers something of a corrective, though none of his characters match Brenda in Barker's film for whom 'Dick is easy to get. You just reach out anytime and you get a dick. What I need is cash', a man 'who will give me money, help me with the things I need, and go away'.[10] LaBute's world of self-referring individuals for whom relationships are little more than a means to an end is seemingly not as aberrant as it might appear.

The pre-credit sequence in *Your Friends & Neighbors* features paintings by the New York artist Alex Katz. LaBute was first alerted to him by a *New York Times* article which suggested the influence he was having on advertising, including Calvin Klein (who would subsequently provide costumes for the film). The aptness is underscored as the language of fashion magazines infiltrates that of his characters. The paintings feature middle-class characters immaculately dressed. Though distant from the work of Edward Hopper, his images suggest something of the same sense of urban alienation as figures occupy the same frame, the same moment, but not seemingly the same experience as one another. This is a world of simulated intimacy and that turns out to be a keynote of the film. The music laid over these images was provided by Metallica as interpreted by four Finnish cellists aptly called Apocalyptica. It was, LaBute suggested, a perfect mix of anarchy and classicism and that, indeed, is a clue to a film in which a sense of ordered style is subverted by unregulated passions.

The film opens with Cary, 'handsome, compact, thirties', seemingly making love to a woman while talking in what he imagines is a stimulating way: 'I think you're a great lay ... no, I mean that [...] I only hope that you like it. [...] I'm serious [...] should I be more tender now.' The shock is the greater when he stops and it becomes apparent that he is alone. He checks his watch and then the tape recorder before pressing the rewind button to listen to himself in the act. In part, it seems, he is admiring his own technique; in part he is rehearsing for his impending encounter with a woman, cutting a few seconds off his earlier record.

There was disagreement over the appropriateness of this scene. As LaBute explained,

> all the way through the post-production process we found that because there were so many related and not necessarily related vignettes that make up the whole we could shift it around like a puzzle and create whole different pictures. This scene danced in and out of the front [of the film] for quite a while and there were almost two camps saying that this should be in the beginning, not at all, somewhere else in the movie. It was almost like an introduction to Jason Patric's character [Cary]. Jason was quite adamant about how strong this would be for the beginning. I think he was right, ultimately. It made a real punch. But it was the kind of thing [that] is completely isolated in the movie. (Director's Commentary)

It certainly obeyed Woody Allen's dictum that that it is vital 'to arrest the audience immediately'.[11]

Ironically, Jason Patric, who played the role, is correct in saying that Cary is the only character not to lie.[12] What Cary feels, however, is chilling, as he screams abuse at a woman who has had the indelicacy to bleed on his sheets. For Patric, however, 'Even in that scene where he pours out the tirade to the girl that's had her period in his bed, in his mind she was on her period and she knew that and she came to him and bled all over his expensive sheets.'[13] And, indeed, as the woman sits hunched in the toilet, Cary excoriates her: 'who in the fuck just gets their period all of a sudden? ... and it's happened all over my bedding! But, no, you knew that and you're twisted to have planned this. I hope to God you've got one of those red biohazard bags in your purse, 'cause you just bought yourself a set of linens! Three hundred and eighty thread count!' (67) A locked bathroom door separates them but clearly they are separated by a great deal more than that. The original shooting script had called for the bloody sheets to be thrown at the window, smearing the glass, a gesture understandably deemed redundant.

LaBute has suggested that this was Cary's one moment of control loss. It is not. This, after all, is the man who interrupts lovemaking to a woman to threaten her with death if she 'ever does that to a guy again – you know, crosses one of us in public', (31) the man who drop-kicks a model foetus. He is attractive, physically fit, a professional whose minimalist apartment suggests a careful attention to detail, a sensitivity to cultural norms. He is sensitive to nothing else. In fact it seems clear that he is a breath away from violence and that he hates women.

Jerry lacks Cary's overt cruelty but shares his self-absorption. We first encounter him in a scene that was originally to have opened the film, a shot borrowed from a Fragonard painting called *The Bolt*. He is seen in costume, performing a scene from Wycherly's *The Country Wife*, in which he is about to make love to a young woman on an elaborate bed. Appropriately enough, as it turns out, he breaks off his tryst to address assembled students. The appropriateness, however, only becomes apparent with time as, later in the film, he breaks off a sexual encounter with his best friend's wife in a bed designedly modelled on the earlier one and, later still, has an affair with the student actress.

Here and elsewhere, LaBute works by just such repetitions, echoes, variations on a theme. He creates a closed world which we enter with little or no back story and leave with no sense of resolution. This is a film in which a small group of people cross and re-cross one another's paths. There is something almost incestuous and inbred about their relationships as they move through the anonymous interiors of a cultivated community of individuals who use the language of intimacy but seem to have little conception of what they might be.

Just as the characters' names are never used so we never know exactly where the action takes place. Indeed, when in one shot a palm tree became momentarily visible it had to be, expensively, digitally removed. This was not to be a film about New York (as it might have been if by Woody Allen) or Los Angeles (where it was, in fact, shot) but about a pervasive modern sense of urban emptiness. These characters are cruel, aware of a sense of failure but unwilling to acknowledge their own agency or complicity. When they say, 'is it me?' what they mean is 'it's not me.' They no longer seem able to distinguish performance from being. Terrified of being alone, they breed their own isolation from the disregard with which they treat those to whom they cling. The failed sexual relationships which thread their way through the film stand as an image of the world they inhabit. The affairs which take place all seem casual and incidental, the product of boredom rather than passion. Betrayal at least offers a frisson, a sense of drama, novelty. And when they are not trying to release their emotional adrenaline, they engage in sexual nostalgia, talking about what for the most part they can no longer do or do with satisfaction.

The Country Wife is a play about sexually predatory men intent on adultery, about, Jerry explains to his students, 'fucking', a remark which forms a segue into the next scene in which he is still performing, though this time in bed with his partner, Terri. As he performs so he maintains what LaBute calls an '"erotic" monologue', the quotation marks around the word serving to underscore its inappropriateness. This time there is no audience of students. He is his own audience, his partner wanting nothing more than for him to 'shut the fuck up'. (5) This, it seems, is only the latest round in a continuing battle. The scene ends as he leaves and she reaches for the television remote-control, the positioning of the television at the foot of their bed perhaps saying something about their relationship.

Jerry's fondness for talking offers a clue to a central concern of the film in that these are characters who spend much of their time talking about sex and relatively little engaged in it. Indeed if language serves as a stimulus it also seems to operate as a substitute. Thus, Mary and Terri both ask their different partners to stop talking, an echo which serves to underscore the ritualistic rhythm of the film, the characters becoming reflections of one another, performing or failing to perform the same acts, saying essentially the same thing, responding to the same sense of a void in their lives.

Barry suffers from the same logorrhoea. After his failure to perform he remarks, 'It's me, isn't it? Of course it is, or you'd be talking.' To which Mary replies, 'Shh, shhh. Please. Please be quiet.' (10) Language, it seems, in such a context, is less an extension of intimacy and more a denial of it, a displacement of spontaneous passion into words, in this case rhetorical questions no more needing a response than he does in sexual terms. Appropriately enough, when he fails in his lovemaking he turns to masturbation. Like the figures in Katz's paintings, they co-exist without really interacting. When Terri subsequently asks Mary if she and Barry could be any happier, her response is ambiguous: '... no', (10) the pause emphasising the ambiguity.

The relationships between Jerry and Terri and that between Barry and Mary are, it becomes apparent, faltering. Barry and Mary seem happily married, settled. They have, it appears, previously been the limits of one another's ambition, settling into their new house as they have settled into their shared lives, except that something is wrong. Like the non-functioning watch that Barry offers his wife to wear 'as jewelry', they are non-functioning sexually. Appearance and function are misaligned. When the foursome meet up, meanwhile, the hostility between Jerry and Terri is barely containable. When he affects to be baffled by the point of a functionless gift, she replies, 'it's a gift, it's not fucking *Medea*,' (14) – *Medea*, with its internecine struggles, being a point of reference in both *medea redux* and the play attended by the characters in *the shape of things*. As LaBute observed, 'you can tell so much about their relationships here because when people are willing to fight publicly you know where they are at. Most people will say "listen, let's talk in the car." But when people let it spill over into an afternoon with friends, it says a great deal about them.' At the same time 'you can feel the pain of the other two people' – '"would you please not do this in my house"' (Director's Commentary) – not least because they are all too aware of the tension in their own lives. Later, as part of a pattern of echoes and repetitions, Barry and Mary themselves expose their faltering relationship in a discussion that takes place in the aisles of a supermarket (a scene which is itself paralleled by a conversation between Terri and Cheri in the same supermarket).

The nature of both relationships becomes apparent when Mary asks Jerry, 'how're things?' and he replies, 'Good. You?' to which she replies, 'Oh, you know ... we're fine.' (17) Not only have we just seen something of the reality of their relationships, but the ellipsis in Mary's reply, the dying fall of 'you know ... we're fine,' (17) is immediately registered by Jerry whose own response, 'Great. Us too,' means the opposite of what it seems. The language says one thing, the tone another. In the context of the scene, both Jerry and Mary have detected something about their mutual failure and mutual need, even if mutuality is precisely what they will fail to find. Jerry, alive to his moment, propositions his best friend's wife who in turn agrees to a meeting with him, though his suggestion that they 'could talk' is simultaneously a transparent euphemism and, to the audience at least, a reminder of his predilection for supplementing sex with language, an indication that she is out of the frying pan and into the fire. Jerry is an improviser, seizing the moment, slipping away from a meeting with his best friend to arrange the details of an affair with his wife: 'He is such a weasel. What a betrayal.'

Cary, by contrast, is 'ferocious. He has that look on his face of disdain for humanity ... he is predatory ... waiting for someone to cross him,' though he articulates feelings which others might suppress. As LaBute has remarked, 'this character has a code, this sense of being always truthful'. (Director's Commentary) In Mamet's *Sexual Perversity in Chicago* (and LaBute himself invokes the parallel in his DVD commentary), it is unclear whether the sexual exploits of one of the main characters, Bernie, have any reality. Cary is different. He is what he purports to be. His speeches are like Iago's soliloquies, unashamed statements of his malevolence. He is the embodiment of self-concern. He exercises in an unfashionable men's gym, as he explains, 'To spite 'em.' Asked who he is spiting, he replies, 'Everybody.' (26)

He is, he explains, 'not one to be messed with. I don't give a shit about anybody. This is my life.' (31) When he encounters Terri in a bookstore, a note tells us that seeing a long, lean woman is 'all the introduction he needs'. (75) When she fails to respond to his approaches, he rounds on her for 'coming off like some dyke bitch'. (76–7) Having seen his earlier vehemence, the threat is palpable. Even this, the strongest, most self-assured and assertive of women, is left stunned by his naked aggression. Disturbingly, this scene provoked applause from a preview audience in the same way that the audience applauded as the male professor struck out at the female student in Mamet's *Oleanna*, a response which suggests the extent to which LaBute had touched an exposed nerve.

There is a purity to Cary's malevolence. As such, he stands in contrast to Jerry who derives his pleasure from performance, though when he takes Mary to a hotel it is none too felicitously stage-managed. He leaves her in the lobby while he negotiates his payment method with the assistant manager. 'Couldn't this work?' he asks, as if he were discussing a play text. 'I do feel optimistic,' he says, somewhat to her bafflement. 'I feel it feels like fate,' (48) he offers, the linguistic infelicity saying something for his own inarticulateness when off text. It is also, apparently, part of his standard operating procedure since Terri later explains that the word 'fate' is 'thrown about our place a lot'. (75) By the time he is ready to shepherd Mary to the hotel bedroom, modelled on the Fragonard painting which had provided the set for *The Country Wife*, she has largely lost such enthusiasm and hope as she had brought to this place.

LaBute recalled a comment by Aaron Eckhart who, in pre-production had asked, '"do you think there is any joy in this?" I said, "I hope not." It was like we were trying to find something that just played out how despairing people can get in their relationships of all kinds because you have a couple living together, a couple married, singles, all the mixes that they try ... There is a thread that runs through the movie of people saying "Is it me?" especially the men. It's enough, they think, to just say it. They don't want to hear that it is them'. (Director's Commentary) 'I tend to hear a false sense of warmth in the way we lead people in sentences,' he has said. '"You know," "I mean," "Listen." People are constantly trying to embellish what they say with this false sense of camaraderie – "I'm with you," "I'm with you on this." A phrase that suddenly started coming up more and more . . . was "Is it me?" These men were constantly asking, without any sense of wanting to know the answer, "Who's doing this?"'[14]

The society LaBute pictures in *Your Friends & Neighbors* is one in which relationships are as disposable as consumer goods and seem to fulfil some of the same functions. When satisfaction is no longer guaranteed by partners, they are thrown away, traded in for another model. This is a market place in which people are on sale or return and in which performances of all kinds are to be monitored for their utility, assessed for their style. When Jerry is asked if he and Terri are staying together, he replies, 'I suppose. I mean, we split the rent. We bought a TV. This huge fucking bed. I mean, we have investments in this.' (34) Terri, likewise, says, 'We had something nice. We paid the bills.' (91) Commitment, it seems, is less emotional than financial.

For Irving Goffman, in *The Presentation of the Self in Everyday Life*, social life was a form of theatre, more especially in America. This is a central trope in *Your Friends & Neighbors* in which the characters carefully sculpt themselves (much as Evelyn would do Adam in *the shape of things*), contrive their own mise en scene, rehearse their lines, deliver arias. Only Jerry is a literal actor, but all the characters self-consciously stage their lives, are anxious for feedback on their performances, are aware of others as an audience. What they demand of one another is what an actor demands of an audience: belief. Or, as Catherine Keener, who played Terri, remarked, 'trust, trust, trust'.

These are characters who appear so completely to have internalised the values of a culture which seemingly privileges appearance over reality, performance over substance, that the real is no longer evident. The most intimate of moments have been infiltrated by the demands to give and receive satisfaction, to maintain a self-image in tune with social norms. And if the audience which is the other person ceases to believe then it becomes necessary to locate a more credulous audience. So, LaBute's characters abandon one partner for another, one audience for another, even if it is themselves, looking for a more positive response, essentially for better reviews.

Thus, the apparently happily married Mary arranges an assignation with Jerry, a man who she barely knows, to whom she is connected, indeed, via the very husband she is about to betray. She jots down a message for him in a book by Camus (at one time at the centre of a debate about commitment and moral values). Later in the film, another message will be written in a book, LaBute having a liking for such repetitions: 'I like the things that recycle themselves. This pays off much much later, toward the end of the movie.' (Director's Commentary) One breach of trust is followed by another as, at the hotel to which he takes her, he charges the room to his school rather than himself. In part it is a way of ensuring that the bill will not come to his own home. In part, his adultery is to be financed by others, and as such is a double betrayal, a tax-deductible betrayal which he rationalises by denying the terms of the contract he is breaching. 'You know what?' he says, 'You're married to him. Okay. Fine. He got there first. I understand that. Totally. Okay? But, so what? That's nothing, right? I mean, it's like, uh ... um, it's not destiny, not "law", is it? It's just chance, really.' (48) In the room, his clothes 'hanging smartly in the closet', their attempts at love-making prove abortive. Jerry, though, is less concerned with betraying his own partner, her husband and his friend than with denying responsibility for the sexual debacle – 'this is not me ... is it me?' (49) The operative word here and throughout the film is, indeed, 'me'. Intimacy is never shared. As Terri remarks, in a characteristic LaBute line, 'fucking is ... fucking. It's not a time for sharing.' (45)

Jerry, though, is not simply concerned to liven up his sex life by a quick affair. When Barry seeks advice on where he might take Mary to revive their sexual relationship, he suggests the same room in the same hotel where he had taken her. What is at stake, it seems, is something more than betrayal. There is an admixture of jealousy, revenge and cruelty masquerading as friendship and concern. His role in *The Country Wife* seems wholly apt to a man who has no objective beyond satisfying himself and consolidating his own self-image, a man for whom women exist to do little more than boost his ego.

Nor are the only relationships in the film those involving men. Cheri, who describes herself as an 'artist's assistant', encounters each of the characters as they visit the art gallery where she works. Each makes the same comment as he or she looks at a picture. We never see that picture, only those who stare at it, the men insisting that it is crooked in one direction, the women in the other. As they stand looking at it they themselves become exhibits in a gallery which fittingly features what appear to be images of fractured people, one showing a woman with her neck ripped open. They all seem trapped in the same rituals, the same behavioural patterns. Cheri is drawn not to the men but to Terri; their relationship, however, seems scarcely more secure. Power always goes to those who care least and power is one of LaBute's central concerns.

Asked by Jerry why things have not worked out, Mary replies, 'Because life is complicated. People can't communicate.' (82) Certainly her relationship with her husband has been destroyed. She is left in despair. If they have been playing games, she is aware, suddenly, that the consequences are real enough. The house that was to have marked a new stage in their life now signals the end of their relationship. Real pain breaks through the social masquerade. In a subsequent scene with Jerry, Barry was to have 'this dirge against humanity', for the first time expressing anger. It was a scene that was out of character and, indeed, he was to have been presented as drunk to justify what was acknowledged as an out-of-character outburst. It was shot but dropped from the final film, his dismay being more effectively expressed through his tentative remarks or silence.

The film thus draws to an end with what is evidently the break-up of the only relationship that seemed to have the sliver of a chance, that between Barry and Mary. They are seen surrounded by packing cases. As for Jerry, he is abandoned by Terri who, to his bafflement, leaves him for another woman. Any distress he feels, however, is only momentary as in the next scene he is seen in bed with the young actress from his play, though even then he breaks off to retreat to the bathroom where he calls his former girlfriend. There is no reply.

The film concludes, as it had opened, with a series of bedroom scenes. In the first, Jerry continues to be discontented with what he has, always reaching for the next relationship. In the next, Terri lies on a bed, aimlessly flicking through cable channels as Cheri tries, ineffectually, to gain her attention. This is followed by a scene in which Barry masturbates as he talks to a woman on a sex line, failing now, as he had at the beginning, to achieve an orgasm. In the first draft of the film, this was to have been the concluding scene. In the end, LaBute chose to end with a scene which some found difficult to take as a vulnerable Mary ends up with the most virulently sexist of the characters, Cary, a mismatch of disturbing proportions. Throughout the film she has been the one who needed companionship, a man who could care about her. She has ended up with someone who cares for no one but himself, a fact known to the audience but not to her. Indeed, it is that fact which makes the final scene so painful. The audience knows what undoubtedly lies ahead. She does not. For all their difficulties, she and Barry had cared for one another. In a desperate attempt to find a solution for her needs she has sought out the one person guaranteed to destroy her.

When she asks him to hold her (the message she had scrawled on the flyleaf of the book she handed to Jerry in her last misguided search for comfort and love) he responds with a sexual assault. When she cries, the man who had earlier assailed a woman for bleeding on his sheets complains, 'you're weeping in my pillow.' She is pregnant, though plainly not by Barry. Now she is with a man who the audience earlier saw drop-kicking a foetus like a football. 'How's that feel?' he asks, having tossed her husband's gift, the non-functional watch he gave her at the beginning of the film, 'unceremoniously on a black nightstand', and rubbing her breasts rather than hold her. 'That's nice,' she replies, rather as Hemingway's Brett does in *The Sun Also Rises* and with the same irony. For LaBute, 'this is as bleak a last series of lines as you will hear. This is his idea of intimacy. She's asking to be held and he rubs her breasts and asks "How's that feel?"' (Director's Commentary)

The film ends with a slow fade in which nothing more is said and, indeed, LaBute has a fondness for silence as he does for emptying the frame of his films, allowing the audience to supply what is not spoken or shown. Where, more conventionally, such moments might be filled with music, he often has a preference for silence. He also resists an easy resolution in his work. Woody Allen, raised on American films, was aware of the pressure for such but explained that he had 'gone on to resolve the films less'.[15] LaBute, too, chooses to work against the American grain, his refusal to offer audiences a curtain call in *the shape of things* being an indication of an aesthetic choice which applied equally well to his other work for stage and screen.

Your Friends & Neighbors was not, he insisted, 'meant to be the statement of the times, but it was a valid statement of the way we get along with each other or don't get along with each other'. (Director's Commentary) The reviews, LaBute confessed, were polarised. For Mick LaSalle in the *San Francisco Chronicle*, *Your Friends & Neighbors* was 'an embarrassing film', a 'sex comedy' that 'tries to be shocking and only manages to be shockingly puerile ... empty, false, insincere and a complete waste of time'.[16] Stephen Hunter, in *The Washington Post*, saw the film as 'a mess', with 'no shape or narrative force', 'theatrically spare', with 'nothing left but character and words'.[17] For J. Hoberman, in the *Village Voice*, *Your Friends & Neighbors* was 'less formally worked out – as well as less politically astute – than the ruthlessly constructed *company of men*'.[18] Writing in the *San Francisco Examiner*, on the other hand, Barbara Shulgasser, while suggesting that 'the movie is mostly a horror story about people who seem genetically incapable of happiness ... trying to live their lives as if happiness were possible,' confessed that the 'tension between the fantasy of satisfaction and the reality of desolation poses an enthralling dramatic situation'. As a result, she confessed, she had taken back 'all the negative thoughts' that LaBute's 'painful-to-watch earlier film engendered'.[19] Responses were largely positive but the sense of unease is evident. LaBute was not a writer critics were finding easy to place.

5 *the shape of things*

Art is not and never has been subordinate to moral values.
Morality seeks to restrain the feelings; art seeks to define them
by externalising them, by giving them significant form. Morality
has only one aim – the ideal good; art has quite another aim – the
objective truth ... art never changes.   Herbert Read[1]

In common conception, the work of art is often identified with
the building, book, painting, or statue in its existence apart
from human experience ... When artistic objects are separated
from both conditions of origin and operation in experience, a
wall is built around them that renders almost opaque their
general significance ... Art is remitted to a separate realm,
where it is cut off from that association with the materials and
aims of every other form of human effort, undergoing, and
achievement.   John Dewey[2]

What's the matter with the truth, did I offend your ears
By suggesting that a change might be a nice thing to try
Like it would kill you just to be a nicer guy
It's not like you would lose some critical piece
If somehow you moved A to point B
Maintaining there is no point changin' cause
That's just what you are
That's just what you are.
          Aimee Mann, 'That's Just What You Are'

John Fowles's *The Magus* concerns a Prospero-like figure who manipulates and shapes the lives of other people who find themselves trapped in a story not of their own devising. In that sense it is concerned with the nature of relationships and art, as it is with the source and substance of power. Despite its mythical air, however, it is as much about the manner in which individuals transform and are transformed as they encounter one another, serving their own psychological needs, devising strategies to attain their ends. Each person in a relationship bears the impress of the other as he or she invites the other to conform to a model which may be at odds with their own sense of themselves. Art, meanwhile, shapes the space around it, offers a version of the real, invites the listener/viewer/reader to respond authentically and morally even if the two are in conflict. *The Magus* was informed, Fowles confessed, by Henry James's *The Turn of the Screw*. In neither work is it easy to distinguish the true from the false. Truth depends on perspective. In both works, the imagination is exposed for its coercive qualities, the artist's role inevitably involving a degree of power, over characters and over those exposed to the work.

Author and authority are not merely linguistically close. There is potentially an act of appropriation involved, a colonisation of the mind and imagination. As Fowles observed, 'There is something slightly shamanic about all writers ... It is the power to put your ideas or your feelings across into other minds. That is power.'[3]

In *The Magus*, the arch-manipulator is a man though, as in so many of Fowles's works, the moral force is a woman. Women are the educators. In Neil LaBute's early work, the manipulator, the source of power, was also male. The response to *in the company of men*, however, was such that he decided to place a woman, Evelyn, named for Eve, the original woman, at the centre of *the shape of things*. Evelyn, it turns out, is an artist who places her work ahead of any other concerns, who shapes the world to suit her own necessities, and is happy to subordinate ethics to aesthetics, to deceive in order to achieve her ends. As LaBute explained in a 2003 interview: 'The idea of a woman being deceptive came from that original discussion with critics and reporters about if women could do that kind of thing. Evelyn, herself, grew out of the discussion about how capable women are of deceit and lying and manipulation.'[4] Manipulation, after all, is not gender-specific. As he explained, 'Everybody has the ability to be manipulative, to be hateful and deceitful. I think they have the capacity for very good, as well. It's just often more interesting to write about one or more people who are being awful to other people because it makes for exciting, dramatic fare.' In a perverse way, though, Evelyn is no less the moral force in so far as she raises the principal moral issues in the play even as, in her role as an artist, she denies any responsibility beyond a commitment to her art, much as LaBute says, 'My business is can I create a world that's possible and could happen? I think that's the only thing I have to do.'[5] Asked whether he thought there was ever a justification for artists placing issues ahead of people, he replied,

> I have definite feelings about Evelyn, and I do understand her.
> I understand her drives. I don't know if I could ever agree with the
> methods that she used, but I understand her feelings ... I can ...
> still think back to when I was a student and can remember
> thinking that theatre was more important than, certainly all my
> other classes and maybe life in general ... I don't know that I
> could personally create at the cost of other people's feelings or
> lives ... But I don't feel comfortable in putting myself in a place
> to judge an artist who does that ... I don't know if art is ever too
> much – is there ever too far that we go.[6]

Asked if there was anything of himself, therefore, in the character of Evelyn, he replied, 'Naturally, some of me has to seep in there ... I know that zeal with which she works, that kind of student righteousness: "I'm so smart, I'm so right, I'm so ahead of the curve." I operated in much that same way, and I had professors who hated me. I'd just dig in and say, "You can tell me all you want, but I'm not changing my opinion, I'll do this my way."'[7]

the shape of things had an unusual history. In 2000, LaBute was one of three writers commissioned by the New York Times to come up with an approach to filming Edith Wharton's novel Summer. What he produced would essentially go on to become the opening scene of the shape of things, though with the genders reversed. The latter opened in

London, at the Almeida Theatre, and then transferred to New York with the same cast. A planned videotaped version swiftly became a commercial film when a film company stepped in, happy to give LaBute freedom of action. The film was then shot in nineteen days, again with the same cast, though the action was shifted from the Midwest to California, where the weather was more reliable for the location shots. The fact that the cast had been together for so long, and hence knew the material thoroughly, meant that it was plausible for LaBute to shoot in a way that retained something of the theatrical feel of the original, preferring, as he had with *in the company of men*, to foreground the characters and language over a self-conscious approach to direction.

The play takes place in a liberal arts college located in a conservative town. In the film version it is called Mercy College, rather too obvious an irony, perhaps, in a work in which mercy is precisely not what is on offer, though the name was originally inspired by a real East Coast university where they had thought of shooting. As LaBute explained, in a commentary to the subsequent DVD release, the California setting had certain practical advantages, but it also made sense 'thematically, in that this was to be about human beauty' and 'there is a kind of beauty myth in California slightly different from other parts of the country.' Evelyn's thesis has a greater plausibility in California (where men and women pump iron alongside the Pacific, visit high-price plastic surgeons and enrol in a variety of religious and therapeutic groups) where the sculpting of body and mind are equally an investment and a way of life. The new setting had another advantage in that it 'suggested a small, lazy, California community' with 'a small town mentality', into which Evelyn comes from the city wearing, in the film version, first a Mao and then a Che Guevara button, an artist turned, in LaBute's words, into 'an art terrorist'. (DVD)

Evelyn, the key mover of events at Mercy College, explains that she has always been 'at someone's mercy'. (117) The implied tension is immediately acted out in the form of a debate over what appears to be the victory of moralists over art. Adam and Evelyn, both college students, he a junior she finishing her MFA, meet, apparently coincidentally, in a museum. To supplement his student loans he is working as a guide/security officer. She is discovered standing near a stretch of velvet rope, with a spray can in her hand, staring up at a massive male sculpture. She steps over the rope. After a moment, she is approached by Adam.

The opening line – 'you stepped over the line' – turns out to be an accurate summary of what follows in a play in which a young woman appears to breach tacit assumptions about the nature of human relationships. In the name of art, ambition, a self-regarding sense of power, she crosses moral boundaries, defies conventional assumptions. She invites trust in order to betray it. Though neither the characters nor the audience suspect as much, she is effectively a confidence trickster seeking to take advantage of the needs she identifies and in part provokes. Behind the seeming randomness of what follows, we subsequently learn, is a measured and coherent plot. What appears improvised and spontaneous is in fact calculation. There is a shape to things. It is simply not that of which others are aware.

She had stepped over the line, she explains, precisely because it was against the rules to do so. She is in the business of transgression. She does rather more than offend against the conventions of a gallery when she steps over the velvet rope which keeps life and art at arm's length, though in doing so she raises questions about the nature of the relationship between the two. She asks how far the artist can go in his or her determination to impinge on the sensibility of the observer. A work of art exists within a framed space. So does the individual, whether in a gallery or not. That frame is determined by the conventionalities of behaviour, tacit assumptions about right actions. What happens when that frame is breached?

She has, she explains, come to spray-paint a penis on the nude statue whose genitals have been covered by a fig leaf (an echo, perhaps, of Wycherley's *The Country Wife* in which a woman remarks that 'I would as soon look upon a picture of Adam and Eve without fig-leaves as any of you, if I could help it.'[8]) She does so on the grounds that 'I don't like art that isn't true,' (8) a statement whose ambiguity is later exposed as the play reaches its conclusion. She is not, it eventually turns out, someone who deals in truth or, rather, she is one for whom truth, like art, changes with point of view. The immediate issue, she insists, is one of censorship. A committee of concerned citizens had called for the statue's penis to be covered up on the grounds that it was 'too life-like' for a god, morality seemingly disguising itself as aesthetic or logical judgement. But then nobody's motives seem entirely clear in a play in which the shape of things is ambiguous and anyway, as Adam notes, 'art' and 'truth' are themselves subjective terms, the subjectivity of art, Evelyn insisting, being the essence of its beauty.

What follows is the seduction of Adam by Eve. In the film version she helpfully features the picture of an apple on her shirt. An innocent is about to be transformed. Told that as an artist she can change the world, Evelyn decides to begin by changing the world of an individual. Adam is the clay she wishes to mould. He is, he confesses at the beginning of the play, 'not anything'. (22) He is the granite block about to be shaped by the sculptress. This Eve is anxious to liberate a literally imminent sexuality. What follows, mythically and in terms of the play, is knowledge, guilt, deception, jealousy. Already, though he is unaware of it, she has begun the process of reshaping him, suggesting that he should change his hairstyle. In the next scene, indeed, not only has he done this but at her suggestion has taken up jogging and working out, even changing his diet. As a result he is thinner, more attractive. Now she sets about changing him on another level. He has begun keeping a diary to which she claims privileged access. She will now be able to infiltrate his privacies. And she resists explanation: 'don't worry about *why* when *what* is right in front of you.' (24)

At the beginning of the play, Adam is a somewhat dishevelled, overweight and not too attractive young man, who cares little for his appearance. In one sense what Evelyn sets out to do is what is presented in a dozen different television shows. She gives him a 'systematic makeover', (117) and not only in terms of appearance. She tries to mould 'the human flesh and the human will'. (119) He is, she finally confesses, a '*human* sculpture'. (118) Her mission, she later explains, is to 'instil "x"' amount of change ... using only manipulation as my palette knife'. (120) Her subject is variously described as 'base material' (119) or 'this creature'. She feels, she finally admits, no more human connection to him than does a sculptor to the stone from which she fashions a shape. He is 'my creation'. (120) She has done little more, she insists, than everyone else does who tries to modify the appearance and person of those they live with or alongside whom they work, though she acknowledges taking this process a little further 'with the artist's reckless pursuit of truth and historical disregard for rule and law'. (120)

While asserting the amorality of the artist, however, she claims that her sculpting of Adam has served to remind everyone of a contemporary obsession with surface. The new improved Adam is 'a living, breathing example of our obsession with the surface of things, the shape of them'. (122) Nonetheless, she claims for herself not so much a moral function as freedom from such concerns: 'I have always stood by the single and simple conceit that I am an artist. Only that. I follow in a long tradition of artists who believe that there is no such concept as religion, or government, community or even family. There is only art. Art that must be created. Whatever the cost.' (138)

In the film version a large banner on the wall of the hall in which Evelyn finally presents her project, the project which has involved the reshaping and deception of Adam, announces 'Moralists have no place in an art gallery.' This is a quotation from the Chinese writer Han Suyin (ironically hardly a heavyweight writer or noted philosopher, being the author of *Love is a Many Splendored Thing*), which echoes Goethe's belief that while art might have a moral effect to demand a moral purpose of art is to invite its ruin. In the lobby are posters advertising productions of Chekhov's *The Seagull* and Ibsen's *Hedda Gabler*. *The Seagull* is echoed in the flyers handed to members of the audience which carry the words, SHE LOVES ME SHE LOVES ME NOT, a phrase from the Chekhov play which is repeated here in a neon sign. In *The Seagull*, Trepliov, a would-be experimental playwright, delivers the line in relation to his mother, as he pulls the petals from a flower, lamenting the lack of love between them. For Bernard Shaw, Hedda Gabler had an intense appetite for beauty but lacked conscience, compassion or humanity. There is, John Gassner once remarked, something 'rather terrifying' about Hedda, rising, as she does, above the conformity of those around her, an 'extremist'.[9] There is more than a little of this in Evelyn.

It is not quite that Adam argues for the morality of art but that he insists on the need for discrimination. For him, art is not what one chooses to describe as such. However, he does feel that the suspension of all moral questions leaves art stranded. Self-mutilation does not become art by declaring it so any more than does the wilful use of other people's bodies by declaring it to be an aesthetic gesture inviting an aesthetic response. His desire that the artist him- or herself should be a 'better person', (133) however, leads him into territory he is unable or unwilling to explore. Ironically, John Dewey, in arguing that art is not what is to be found in a gallery insisted that, historically and globally, art is 'everything that intensifies this sense of immediate living', and Evelyn would doubtless have been pleased to know that for Dewey this might include 'Bodily scarification'. (6)

Art abstracted from human experience is, John Dewey suggested, art drained of true significance. The function of the critic was thus 'to restore continuity between the ... intensified forms of experience that are works of art and everyday events, doings, and sufferings that are universally recognized to constitute experience. Mountain peaks do not float unsupported; they do not even rest upon the earth. They *are* the earth.' (3) He was resisting, in other words, the lifting of art out of the continuum of experience. Those who would later use their own bodies as the site of their art were, arguably, merely carrying that principle to its logical conclusion, cutting their bodies as a sculptor cuts the clay or shaping the space around them by their presence. Neil LaBute's *the shape of things*, among other things, explores the assumed division between art and life, taking entirely literally assertions of the intimate connection between artwork and human experience. There is a game being played but the game has real consequences because it implicates individuals, and one in particular.

Shakespeare plays with the idea of a woman turned into a statue and re-animated (in *The Winter's Tale*), a piece of trickery which is not without its relevance to *the shape of things*. Bernard Shaw constructs *Pygmalion* around the idea that a human being can be reshaped and admired as the product of the applied skills of a man for whom the venture is no more than a product of his hubris. In Hitchcock's *Vertigo* the psychologically disturbed protagonist allows his needs to be manipulated by those who construct a woman who matches his memories of a woman he lost. There is at the heart of art a metamorphosis, an act of transformation as what is imagined is given form. And transformation, as Kafka acknowledges with Gregor Samsa, may carry a threat as well as a promise. *the shape of things* tips its hat to Shaw. As LaBute remarks, 'there is something of that Pygmalion sensibility in that desire to mould something. But while Pygmalion is driven by a kind of love, there's far less of that here because ... love is something other than the figure that's being moulded. It's the work that she does.' In the play he invokes Kafka while he has acknowledged the relevance of *Vertigo* ('I didn't go into it thinking that, but that kind of sense is certainly in there'), though 'there's less of the beautiful mood that's evoked in that.'[10]

Beyond the story of a confidence trickster, then, lies a debate about art and its relationship to experience, about the power which comes with transformation and about the extent to which character is itself a performance and identity a construct.

For Adam, art that reaches into other people's lives as though everything were available for appropriation, art generated less by an interest in form than by personal inadequacies, becomes a kind of therapy whose price is paid by others.

> if i totally miss the point here and somehow puking up your own little shitty neuroses all over people's laps *is* actually art, then you oughta at least realize there's a price to it all ... somebody pays for your two minutes on cnn. someone always pays for people like you. and if you don't get that, if you can't see at least *that* much ... then you're about two inches away from using babies to make lamp shapes and calling it 'furniture'. .... anybody can be provocative, or shocking. Stand up in class, or at the mall, wherever, and take a piss, paint yourself blue and run naked through a church screaming out the names of people you've slept with. is that art, or did you just forget to take your ritalin? there's gotta be a line. For art to exist, there has to be a line out there somewhere. a line between really saying something and just ... needing attention. (132–3)

Both Adam and Evelyn quote from Oscar Wilde, Adam recalling his observation that 'all art is quite useless', Evelyn presuming he would have preferred, 'insincerity and treachery seem inseparable from the artistic temperament.' (134) The quotations are deployed as part of their argument but they are hardly irrelevant to a central concern of *the shape of things*.

Apart from anything else, the play raises questions both about the manipulative nature of human relationships and the manipulative nature of art. What the artist serves is the end product. Often, people's lives are shamelessly appropriated by the writer, as their images are commandeered by the artist. It is not the truth of those lives that matters, but the truth of the work. There is nothing moral about the process of creating art of any kind. As W. G. Sebald observed, 'Writing is by definition a morally dubious occupation, I think, because one appropriates and manipulates the lives of others for certain ends.'[11] As LaBute has said, 'I know who Evelyn is, I understand her. In fact you could look at the piece and imagine it's as much about writers as it is about fine artists because writers in general are fairly cannibalistic, are vampiric and looking to take from some other source, so I see that in myself. So I can use a situation in the paper or a conversation with a loved one and feel it emotionally, but also looking from the point of view of boy, I'd love to poach a portion of that and feed it into my work.'[12]

Evelyn both appropriates others to create her art and displays a disturbing sense of detachment, which makes her seem no more than a Machiavel but potentially underlines her status as an artist. Like a writer, she remains detached from the lives of those she creates and there is, arguably, an amorality to art. When, in *Something Happened*, Joseph Heller has a man accidentally kill his son – an extraordinarily painful passage to read – there was, he confessed,

> a smile on my face ... I had had that down in my notebook for years before I came to it ... I treasured it like a miser, a rare diamond. The same thing happened in *Catch-22*. In that novel, towards the end, I describe in detail the death of a rear-gunner called Snowdon, who had been dying all through the book.

88

I remember this vividly. I wrote that scene as about six hand-written pages in one evening. I knew it was right and I sat back and wanted to laugh ... it is a part of the book that I hoped would bring readers almost to the verge of tears when they read it. There is something cold and manipulative in writing those passages in a novel in which I intended to have an emotional effect upon the reader.[13]

W. G. Sebald has remarked, 'I think Graham Greene said some-where that most writers have a splinter of ice in their heart. This seems to me a very perceptive remark because writers have to look at things in a certain way. There is this horrible moment when you discover, almost with a sense of glee, something that, although in itself horrid, will fit exactly with your scheme of things!'[14]

Asked if he would define what Evelyn does as art (her trans-formation of Adam turning out to be a project for her masters thesis), LaBute replied:

Sure I would. I would define it as art because she's defined it as that. I wouldn't disagree with her that it's art. So I think it's good art? Or useful art? There [are] three statements Goethe said and the last one was, 'was it worth doing?' I suppose that would be the big question for me. I don't devalue it as her work and if she believes it ... it's such a fine, subjective line. I certainly believe in that side of the argument, that it's so subjective that they can both be right. He can see it as shit and she can see it as art and neither one has to be wrong about that, so whether he sees it as art is different to whether I would do it.[15]

As he explained elsewhere,

I'm big on the argument the film proposes about subjectivity ... This [picks up glass of water] can be art because you made it, or it can be a glass of water to me and I can think you're a loon for calling it art, and we could both be right. So I'm big on 'I'm okay, you're okay' but if pushed, it turns quickly into 'I'm okay, you're a piece of shit.' Because ultimately ... I'm happy to come out even, but if forced, I want to come out on top. And that's what was happening up there, two people who are having an argument about something, where one's having a breakup and one's having a discussion about art – we often just see things through our own lens and it's difficult to understand what somebody else is saying when we're so driven to take care of our own need.[16]

Has Evelyn, however, not also paid a price? Surely, the arch-manipulator, betrayer of trust, calculated seeker of advantage, faces something more than a possible reprimand from the Dean for her actions. Her version of the artist is one that disavows 'religion or government, community or even family'. (122) Art must be created 'whatever the cost'. (122) But is it the art she serves or the grade she is hoping to secure through it in what is, after all, her thesis project, a means to an end? If Adam is socially isolated as a result of her ministrations, does she face much less having publicly displayed her capacity for treachery, her willingness to make public the most intimate of exchanges? As she leaves, she claims to be about to 'hook up with some guys from my department', (135) but it hard to believe that 'the guys' or anyone else will put much faith in her now. Certainly no one turns up at the reception which follows her exhibition.

LaBute himself claims to have noticed the extent of the price she pays, in part, at least, as a result of the shift from stage to film. Nor was it a matter of changes in dialogue. If the close-up gives a certain power to the director, as he pre-empts the choice of audience attention, it also cedes authority to the actor. Speaking of Rachel Weisz, who played the role of Evelyn, he says,

> I think she altered the course of the film ... she knows what the camera is capable of ... suddenly there's a switch in the story – I started to get a sense of what it had cost this young person, what she had perpetrated on this other guy. And Paul [Rudd] immediately spotted this and said, 'What is she doing? She's pulling the sympathy away from me.' And I realised that but it actually balanced the argument in a way that we hadn't seen before, so I let her do this and she changed the course of something we'd been doing happily for eight months and made something new and, I think, equally valid and exciting.[17]

The argument is, of course, hardly balanced but an element of ambiguity was already inherent in the text. Adam, after all, is scarcely innocent. He readily collaborates in his own seduction. His version of love is not without its masochistic dimension as he equates a surrender of will and moral judgement with personal commitment. His character is moulded because it is obligingly plastic. In one sense he might seem to do no more than make those adjustments necessary to accommodate the desires of others, except that this involves the deceit, betrayal and, ultimately, abandonment of his friends. In the final moments of the play, and following his public humiliation, he remains dependent on Evelyn. She has only to suggest that one of the things she once whispered in his ear was true – as opposed to everything else about herself and their relationship – for him to put on the cassette, on which she had insisted he record their love-making, and spin it back and forth in search of this elusive moment of supposed truth. He does so wearing the jacket she had once forced him to abandon, like a comfort blanket, if also a gesture of independence, but, the stage direction tells us, '*what is being said remains elusive. Unheard. He continues.*' There appears to be no substance to her remark or, indeed, to him.

But there is something else about this transformation. It is not merely that she has reshaped him but that she has reshaped him according to a particular paradigm. A young, Jewish, neurotic, vaguely bohemian young man is slowly changed into an apparently non-Jewish, middle-class, middlebrow preppy figure who could easily pass muster in this conservative town. But there is surely something altogether recognisable about this drift towards conformity. It scarcely takes a manipulative figure to effect such a transformation. What Evelyn does to Adam is what society does to most. If there is a way of behaving or looking that is more likely to bring about the satisfaction of desires – whether real or invented, sexual or social – then this is a price paid by more than Adam.

And who is Evelyn? She offers Adam one version of herself. She is, she explains, twenty-five years old, with a history of self-mutilation, and at the age of sixteen had had a nose job as a birthday present from her Jewish parents. At the end of the play she insists that she is twenty-two, non-Jewish and, despite what appear to be the scars on her wrists, had never mutilated herself. Which is the truth? And who is the real Adam, the clay from which Evelyn sculpts or the finished product? These are shape shifters.

Nor is Evelyn the only manipulator or deceiver. Adam's old room mate, Phil, has had an affair with his fiancée Jenny's namesake and seems anything but committed to his impending marriage. Jenny, meanwhile, is seduced by the new Adam so carefully constructed by Evelyn. Even as Adam is declaring his love for Evelyn he and Jenny are having a brief liaison which prompts Phil, in turn, to respond to Evelyn's overtures. This sexual dance may be orchestrated by Evelyn but she is not the only mover. Nothing is quite what it seems while betrayal appears a natural instinct. Asked by Evelyn to abandon his friends as evidence of his love for her, though in fact as part of her plan to reconstruct him, he does so with surprising alacrity.

LaBute is fascinated by the sacrifices individuals are willing to make in return for very little, for momentary satisfactions, the evanescent thrill of power, for what seems like love but which often appears little more than social convenience or an antidote to tedium. In a sense this is to say that he is fascinated by the gap between stimulus and response. Sometimes that gap is a moral one, sometimes little more than a failure to understand or engage with the notion of consequence. Some restraining force seems to be absent. What is lacking is empathy but beyond that a sense that there is any human imperative that supersedes self-interest. It is hard to think of a relationship in his work, outside those in his film adaptation of *Possession*, that is anything more than a misalliance. As he has said, 'A lot of those people ... are fuelled by not knowing how to communicate – they're over-communicating or under-communicating. They try to get their needs met, but they don't know exactly what they are looking for. So they stumble along and try these outlandish ways of making it happen.'[18]

On one level, *the shape of things* is plainly about a woman's manipulation of a young man to serve her own ends and, beyond that, of an artist's willingness to subordinate everything to her art. There is, however, something more than that. William Carlos Williams once remarked of his writings that, 'they are things I write because to maintain myself in a world much of which I didn't love I had to fight to keep myself as I wanted to be.'[19] The work is not free-standing but a claim on significance and meaning. As Wallace Stevens observed, 'The imagination is the power of the mind over the possibilities of things.' (1) In *the shape of things*, Adam seems shapeless before Evelyn imagines him into being and in doing so she herself stakes a claim to create not only him but herself. She acts. Where Adam seems adrift, she seizes control. She exists through acting on others and for her language is as much a tool of art as her ability to transform a man happy to surrender his will to hers.

She is an artist of language. Indeed, this is her primary tool. In her hands words are wholly malleable and in that she is entirely human. As Jean Piaget notes, 'if the function of language were merely to "communicate", the phenomenon of verbalism would hardly admit of explanation. How could words, confined as they are by usage to certain precise meanings (precise because their subject is to be understood), eventually come to veil the confusion of thought, even to create obscurity ... and actually prevent thought being communicable?' (11)

Language is precisely designed to be malleable. Evelyn lies but does so in order to transform Adam into a form she has first to imagine. And, the humiliation aside, is his final state worse than his initial one? Like the original Adam he has been gifted sexuality and knowledge, knowledge that radical transformations are possible. As Clyde Kluckhohn has said, 'language is an instrument for action ... We use words to promote our own purposes in dealing with others. We build up verbal pictures of ourselves and our motives. We coax, wheedle, protest, invite, and threaten.' (14) Evelyn obligingly confesses to the fact that she had 'coaxed' (120) Adam.

If it be objected that Evelyn is purely selfish then this is perhaps to say no more than that she is indeed an artist. In his book on the rhetoric of the imagination, James E. Miller Jr. quotes from Hermann Hesse and Georges Simenon. In *Demian*, Hesse writes: "I did not exist to write poems, to preach or to paint, neither I nor anyone else. All that was incidental. Each man had only one genuine vocation – to find the way to himself.' (112) For Simenon, 'if a man has an urge to be an artist, it is because he needs to find himself. Every writer tries to find himself through his characters, through all his writing.' (115)

For all Evelyn's self-justifications, her pretended objectivity with respect to her 'project' (even as she confesses to the subjectivity of art), there are hints of an altogether different reason for her actions. There are moments when a different Evelyn bursts through. Not merely does she refer bitterly to her own sense of victimisation in her youth and thereafter, but, speaking of Phillip she says that, 'the only thing that would help him is a fucking knife through his throat.' (43) The very disproportion of her response suggests something she cannot or will not articulate.

If Adam has been turned into a work of art does that mean that he is not real and that the former Adam had been? Because he has been shaped by Evelyn is he different from the Adam who had simply been shaped by an upbringing that had brought him to this liberal college in a conservative town? And has she, perhaps, not indeed done him a favour? He was, he confesses, 'nothing until you started dicking around with me. I admit it. No-thing.' (124) But, he insists that he was 'absolutely fine with that,' though in fact she seems accurate enough when she says that he had had no friends, Phil and Jenny aside, while even their friendship seems to have been more tenuous than it first appeared. Now, she asserts, he is 'a more desirable person ... people begin to notice you.' Is it deceit, then, that is the root of our potential objection, the fact that she failed to spell out her intentions, or that she served her intellectual rather than emotional needs, let alone her taste for power? Since in ordinary relationships people are not necessarily even aware of the transformations they nonetheless work to effect, thereby deceiving themselves, it is difficult to establish a distinction. As to the distinction between emotional and intellectual needs, this is surely difficult to specify, each frequently masquerading as the other. Who is to say of Evelyn that her motives are as she presents them? Indeed she hints at aspects of her own past that have made mastery of her situation a compensatory necessity. As she has sculpted him so she has sculpted herself. She confesses to having 'manufactured' (122) her emotions. If she creates 'strong moral ambiguity' in Adam, so she does in herself.

She has, she suggests, always been in thrall to others and, indeed, remains so in so far as her work is to be graded and any infraction liable to attract a summons by those in authority. There is a hint of something in her youth, which she fails to specify but which explains, perhaps, her desire to manipulate others, to behave without mercy. Given her unreliability, however, it is difficult to know whether this, in turn, is a further piece of deception. After all, she says of herself that 'I'm a very straightforward person,' (125) as F. Scott Fitzgerald's Nick Carraway had insisted that he was the most honest person he knew, a man with the capacity to deceive himself as well as others. Both are unreliable narrators. If Gatsby was self-invented he is invented anew by Carraway who constructs a figure ultimately to serve his own ends. The Gatsby we see is the Gatsby Nick chooses to present, physically attractive, morally insecure. But for Carraway and Evelyn alike, morality is beside the point while, like Gatsby, Evelyn tends to see life through a single window.

As Adam becomes more desirable so he accretes power and with power seems to come a moral ambivalence. He lies, betrays, deceives. It is as though the more he conforms to a model of the desirable the greater the licence he feels able to claim. As LaBute himself has said, 'I think that's part of what [Evelyn] is putting forward [though] I didn't see this necessarily when I started this, but the more conventionally attractive he became, the more opportunity he was afforded, and the greater chance he had of stumbling . . . I don't think it's a crazy notion to say that we are driven, in American culture, by a lot of those things.'[20]

The audience, in stage and film versions alike, have been seduced in the same way as Adam and feel something of the same ambivalence. For all that Evelyn has taken advantage of him, the end product is more attractive than the original as a portrait is liable to offer an idealised version of its subject, and the audience registers this fact. There is a trade involved and, beyond the moment, it is by no means certain that Adam has come off second best. While being remodelled he has presumably learned something not only about others but also about himself. As LaBute has said,

I think he's . . . victimized without being a complete victim. I don't feel as if everything that's happened to him, he's been

completely at the mercy of Evelyn. I think there are points along
the way where he's given an opportunity and he fails. Jenny goes
so far as to kiss him – he didn't have to kiss back. He didn't have
to lie to his friends, he didn't have to say I'll give my friends up.
He didn't have to lie when asked about what happened to his
nose. [There are] a lot of lies and treachery that Adam begins to
foster on his friends. I can't see him as a complete victim. It's also
hard because when you look at him, the changes have been pretty
positive in terms of what we think of as handsome and fit and all
those things. It wasn't like she was saying, 'Hey, look, I want to
see just how far I can make this guy fall apart, so I'm going to get
him to stop running and wear more slovenly clothes.' Because in
a traditional sense, since he looks better in the end, we tend to
think he's a better person. But as Evelyn points out, that means
nothing. (Director's Commentary)

That final remark, of course, underscores the moral ambivalence of a
piece which seems to offer the portrait of a Machiavel, an Iago, but
which is finally about something more than a manipulative personality, a study in power.

Adam, meanwhile, lies about his plastic surgery out of embarrassment that he should have resorted to it and done so at Evelyn's urging. He
betrays his friends because the end seems to justify the means. Which is
the real Adam, the dishevelled, naive, vulnerable, uncommitted, inex-
perienced student or the stylish, sexually experienced, attractive young
man whose love for a woman seems to have rescued him from an
unfocused and apparently vacuous existence even as it has validated
behaviour that would once have dismayed him? He remains vulnerable,
to be sure, but this is the vulnerability of commitment rather than
innocence. He has, in other words, become wise in the ways of the
world. But are these characters any more or any less than actors. Evelyn
is playing a role, to be sure, but are the others not?

As Erving Goffman observed in *The Presentation of Self in
Everyday Life*,

> When an individual plays a part he implicitly requests his
> observers to take seriously the impression that is fostered before

them. They are asked to believe that the character they see actually possesses the attributes he appears to possess ... that, in general, matters are what they appear to be ... At one extreme, one finds that the performer can be fully taken in by his own act; he can be sincerely convinced that the impression of reality which he stages is the real reality ... At the other extreme ... the performer may be moved to guide the conviction of his audience only as a means to other ends ... When the individual has no belief in his own act ... we may call him cynical, reserving the term 'sincere' for individuals who believe in the impression fostered by their own performance. It should be understood that the cynic, with all his professional disinvolvement, may obtain unprofessional pleasure from this masquerade, experiencing a kind of gleeful spiritual aggression from the fact that he can toy at will with something his audience take seriously.[21]

This would seem to be precisely the distinction between Evelyn and Adam, except that Goffman's reference to 'the impression of reality', to an apparent sincerity, alerts us to the extent to which he reminds us that the real is itself permeated with performance. Indeed he recalls that the word 'person' owes its derivation to the word for mask and that our sense of ourselves may be intimately related to the version of ourselves we choose to present to the world. It is in that sense that he invokes Simone de Beauvoir's observation that when a woman makes herself up, wears particular underclothes, dyes her hair, 'she is, like the picture or the statue, or the actor on the stage, an agent through whom is suggested someone not there – that is the character she represents, but is not ... she strives to identify herself with this figure and thus to seem to herself to be stabilized.' (65) This is not a distinction between reality and artifice, appearance and being, but an acknowledgement of their interpenetration.

LaBute has said of Evelyn, who consistently deceives Adam and misrepresents her past, her feelings and her intentions, 'I consider her to be a very truthful person, in fact she tells the truth when you don't necessarily want to hear it. But I knew within the parameters of what she was doing, she would have to lie.' How, then, is she truthful?

Adam, meanwhile, who seems the innocent victim of her contrivances, is apparently happy to adopt a new persona, lying with a seemingly spontaneous ease. Truth, then, as LaBute insists, 'is such an elusive thing'. At what point does the performed self become the self? When the film version moved the action from New York to Los Angeles, it seemed particularly appropriate to him 'because the heart of the thing is obviously theatrical'. That notion would extend to his approach to the filming itself, with theatrical sets and, as he explained, 'movement limited within the frame'.

In the theatre, that theatricality was underscored by his staging of the scene in which Evelyn finally presents her 'thesis' to those assembled in the art gallery. As he explained, 'When that scene happens in the play, the fourth wall is abandoned and the actors go and sit in the theatre and her audience for her exhibit becomes the audience who's watching the show.' When she asks those who had seemingly assembled for her exhibition if they have any questions, the theatre audience is invited to take part and frequently, both in London and New York, did so: 'Whether that was, "Hey, you want to do that to me?" or "Can I ask you out?" Sometimes, "Why are you such a bitch?"' This, of course, as he confesses, is precisely what is not possible in cinema.

> The audience is now watching an audience watch her rather than actually just watching her. When I realized that was going to be the case – that I didn't want her talking to the camera the whole time, I thought, 'How am I going to replace that very fun theatrical trick?' Well, I couldn't, ultimately. I used it once – there's a moment when she looks into the camera and flips off the audience in essence, but that's the only time I broke the fourth wall ... so what worked as kind of a performance piece suddenly became less than that on screen.

The 'flip off' consists of her lowering her microphone, staring at the camera, raising the middle finger of both hands and mouthing the words, 'Fuck You.'[22] For LaBute, 'the theatrical quality' of the scene in the stage production was 'so great that I just couldn't capture it [in the film]. So, I felt that the punch of this scene was still intact, what had happened', between Evelyn and Adam, 'but the feeling that that elicited by actually having her do it right to your face was impossible to replicate'. (Director's Commentary)

The meta-theatrical gesture in the stage version served to draw attention more directly to the performed nature of experience as, individually and collectively, the audience were turned into actors, pulled into the play which a moment earlier they could observe as if there were a protective membrane between them and what was enacted. For LaBute, the moment that audience members realise that they too have been deceived by this woman is akin to children's theatre 'seeing the bad person coming up behind the hero ... you want to scream out loud, "Watch your back!"'

It also served as a reminder of the fact that the play itself is no less a construction than the project that Evelyn undertook, that it invites a moral collusion which is on a par with that invited by Evelyn as she turns private experience into public art. But if the audience is collusive it is also deceived. It effectively re-enacts the process which Adam undergoes. As LaBute has said, 'I ... wanted it to be a painful thing, because I want you to like Adam. Yeah, he makes some bad choices along the way, but I still want you to like him, because that makes it more painful for the audience when you find out what's happening to him. At the same time it's happening to him, it's happening to you. You've been lied to the whole movie as well. It's not as if she's let you in on it. Somebody may guess it, but for the most part she's lying to everybody including the audience.' (Director's Commentary)

For LaBute, Rachel Weisz's approach to her character 'changed from the stage which is a very presentational medium where you have an audience who essentially become her audience for her thesis project'. She 'worked the crowd like a lawyer or a circus clown. She was able to state her case with the very audience she has misled in a really seductive theatrical way.' With the film it was necessary to find a different approach. But if film closed down one possibility it opened another. As he explained, 'she probably played her final scene with greater emotion than she ever did in the theatre ... a camera can go right up into her face and detect flickers across the eye or a wiped-away tear in a much more, almost violent, way than you can in the very confined, non-changing space that is a theatre.' As a result 'there was a much greater split between who was right and who was wrong in the stage play' as opposed to the film, in which viewers are 'very torn emotionally' and 'the gray areas' were emphasised.

Speaking of Rachel Weisz's film performance, LaBute remarked, 'even in her eye it is almost as if she is about to cry. On stage you didn't feel that. She was so cold. And cruel about it ... It was a really strong, powerful performance. But here [on film] that ambiguity is how does she really feel about [Adam]?' (Director's Commentary)

That aside, in moving from stage to screen *the shape of things* changed relatively little. LaBute's fondness for retaining aspects of theatre, a product of necessity in his first film, here had an added significance in a work in part concerned with performance. Rachel Weisz has said that 'all of Neil's films are like plays ... in that the characters get to speak a lot and the camera doesn't move around very much ... Neil's films hold the two-shot and the two people talk in that two-shot for maybe ten minutes. There's no editing, so that's what makes it seem play-like.'[23] The two-shot is, perhaps, in part a reflection of the dynamic of *the shape of things* in that six of the ten scenes involve two characters in conversation. It is primarily the nature of these relationships which compels, their privacies only breaking surface in the penultimate scene in which Evelyn consciously chooses to deny the division between private and public, art and life, as all four characters find themselves an audience to their own lives.

LaBute has remarked that 'We are accused of being theatrical but if you saw this in a Mike Leigh film you'd just think it was cool. It is interesting the path that a play takes, something that has had a genesis as a play and that then goes over to being a film. If you want to retain that, to give people a flavour of it rather than pretend that it didn't exist in another form, I don't think you can escape it.' The paradigm is Mike Nichols' film of Edward Albee's *Who's Afraid of Virginia Woolf?* which, with the exception of an unnecessary scene set outside the claustrophobic environment of their living room, carried over the single set of the play. For LaBute, the effect is to put the emphasis back on the writing and the acting, something he, himself, favours: 'I am just always drawn to the actors and what's being said.' (Director's Commentary) By the same token, he avoided complicated camera moves:

> They're just little push-ins and slides from one end of a room to another. It really makes sense for a film of this kind. I try, as often as I can, to not call attention to myself, to not have mood music, to not overcut, not say, 'look at me, look at this crazy, clever shot.' I think that directors have to find a way to overshoot a scene that's been underwritten. Even though it's my own writing, it's nice to work on something that has a lot of writing. Movies used to have tons of dialogue ... In the last thirty years we've been relying much more on effects and spectacle rather than good solid writing.
>
> People mistakenly think that shooting a long take ... is saving you money. But the fact that you're doing all these lines means that if you make a mistake you've got no coverage, you've got to go back and do it over and over. So there is no saving in terms of money. It's an aesthetic choice. You either like it or you don't. For me, I like those things when actors get to act together all the time rather than just feeding lines off-camera to each other. (Director's Commentary)

He resists the temptation to 'open up' the picture, to seize on the supposed freedom of film, choosing, instead, to film in a way that far from concealing its theatrical origins, underscores them. 'People are moving in and out of frame,' he explained,

> and the frame never moves. I'm a big fan of that. I know that people can look at this kind of film and think, oh, it's too talky or it's too much like going to the theatre. I can never see that as a negative thing. I so love going to the theatre that I want to embrace that. And I love using the wide screen, anamorphic lenses, to shoot this very intimate movie because you force people onto the side of the screen and I leave all this empty space which I think is beautiful. (Director's Commentary)

It was an observation which served to emphasise his debt to Woody Allen. Speaking of his film *Manhattan* he remarked that it had occurred to him that it would be 'fun to work in black-and-white [as LaBute had wished to shoot *in the company of men*] and it would be fun to work in anamorphic, in real wide-screen ... it would be very interesting to do an intimate picture like that.'[24]

It is tempting to think that he also derived from Allen his fondness for allowing actors to leave the frame, a device which he first tried in *Annie Hall* but which he thereafter used in a number of films. In *Annie Hall*, 'Annie and Alvy are talking and arguing, and then I leave the frame to get some books. Then she leaves the frame and there's nobody at all in picture ... in *Husbands and Wives* the camera is just fighting for its life to keep the characters in frame.'[25] LaBute uses precisely this technique in *the shape of things* and in *Your Friends & Neighbors*.

In the final scene, Adam confronts Evelyn. The sparse audience to her presentation has now entirely withdrawn. It is a confrontation in which neither character wins but Paul now emerges as someone with decided opinions, especially about the morality of art (a scene cut somewhat in the film version). 'I am happy,' LaBute has said,

> that we've ended the way that we do, that there is no resolution here, that there is no scene of him getting a chance to talk to Jenny and say 'I am sorry,' or seeing Evelyn break down after being what people might consider a horrible person. I don't. It's hard for me to look at her and say that she is a horrible person. I think what's nice about this piece is that it gives equal time to both sides ... I don't believe in her methodology, but I understand her drive to create, to make something artistic and that to her as a student it is more important than anything else, more important than [Adam's] feelings. I don't believe that as a person but I absolutely believe that she does. And you have to be true to your characters. I am not here to be true to the audience ... characters sometimes go unpunished, because that is the way things work out in life. (Director's Commentary)

6 *The Mercy Seat*: a crucible of conscience

I should've known
It was coming down to this
I should've known
You would betray me but without the kiss
I should've known
The kind of set-up it is.

I should've seen the cracks in the ceiling
And the mirror covered up with dust
But I was busy talking on the phone
I should've seen the obstacles but I said,
This house was built for us
Hello
Is anybody home?

I should've known
The minute that we hit the wall
I should've known
The writing was upon the stall
I should've known
'cause Rome was starting to fall.

> Aimee Mann, 'I Should've Known'

When the *Titanic* set off from Berth 44 in Southampton on
10 April 1912, it carried a seaman by the name of Thomas Hart, except
that it was not him because he had lost his discharge book in a pub and
never sailed on board. Who his counterfeit might have been was never

known. Yet another sailor smuggled himself off the ship at Queenstown and hence appeared in the list of the dead. He lived on, it is assumed, though under what name and embracing what fate was never discovered. One of the passengers called Michael Navratil registered as Hoffman, the better to effect the kidnapping of two children. And he was not the only one on board to attempt a kidnapping. When the ship sank and fifteen hundred of its two thousand passengers died in the ice-cold waters of the North Atlantic there was one at least who thought to grasp the moment. Mrs Leek Aks saw her ten-month old son, Frank, wrenched from her by a steward and passed down to Elizabeth Nye, already in a lifeboat. When Nye reached the *Carpethia* she claimed the child as her own. Did people change their character in a single moment that night, or reveal it to themselves and others? Which the mask, which the true self? At the very moment of disaster there were, it seems, those who decided to seize their chance, finding advantage where others were overwhelmed.

On 11 September 2001, at 8.46 EST an American Airlines Boeing 767, flying from Boston to Los Angeles, crashed into the North Tower of the World Trade Center in New York. Seventeen minutes later, a United Airlines 767, also flying from Boston to Los Angeles, crashed into the South Tower. At 10.05 the South Tower collapsed, followed twenty-three minutes later by the North Tower. Grey ash spread out across the city and up into the sky, turning the sun blood red. 2,752 people had died, though it was to be many weeks and even months before the details of who had lived and who had died was clear. And even then the information was incomplete.

On 3 October 2001, Carlton McNish reported that his wife had died at the World Trade Center. He filled out an affidavit in order to receive a death certificate and his wife's name was added to the list of missing. A memorial service was held and he received over $100,000 from charities. McNish is now serving time for grand larceny. There was no Mrs McNish. In 2002, a Manhattan woman was also charged with grand larceny, falsely claiming that her father had died in the disaster. In 2003 Patric Henn received $68,000 from the Red Cross having claimed that his partner had been killed in the attack. When police concluded that the partner had never existed, a warrant was issued for his arrest. In 2004 Terry James Smith was found guilty of defrauding the American

Red Cross and others of \$136,000 by falsely claiming that his wife had died in the World Trade Center attacks and that he had ten children to support. His wife was in fact living in Jamaica and was supporting a single child. He gambled the money away in San Diego and Las Vegas.

9/11 spawned a disturbing number of criminal cases as it slowly emerged that FBI and other government officials had stolen artefacts from Ground Zero, that bogus charities were set up, false claims submitted (including some of the claims for nearly three hundred thousand air-conditioners and vacuums to deal with contaminated air and dust), family members invented only to meet a fictional and ultimately lucrative death. At a moment of trauma, and shortly thereafter, there were those whose minds were focused not on a shared pain, the desire to help or mourn, but on the opportunities unexpectedly and fortuitously opened up by disaster.

Not least among their number was an American administration heavily influenced by those who in the 1990s had been part of the Project for a New American Century and who now found themselves in a position of power. Hence, virtually the first direction given by President George W. Bush was to explore the supposed involvement of Iraq, that country having been high on the list of the neo-conservatives. The effect was to convince a high proportion of American citizens that 9/11 had involved a state with whom they would, in truth, soon go to war. Private exploitation of catastrophe plainly had its parallel in a public exploitation. The question is, do both have their roots in the same impulse? Is human nature naturally attuned to casuistry and self-interest? Is a natural empathy balanced by an equally natural impetus to exploitation? Are there no limits to which we will not go, individually or collectively, no betrayals of which we may not be capable?

In England, as people watched transfixed at the sight of both towers ablaze and people leaping to their deaths, a senior adviser to the British Secretary of State for Transport, Local Government and the Regions sent a memo suggesting that it was 'a very good day to get out anything we want to bury'.[1] A calamity was to be embraced as an opportunity.

LaBute was not in New York on 11 September. He was in Chicago getting ready to fly to New York to start rehearsals for *the shape of things* on the 13th. All flights were cancelled and he had to take the train. While horrified by what had happened, in common with all those people stranded around the country, he was also irritated at the delay. He was not alone, nor was 9/11 the only trauma which sparked such momentary apparent unconcern. In *The Discomfort Zone* Jonathan Franzen confesses that flying back to New York in 2005, in the immediate aftermath of a hurricane that had devastated New Orleans, 'I worried that Katrina's aftermath might create unpleasant turbulence on my flight.'[2] It was possible, it seemed, to be simultaneously moved by other people's pain and to detach oneself from this and respond on another level. As LaBute later remarked of his irritation on that day, 'I remember thinking, "Ooh, that's not a very good thought to have" ... I knew it wasn't right, but the thought had already come out.'[3]

In March 2002, however, he found himself on a plane, for a vacation with his children, and for the first time thought what someone might do if they had a chance to draw a line across their lives and begin again. The events of that September Tuesday were to be not the subject but the necessary pre-condition for the play he now wrote: *The Mercy Seat*. After a series of plays/films set in anonymous places at indefinite dates, here was a work that required a specific location and timeframe.

The single set of *The Mercy Seat* is covered in dust, the residue of the towers and a constant reminder of what has happened. This was not, he explained, to be 'a play that concerns itself with the politics of terrorism ... but it is a particular kind of terrorism: the painful, simplistic warfare we often wage on the hearts of those we profess to love'.[4] The irony, of course, was that a play in which a character exploits 9/11 should be a play that could itself be accused of doing the same. It opened, in New York, just fourteen months after the attack and he was nervous that New York audiences would resist a work that turned on this traumatising moment but which seemed to exist to one side of the flag-waving celebration of solidarity that for a while had appeared the only legitimate response to an external assault.

Indeed, one of the two actors he cast, Sigourney Weaver (the other being Liev Schreiber), had just been appearing in another play, Anne Nelson's *The Guys*, which precisely expressed that mood. Anne

Nelson, a journalism professor who had never written a play, had been asked to help a New York fire captain write eulogies for eight of his men who had been lost in the attack. A chance meeting with the artistic director of the Flea Theatre, whose audiences had plummeted from ninety per cent to five per cent following the attack (it was situated five blocks from Ground Zero), resulted in a work for two characters, based on Nelson and the fire captain. Staged just three months after 9/11, it was a play about healing in which the two people bring out the best in one another as they celebrate the lives of those who have been lost.

The contrast with LaBute's play could not have been greater. *The Mercy Seat* also features two characters but it is not a work about healing, or the need to come together. It is a play about deceit, betrayal (Liev Schreiber's last Broadway appearance, ironically, had been in Harold Pinter's *Betrayal*), cruelty, the slow, and not so slow, attrition of love. Ground Zero became not simply a place but a metaphor. In *The Mercy Seat*, LaBute explained, he was 'trying to examine the "ground zero" of our lives, that gaping hole in ourselves that we try to cover up with clothes from The Gap, with cologne from Ralph Lauren, with handbags from Kate Spade. Why are we willing to run a hundred miles around simply to say to someone, "I don't know if I love you any-more?" Why? Because Nikes are cheap, running is easy, and honesty is the hardest, coldest currency on the planet.' (Preface, p. x)

The reference to The Gap is not fortuitous. Elsewhere, he recalled that when the rubble was cleared away from one of the fire engines, neatly folded piles of clothes from The Gap were found. Before the true seriousness of things was known, even firemen, who were to be elevated to the role of heroes, were not averse to taking advantage of a moment of anarchy, firemen being no more or less than human beings. LaBute considered writing an insert for the programme outlining this incident but thought better of it, as well he might since the play itself is a demonstration of precisely that kind of moral ambivalence, a prioritising of the self even at a moment of maximum stress which seems to demand solidarity. Plainly, *The Guys* and *The Mercy Seat* were at opposite ends of the spectrum and Sigourney Weaver was faced with a radical change of direction.

Speaking in 2003, LaBute observed that

Time has proved me right, you know ... In the two years since 9/11, there have been a number of people who either used the day to disappear or to capitalise on it in some way, usually monetarily. With an event like that, the problem is the American media tends to make it simpler, they create a unified response. All over CNN it was 'America attacked! America responds! America unites!' All that sort of thing. I just knew it couldn't be all that simple, that this story was made up of thousands of small stories, and not all of them had to be courageous.[5]

In a preface dated October 2002, LaBute explained the origin and intent of the play. Its sometimes defensive tone says something about his concern for its reception. 'I don't know exactly why I put fingers to keyboard on this one,' he noted. 'It was rewarding and painful to be part of. I love it and I hate it. It is what it is. So be it.' (x) These are odd remarks justified by the sensitivities he suspected he might be offending, as if he were appropriating a national disaster for his own ends, as Evelyn, in *the shape of things*, had justified her appropriation of another person's life in the name of art. The act of writing the play was thus close in spirit to the play's subject which is also, in part, concerned with appropriation. When it opened in New York, the reaction was mixed.

As he explained, 'There was a sense in New York especially of it being too soon to have artistic work that was dealing with what happened, and certainly too early for work that was at all sceptical of how a survivor might have dealt with that day in a dishonourable way. Many people seemed to appreciate the play for what it really was – a relationship drama that played out against the backdrop of a larger disaster – but many people felt that I was peddling in dirty laundry or trying to make a dime off somebody else's sorrow.' Understanding the sensitivity of the New York audience in particular, he nonetheless insisted on the legitimacy of his play and in doing so staked out his essential philosophy as a writer: 'I think we're far too afraid of pain in life – I know I am – and so that's why I find myself pushing it on the page. Trying to see where somebody else might take it, how they react, if there actually is a way to rise above some of the crap that I throw at these characters. My plays often end up being a crucible of conscience.'[6]

The Mercy Seat was not the only work responding to 9/11. In November 2001, Paul McCartney wrote 'Freedom' while two months later the country-and-western singer Alan Jackson wrote 'Where Were You When the World Stopped Turning?', feeling guilty as he did so for fear he might be seen as taking advantage of other people's suffering. In March 2002 came Neil Young's 'Let's Roll', a celebration of those on board United Airlines Flight 93 in which the passengers had fought back. In July, Bruce Springstein released 'The Rising', based on his conversations with 9/11 widows. Most works were celebratory or commemorative, though Eric Fischl's 'Tumbling Woman', a sculpture inspired by those who leaped from the Twin Towers, was removed from Rockefeller Center following protests. The first novel to engage the events, Extremely Loud and Incredibly Close, by Jonathan Safran Foer, appeared nine months after the Towers fell. Frederic Beigbeder's Windows on the World was published in 2003 and Don DeLillo's Falling Man in 2007. Writers, musicians, artists were by no means silent, but they were, perhaps, nervous. Emotions were still raw. In LaBute's case, though he was ostensibly not so much addressing the 9/11 cataclysm as using it as a context, a plot device, the human dereliction and failure of love at its heart being a microcosm of that more profound betrayal of human instincts which provides his setting.

The Mercy Seat is set in New York City 'not long ago', an odd description given what turns out to be the specificity of the context. It takes place in a spacious loft apartment whose stylish furniture is covered in white dust. Through the window, buildings are visible. There is an amber haze in the air. It is just after four in the morning. A man, Ben Harcourt, thirty-three years old, sits staring straight ahead, with a cellphone in his hand. It rings repeatedly. In the context of 9/11 it was an iconic sound, unanswered phones offering chilling evidence of the dead. After a moment, Abby Prescott, a stylishly dressed woman enters. She is described as 'about forty-five'. She, too, is covered in dust and begins putting groceries away until she can no longer stand the sound of the telephone and switches it off.

The towers have fallen and at first both characters seem to some degree in a state of shock, but their indecision and tension turn out to have another source. The catastrophe has merely created a new context for a long-deferred decision. The two are lovers and the calls, it transpires, are from Ben's wife, desperate to contact him. Plainly, to answer the call is, as Abby points out, 'the decent thing to do', (7) though in the context of an adulterous affair and her assumption that, before the attack, he had been about to call his wife to announce that he was leaving her, the word 'decent' is as ironic as it had been when Cary used it in *Your Friends & Neighbors*.

It was, LaBute said, a play 'about two New Yorkers who face down one another and their own selves on a long, dark morning of the soul. I hold the mirror up higher and try to examine how selfishness can still exist at a moment of national selflessness.' (x) That is, indeed, the thematic heart of the play, though the dark morning of the soul seems precisely what is squeezed out by the selfishness, even as the tears that are shed are a marker of something more than a personal drama. This is despite the fact that only one of the characters, Abby, chooses to give attention to what lies just beyond the window or to the dust which is evidence of something more than pulverised buildings. Certainly, audiences were aware that the nation had been at a moment of decision even as they were invited to watch a couple whose own dilemma was a reminder that public catastrophe had not obliterated private dramas.

Ben has clearly not stirred from the apartment. Abby, however, has and brings back news from the outside world. She does have a sense of the momentousness of what has occurred, even as her account of the anarchy beyond the windows comes back, seemingly inevitably, to their personal dilemma: 'the world has gone absolutely nuts out there [. . .] No idea what's happening, no one does, the army patrolling around – there are people in camouflage on the Brooklyn Bridge – and you're, I don't know, just ... don't know where you are.' (10) She accuses Ben of failing to react to either crisis in their lives, indeed of being indecisive by his very nature. But, beyond that, she feels a sense of disgust at a man who could see what has happened as an opportunity, 'a meal ticket', (12) who, after the shock, realised that he could simply disappear with Abby, joining the list of presumed dead and thus avoiding the confrontation with his wife which he is apparently unwilling to contemplate.

What Abby realises is that his indecisiveness is rooted in a lack of commitment of any kind. He remains in the apartment because to emerge would be to prejudice what seems his newly formulated plan to disappear. He must not be seen. They have discussed the attack, expressed their sense of relief to one another and the subsequent guilt at feeling such relief. But he is seemingly incapable of registering the full shock of the event not least because private issues take precedence. He falls back on a rhetoric whose falsity is a sign of something more than the incapacity of language to register trauma. For her part, Abby describes seeing a woman on the street fixing photographs of a young man on light poles, buildings, cars, with the slogan '"Have You Seen Him?" and a phone number.' (14). Implicit in this, of course, is his own failure to answer the telephone, to put an end to his own wife's fear and anxiety. Yet Abby, too, is complicit in this. As he points out, she has no more laid aside her private life to help people than he has. She has, after all, been urging him to abandon his wife to serve her own desires. Beyond that, there is a truth to the answer he offers to his own question,

> do you think we're not gonna rebound from this? And I don't just mean you and me, I'm saying the country as a whole. Of course we will. We'll do what it takes, go after whomever we need to, call out the tanks and shit, but we're gonna have the World Series, and Christmas ... We do it every year, no matter what's happened or is going on ... the American way is to overcome, to conquer, to come out on top. (16)

LaBute is prone to suggest that his plays are about relationships rather than commentaries on society. They are certainly concerned with the former, but they are also about the latter. A year on from 9/11, as audiences were aware, business in America, if not quite as usual, was still business. Patriotism required something more than a reactive retribution, and the usual distractions were available. Ben's self-justifying cant aside, there was also a disturbing truth in the ease with which other people's deaths had been accommodated, life had continued. Ben is merely faster off the mark than others, resentful that she would suggest disqualification simply on the grounds of the speed with which he has reacted.

There is, though, a subtext to their conversation. The tension between them derives from something more than her resentment at his apparent indecision. Indeed the surprise is that they had ever been drawn to one another in the first place. The gulf between them is more fundamental than a matter of the twelve years which separate them, twelve years which mean that they share little in the way of common cultural referents. They have profoundly different sensibilities. For him, knowledge for its own sake is 'useless . . . crap'. (19) There is no percentage in it. For her part, she is more than his intellectual superior. She is his actual superior, though he prefers the word colleague or co-worker, being resentful that she has never promoted him, resentful, indeed, that she beat him to her current job.

Whatever it had once been, their relationship now seems little more than an armed truce, an unequal battle in which his every utterance is an explanation of his inferior position. There are echoes of *Who's Afraid of Virginia Woolf?* in their linguistic battles. When Ben accuses Abby of wearing the slacks around here she replies, '*somebody's* got to,' (37) as Martha, in Albee's play, remarks, 'I wear the pants in this house because somebody's got to.'[7] Ben invokes his real twelve-year-old daughter as a weapon, imagining her crying for her father, as George and Martha had invoked their imaginary child. In the person of Ben, however, we are plainly dealing with a man lacking both in sensitivity and irony even as he lays claim to transforming himself.

He confesses to his weakness, to the fact that he has effectively faked his way through life, seizing the main chance without ever being in command of that life. Now the '*apocalyptic* shit' has given him a chance to 'erase the past . . . wash away a lot of the, just, rotten crap,' a chance which Abby insists is tainted because it is unearned, because he is once again being opportunistic. In contrast, she does have scruples, though not, oddly, about Ben's family. As a company executive she feels guilty that what she is doing is sexual harassment, a subject on which she has delivered lectures while conducting an affair with an employee, as she simultaneously suspects that their affair is his revenge on her for her elevation. It appears that she wants commitment, the very thing he cannot offer. A lengthy discussion of their sexual practices turns around the suggestion that it is itself evidence of evasion. His favourite word, meanwhile, is 'whatever', a linguistic shrug of the shoulders that will recur in a subsequent play about emotional dereliction, *The Distance From Here.*

On the other hand, for all of her complaints about Ben's lack of commitment, Abby remains remarkably unmoved by the events that have transpired outside her windows. She may invoke the dead, 'some of them our associates', (49) and confess to a sense of guilt, but this has not been sufficient to disable her emotionally let alone provoke her to try to discover who has survived and who not. Instead she spends her time talking to a man she suspects of being worthless, scoring points, accusing him of failings of which she is no less guilty for being articulate and seemingly morally sensitive. Her redemption is that she knows it. When Ben asks why she invokes the dead, she replies, 'I think I accidentally started to feel something for a moment. Sorry.' (49) Her irony, though, is not quite sufficient as a response, even if it stands in contrast to Ben's insistence that he is moved by the fact that people have died who he had 'had *coffee* with . . . I mean, all those guys from maintenance.' (50)

There is no pretence on LaBute's part that this is an equal contest – and there is a contest underway. Ben is disquieteningly insensitive, unaware of his moral crassness, liable to blurt out self-condemning remarks. When a neighbour, whose husband may have died, calls in search of milk for her children he is happy for her to have it because 'I don't even like 2 percent.' (52) The question is why LaBute chooses to make this such a one-sided relationship. Nothing we see can explain the attraction we are asked to believe Abby has felt and seemingly continues to feel. She had, she insists, wished to run away with him from the first moment they met. But that was three years earlier. Everything we learn in this play suggests that this is highly implausible. He picks up few of her cultural references (confusing Guy Burgess with Anthony Burgess). Intellectually, he stumbles along several paces behind her. He never shows the slightest concern for her feelings and has plainly equivocated throughout their time together. Even his idea of sex is self-serving, an expression of his desire to dominate and humiliate. Nor does that last offer an answer in that there is no reason to suspect that she is in search of humiliation.

Betrayal is plainly not a function of intelligence, age, gender or even moral sensitivity. It is an available option if not a default setting. In Camus's *The Fall*, the central character, Clamence, remarks, 'I, I, I, is the refrain of my whole life and it could be heard in everything I said.'[8] Arthur Miller, in responding to that book, has his central character in *After the Fall* ask, 'In whose name do you ever turn your back but in your own?'[9] *The Mercy Seat*, for all the seriousness of its setting, forswears the kind of existential angst of Camus and Miller, but there is a moral debate at its heart which has to do with the implications of a human nature that can perpetrate an event such as 9/11 but also break a human contract which is altogether more intimate.

Only now does Ben confess that his desire simply to vanish, to simulate his death, is inspired by a wish to avoid responsibility for mortgage payments and a potentially ruinous divorce settlement. Low cunning rather than passion provides his motivation. As to her career, he suggests that she should abandon it, though not before calling in sick so as not to lose out on the possible bonus of sick pay, a suggestion which is, perhaps, a step too far by LaBute as Ben obliges by plunging ever further into the moral abyss, articulating thoughts which even he was more likely to keep to himself. Cary, in *Your Friends & Neighbors* was content to express his cruelty and contempt because he was unashamed. Ben, by nature, is a ducker and weaver, unwilling to commit even to his own failings.

Finally, Abby presents him with an ultimatum. She is prepared to go with him but only on condition that he call his wife to tell her he has survived and to explain that he is leaving her, as she believed he had been about to do before the disaster. Confronted with this demand, he agrees. When he dials the number, however, it is Abby's phone that rings, not his wife's. The call he had been about to make a day earlier had been to break off their relationship, a decision he had revoked only when life, or the death of others, seemed to have played into his hands. Now that she wishes him 'to purge all my sins for some un-fuckingfathomable reason', (67) to choose between his children and her, he finds he cannot go through with it.

Abby bows to what now seems the inevitable. She will return to work. Whether he does or not, she explains, is for him to decide, though, she insists, she will show him 'some mercy' and not inform on him. She leaves the room while he sits looking at his cellphone as it repeatedly rings.

Mercy is in short supply in a play in which just beyond the windows of the set, and plainly in the forefront of people's minds, nearly three thousand people have died (higher numbers are quoted in the play as they were at the time). There was none for those who were burned, leapt to their deaths or died in the down-rushing plunge of buildings which turned to dust even as they fell. For much of the play, Ben offers little in the way of mercy to those he is seemingly willing to abandon, no mercy either for the woman he purports to love, a love he finds it so difficult to articulate. She, too, seems unrelenting, allowing no consoling lies. Yet the play itself is a form of confessional as little by little the truth of their feelings is exposed.

LaBute has explained that the play's title is a biblical reference. 'The Mercy Seat', he has said, 'was the top of the Ark of the Covenant ... that in the temple was the one space where God could come and man or the priests could speak before him ... I think, hopefully, both of them are at some point kneeling before it. They are throwing themselves at the feet [of God] looking for mercy.'[10] The play certainly has three epigraphs, two of which pick up this reference. One is from a church hymn:

> Approach, my soul, the mercy-seat,
> Where Jesus answers prayers;
> There humbly fall before his feet,
> For none can perish there.

LaBute's comments notwithstanding, it is hard to read this anything but ironically when unanswered prayers went hand in hand with unanswered telephones, not only Ben's but those which rang throughout a city whose connections were severed forever. In terms of Ben and Abby, though they do confess and end by turning away from their betrayals, it is hard to see this as redemptive. Both were prepared to go ahead with their lies and acts of desertion. They only choose not to because the logic of the tension between them becomes unavoidable. They ultimately do the right things for the wrong reasons.

The second epigraph is from the Australian musician Nick Cave:

And the mercy seat is waiting
And I think my head is burning
And in a way I'm yearning
To be done with all this measuring of truth.

Certainly, the game of truth and illusion that they play, like that which George and Martha play in *Who's Afraid of Virginia Woolf?*, is painful and the conclusion far from unambiguous. 'The Mercy Seat Lyrics' of Nick Cave concern a man on death row, in the presence of death, whose hand is tattooed G.O.O.D. and whose wedding ring, 'a long-suffering shackle', is inscribed E.V.I.L., a man who insists first on his truth and then on his dishonesty. Ben and Abby also exist in the presence of death and equivocate. There is a bleakness in their separating as there was in their coming together, hence the force of the third epigraph, from Edna St Vincent Millay:

A wind with a wolf's head
Howled about our door,
And we burned up the chairs
And sat upon the floor.

Beyond the door is death, within, the death of a relationship. A relationship that has gone cold is warmed only by the friction of its own disassembly. *The Mercy Seat* was not written because he felt '"I must weigh in on this; I must say something about that terrible day." What came out was ultimately another relationship play, about two people who proved that their own problems were far more interesting and important to them than the lives of three thousand other people who passed away.'[11] But that was precisely a way of writing about that terrible day in that the human meaning of 9/11 was not susceptible of the simplistic uses to which it was put.

9/11 was not an assault on goodness by evil. People did not become heroes by dying. It was not reducible to flags flying in the wind or politicians uttering dangerous platitudes later to be converted into strategies as the real was transformed into the real politic, nearly three thousand deaths becoming a justification for many thousands more. It was about the sudden death of men and women whose individual stories were fused into one by the heat not simply of two exploding aircraft but of a desire to create a master story. Ben and Abby differ from those others only by being alive. Their love and their betrayal of love, their cynicism and their guilt, confessions, retractions, lies and truths are the common currency of human nature. They survived; others died. Ben's return to his wife is not a restoration of order or a rediscovery of commitment. His reasons for returning are no better than his reasons for leaving. Indeed it is not even clear that he will return, the play ending as he stares at his cellphone which 'rings and rings', a desperate attempt to reconnect to which he has not responded as the stage fades to black. As for Abby, she wraps a scarf around her mouth and steps out into a world in which the dust of broken lives still blows in the air of a September morning. Nothing is really resolved. The connection between them is broken, as was that between those who died in the Twin Towers and those who lived on and who listened to ringing phones hoping against hope that a connection would ultimately be made.

The Distance From Here

There is nothing that competes with habit
And I know it's neither deep nor tragic
It's simply that you have to have it

So you can make a killing
Oh you can make a killing
Oh you can make a killing

Aimee Mann, 'You Could Make a Killing'

LaBute has spoken somewhat cryptically of his upbringing, hinting at brittle relationships within his family and a bleak social world beyond it, but his plays, while focusing on a certain human disregard had done so in the context of what he himself conceded were 'fairly privileged, white collar, white bread men and women'.[1] Now, in *The Distance From Here*, with its alienated male characters, Darrell and Tim, he turned his attention to those alongside whom he had once sat in school, those who never seemed to have had a chance, giving up early, pressed to the margins. These were not so much failed dreamers as those who seemed to have settled for what they had. 'Whatever' is their constant refrain, as it had been Ben's in *The Mercy Seat*, and the play carries an epigraph from Kurt Cobain: 'Oh well, whatever, nevermind' – except that a frisson of violence suggests something more than resignation.

As he says, recalling his own schooldays, 'I sat next to a bunch of boys like Darrell and Tim in woodshop and algebra and study hall and watched them simmer and burn and consistently pull down a solid D– in nearly every subject. They knew, even at sixteen, that they had absolutely no hope in this life and they were pretty pissed about it. Pretty damn pissed indeed.'[2] Paul Rudd, who played the part of Darrell, also came from such a background: 'this is a prime example of what tons of kids do every single day, just sit and pass time in the mall. I grew up with my character, Darrell. A lot of my buddies in high school were like those guys, those who didn't really have any sense of direction.' (SBS) The picture that emerges from *The Distance From Here* is of a group of teenagers who sense their exclusion but affect not to care. Two of them have not yet entirely given up on the possibility of escaping their situation, but the third – misogynistic, racist – looks for meaning in a spasm of violence which is his only route to self-definition, like Richard Wright's Bigger Thomas, in *Native Son*, seeking to raise himself above his circumstances by proving himself capable of the unthinkable.

Not the least depressing aspect is that these lives seem to replicate those of their elders. The family is a familiar icon of national life in the United States, frequently invoked as the source of values. In *The Distance From Here* (first performed in London's Almeida Theatre in May 2002), it is seen as attenuated, broken, drained of function. For LaBute's characters there is something frighteningly hermetic about their social and psychological environment. Abandonment, betrayal, cruelty seem natural instincts. Alternately vulnerable and predatory, they circle one another like the caged animals which provide a central metaphor in the play. Sex is less likely to breed intimacy than alienation. It becomes the site of further betrayals. Abortion, miscarriage, abandoned and murdered babies suggest a biological and spiritual cul-de-sac. Behind and ahead is a blank wall as if they were condemned before their birth.

These are people who work as cleaners or in a dog-food factory and who bridge the time between bouts of sex or spasms of violence with endless cigarettes, burning up their money and their lives. They sit watching the blue-silver flicker of the television as a baby cries somewhere, unattended, or encounter one another in strip malls or public spaces which edge towards a dereliction that reflects their own increasing desolation. Out in the garage is a car leaking fluid. Inside is a scatter of people leaking energy and will. This is a world in which

fathers have moved on. Abandonment seems a keynote. Where a substitute has moved in he watches with equal, and predatory, interest a
mother and her daughter, each seeking in him some answer to a
question they can hardly formulate. In town is a school where the
lessons learned seem to have little to do with their lives. If they are not
in detention, the pupils are hanging out, shoplifting, working in fast-
food outlets, drifting through a blank urban landscape, a world of
concrete walls and broken signs.

These are people, LaBute confesses, from whom he was tempted
then and is tempted now to turn away, because of their air of menace,
because he shares nothing with them (not even a common past since
he was never part of their world), but also because they represent an
implicit accusation. His own accomplishments seem the greater in
comparison with the distance he has travelled from them. He is free;
they are trapped. He is articulate; they can barely voice their needs or
hopes. If his America has turned, by the classic combination of talent
and luck, into precisely the American dream of possibility, theirs is a
place where they are mocked by such myths. For the most part they
lack what is necessary in the race to be first in a society in which
second place is no place at all. They give up before they begin because
they see no purpose in striving for what they cannot believe will be
theirs. With dead-end jobs or no jobs at all, they settle for fast food and
slow lives. Their teenage offspring, living in families which have
redrawn their boundaries with each defection, attend schools, or
more often fail to attend schools, where a failure to learn is a badge
of honour and those who try are objects of contempt. The language
they speak, meanwhile, reflects a poverty of spirit even if occasionally
they are capable of an ironic lyricism as they describe memories or
hopes which for a second transcend their circumstances. This is that
other America, the one in which the pursuit of happiness is an abandoned project.

As his earlier plays suggest, however, cruelty and betrayal are
not functions of class. *bash*, *in the company of men* and *Your Friends
& Neighbors* hardly offer a picture of a communal America. The urban
office is no less bleak than the suburban shopping mall. This is a
society in which self-interest trumps any sense of community. What

differs is the quality of the boredom: in the case of his upper middle-class characters a kind of ennui, in the case of these by-products of the American system, routine, habit, a lack of purpose. In the earlier plays sex is a weapon, a sign of power, a lifestyle choice. In *The Distance From Here* it is an opiate, an act of aggression, a prelude to abandonment. In *The Distance From Here* an act of infanticide occurs but we have encountered this before in *iphegenia in orem* and *medea rex*. There, though, the deaths were reported. Here it is staged. What is missing at all levels, in the lives LaBute now stages, is a sense of transcendence, any basis for moral discrimination.

It is not for nothing that the play opens with Darrell and Tim at the zoo, playing hooky from Washington High School where they are juniors (LaBute went to school in Washington state). Like Eugene O'Neill in *The Hairy Ape*, LaBute offers a portrait of people trapped in part by a society whose myths do not extend to the losers. Like Edward Albee's *The Zoo Story*, *The Distance From Here* stages the lives of those divided from one another by the bars of indifference, except that O'Neill offers his play as a political parable and Albee his as an indication of the possibility of redemption, complete with Christian iconography. When LaBute describes *The Distance From Here* as his attempt at a resurrection there are no religious implications. He is simply indicating his desire to reach back to those who were dead to him in order to offer them the retrospective gift of attention. It is his attempt to give shape and form to his scattered memories of those whose irrelevance to his life had until then left him indifferent to their fate, even as he in turn accused them of indifference. As he has explained, '*The Distance From Here* is some sort of effort on my part ... to acknowledge a kind of person I've always known well but consciously and constantly marginalized.' (8)

Darrell, who LaBute describes as a teenager with long hair, cunning eyes and a downward twist to his mouth, tosses the last of a candy bar to an unseen ape, ignoring or provoked by a sign which urges visitors not to feed the animals. His companion, Tim, has, we are told, 'a softer look about him altogether', though Darrell implies that his father had been in the habit of chasing him around the neighbourhood with a hammer, a father who, like Darrell's own, is now absent. (11) It quickly seems clear that Darrell is the alpha male, though his remark of one of the monkeys that "'s a *bullshit* life! 12 × 12 pen's your kingdom and you don't know shit about <u>whatever</u> .... Picking at herself like she's got a *lifetime* ahead of 'er' (12) increasingly seems an accurate summary of his own life: he divides his time between an unprepossessing living room, a shopping mall, a parking lot and the zoo, no less baffled than he assumes the apes to be. 'Fucking *simians*', he shouts, 'they just don't get it, do they?' (19) The parallel is underlined later when Darrell is described as giving an 'animal roar'. (71)

LaBute has said that his play is an attempt to capture teenage rage 'in a story about families. Shattered families, to be sure, but families all the same. The absent fathers that haunt the pages of this play are not the only "missing persons" here.' Emphasising the symbolic significance of the opening scene, he insists that 'emotionally, Darrell and company went AWOL a long time ago. Darrell, his friends, and the other characters of this story are banging their collective heads against the bars of their cage, not exactly sure whether they're trying to get out or to get back in.' (8)

The play largely alternates between alienating public spaces and the living room of Darrell's house where he lives alongside his mother, his stepsister Shari (whose baby's father makes no appearance, not least because she is not sure who it is) and a stepfather, Rich, who affects a macho relationship with him (even as he fails to tell him that his own birth father has been trying to reach him and withholds money his stepson tries to borrow). At twenty-one, Shari is already showing signs of following her thirty-eight-year-old stepmother Cammie, in more ways than one. Irritated by her baby's crying, she turns up the stereo and leaves it to cry. Acknowledging Cammie's observation that 'you just feel like knocking the shit outta them,' (21) she justifies ignoring the child's needs on the grounds that it will prepare it for a life in which people do not get what they want and look in vain for help. Her own desperation, though, seems clear. Her stepmother is the only person to whom she can turn, though it becomes apparent that she is having a sexual affair with her stepfather ('Whatever you wanna call it – "wrong", some kind of *betrayal*, fine – it's still nice, ain't it?' he observes) (120), even as she is drawn to her stepbrother, looking for some consolation. Rich, meanwhile, pretends to resent her presence. Her child's crying, he says, makes him wish 'to *punt* that little fucker into the next county', (43) as if he were a distant relation to Cary in *Your Friends & Neighbors*. In part he is reminiscent of Stanley Kowalski, in *A Streetcar Named Desire*, entering swinging his lunch pail and stripping off his sweatshirt. The sexual charge between him and Cammie is clear. What he lacks is Stanley's shrewdness.

When Darrell talks about his absent father, who had served in the Gulf War, it is to recall a bizarre but violent story. His father had been flying in a helicopter when it encountered a flock of birds. 'He said they must've killed thirty or so of these birds and that was the *best* thing that happened while he was there.' (33) For his part, Darrell feels torn between admiration for what he takes to be the adventure of military service and contempt: 'Bunch a *birds*, who gives a fuck.' (33) Since he is sitting at the time on a wire bench in front of an anonymous concrete wall in a shopping mall whose sign is missing several of its letters, and contemplating whether or not to steal some more CDs, his own life seems hardly more purposeful. Meanwhile, his girlfriend, Jenn (herself from a loveless family in which her father screams obscenities), evidently cares more for the reluctant Tim than she does for Darrell, whose jealousy plainly scares her even as she is equivocal about her own feelings. 'A little trust, maybe, Try that,' (67) she says to Darrell, in a play in which nobody trusts anyone.

Rich, too, had served in the Gulf War and carries a tattoo that marks the number of Iraqis he killed: 'And that's not villagers, any mistakes we made. All those are *confirmed* kills. Bona fide sandniggers.' (82) This is the generation ahead of Darrell. The stories they tell are of xenophobia, violence and paedophilia. Rich explains that he had been offered sex by a girl aged ten or eleven, and her mother, though she had run off with the dollar deposit he had given her. These are Darrell's models. This is the society that seemingly finds a place for their class only as agents of power. Even Rich, though, is not without a sense of something missing from his life. His principal memory of his time in the service is not the killings but a moment of beauty when he flew a kite high in the sky of Saudi Arabia as if this were a symbol in some way of everything out of reach to a man who is a foot soldier of capitalism and whose days are largely filled with routine work interrupted by hours spent in front of a television set or at sports events.

Asked whether the idea of absent fathers in the play might have its roots in his own situation as a child, LaBute confessed, 'it's definitely there. There are, absolutely, absent fathers throughout the piece and the weight that they are accorded certainly came from the upbringing I had with a father who was often on the road and the [fact that] his homecoming was always conflictual. What mood would he return in? Was it going to be a good day or a bad day, depending on how he feels? And I think that hangs over the power structures that are in the play. Darrell is the strong one in his relationship with his girlfriend and his friend Tim, but when Rich, the newest boyfriend of his mother, is around he is not the alpha male any more.' (SBS)

For Darrell, nothing has value. School is a humiliation, education an irrelevance, family life non-existent. When he asks his mother to confirm a childhood memory, she replies, 'I don't recall much about you ... I mean, just you as an individual – you never really made that big an impression.' (104–5) He picks up fragments of knowledge, at times deploying a language at odds with his anti-intellectual stance. He is not innately stupid; he has simply decided that there is no purpose in playing a game he has convinced himself he cannot win. His streetwise language, his pose of indifference, conceals a vulnerability he can never express. He needs the 'friends' he abuses. He is not unaware of the vacuity of his existence, that the future appears to offer him nothing, but affects not to care. To cheat, to steal, is his way of winning a victory over a system in which he can see no other way of succeeding. He mocks Tim for working, more especially in a fast-food store which deals in Chinese food, his vague xenophobia offering him the only superiority he can claim besides his physical strength. The result is a bitterness that edges towards violence. When he believes himself to have been mocked in class for his failure, he fantasises beating his twenty-five year-old woman teacher, 'find her, edge of park somewheres ... trying to start her car, bad *distributor cap*, some shit like that ... and just beat the <u>fuck</u> outta her ... fuck-her-up.' (72–3)

124

In some ways the play which most comes to mind in the context of *The Distance From Here* is not American but British. Among those British playwrights LaBute has confessed to admiring is Edward Bond, a man with fierce political convictions who, in a series of plays, offers a searing portrait of human cruelty, a cruelty which always has a social, political, historical context. In *Saved* Bond stages the lives of those alienated from themselves, effectively abandoned by a society on the make and happy to discard those with no purchase on their world. The ambiguously named *Saved* is set, Bond explained, in a brick desert, a bleak urban world whose open spaces are merely the site of meaningless encounters and a crude violence. Its characters are very close in spirit to those portrayed in LaBute's play, most obviously when it comes to the murder of a baby.

For Bond, there is a politics to his portrait of alienated individuals. Violence is not innate but the product of a particular society. In response to a sceptical reviewer in 1960s Britain he invited him to join him on the streets where he would show him 'something unforgivable'. He was about the business of confronting audiences with their own complicity in a social and political situation that was potentially rectifiable and in so doing was balancing the scales, art, in his view, having for too long primarily served the purposes of an elite. 'Just as history abandons certain classes', he argued, 'replacing feudalism with capitalism, for example – so art abandons certain classes.'[3]

For Bond, part of the function of literature is to make society self-conscious. He is a socialist writer for whom the transformation of society is an urgent necessity. Art offers both a rational analysis and a reminder of possibility. It locates human action within history (his plays range over time and space). LaBute seems to have no such presumption. Certainly the prefaces he writes to his published plays are not, like Bond's, statements of a political aesthetic. He is not an ideologist intent on tracing the nexus between capitalism and a brutal social environment. A certain version of America does emerge, in which self-interest is proposed as a central motive, a sanctioned myth, and individual relationships are shown as having been infiltrated by such values. He is not, though, proposing a political response. He does not write *The Distance From Here* because art has abandoned the class he writes about, but because he has. He has a sense of unfinished business, some dereliction of which he can accuse himself.

At the same time, though he has been described as adopting a scientist's detachment (and his unwavering gaze is certainly part of his appeal), there is a sense in which the spiritual and moral depletion he documents invites something more than a simple acknowledgement. Human nature may transcend history (though all LaBute's plays, unlike Bond's, occupy the near-present), but it is various. The space between the play's action, the characters' behaviour, and audience reaction is an indication of values outside the play which may seem to have been evacuated within it.

The climactic moment of *The Distance From Here* comes at the penguin pool, with its plexiglass wall set on a concrete barrier 'which separates the animals from visitors to the zoo'. (105) It is a description that recalls Jerry's speech in Edward Albee's *The Zoo Story* in which he speaks of 'everyone separated by bars from everyone else, the animals for the most part from each other, and always the people from the animals'.[4] Certainly, in a play in which the spaces between people are the greater the closer they are forced together, the zoo seems to carry paradigmatic force.

Darrell, Tim and Jenn stand beside the pool, whose surface is frozen, brought there by Darrell for a purpose as yet unclear even to him. Inside a bag, he carries his sister's baby which soon begins to whimper. He is, he explains, going to ransom the child, though not to its mother. He is going to ransom it to Tim and Jenn in return for confirmation of a story he has been told, the story of Jenn's sexual humiliation by a black man. At one moment he even threatens to throw the baby like a football, an echo of Rich's earlier remark and a suggestion that he comes from a sub-culture in which each generation risks merely following in the footsteps of the last.

Little by little, the story emerges. Jenn had found herself pregnant by Darrell, at a time when his mother had sent him away. Believing that the pregnancy could be ended by repeated punches in the stomach, she traded sexual favours in return for the assistance of the only man prepared to help her. LaBute recounts hearing just such an urban myth while at school. As he observed, 'That story stayed with me for a long time, right up until I wove it into the dramatic fibre of this play. I hope', he adds, 'it has finally left me now, a part of this world and no longer a frightening image from my teen years.' (8) Darrell responds by hurling the baby to its death in the pond and beating both Tim and Jenn before setting out on the road to nowhere in particular.

In the final scene, time has passed. Tim and Jenn return to the penguin pool. He intends to go in the water and find the baby, though why is not clear. They both confess to vague dreams of escape, even as they are drawn back to this place. It seems clear they will never leave the world into which they have been born. Nobody is going anywhere. Once again, LaBute's habitual closing direction, 'SILENCE. DARKNESS', is something more than a production note. It has a moral and psychological force.

For Edward Bond,

> the idea that human beings are necessarily violent is a political device, the modern equivalent of the doctrine of original sin. For a long time this doctrine helped to enforce acceptance of the existing social order ... But because the idea of god is incompatible with modern science, science has been mis-used to formulate the doctrine of necessary human violence. This is a political invention, not a scientific discovery ... The consequences are heard in bar room chatter, 'We throw babies against the wall because we're animals at heart,' and seen in the Conservative MP who, some time about 1970, wanted young offenders publicly exhibited in cages.[5]

He does not deny a history of violence. What interests him is why it exists. To him, 'violence is contingent not necessary'. It is not a product of urban living but a product of 'situations in which people are at such physical and emotional risk that their life is neither natural nor free'. (11) Human nature, he insists, 'is not fixed at birth, it is created through our relation to the culture of our society' while 'we create our self-consciousness through our social relations, and our self-consciousness is not primarily the fruit of private introspection but of social interaction'. (12) Violence 'is not an instinct we must forever repress because it threatens civilised social relationships; we are violent because we have not yet made those relationships civilised'. (12) Some are violent, he suggests, because they 'pass most of their life as spectators not only of sport but of almost everything else, people whose political role is being a ball and not a player'. (13)

Such observations seem to bring us extraordinarily close to the spirit of *The Distance From Here* with its caged characters, tangentially related to their culture, whose failed social relationships impact on their sense of self and who spend much of their lives not only as passive observers of sport and television but of their lives. For them, violence is a form of language. Darrell and Tim exchange playful punches, which always threaten to devolve into something more serious. Rich slaps Shari as an intimation of intimacy and, finally, Darrell kills a baby in a gesture which compacts a lifetime of frustration. He has a liking for the words he inadvertently picks up at school but has no context for them. They give him no ownership over his life or world. Action short-circuits his need to communicate feelings he can otherwise not express. However, where for Bond violence is a product of a class society and almost certainly a necessary tactic in order to bring about a classless society, LaBute seems to have no such agenda. At the same time, he plainly does suggest that his characters are a product of a system content to relegate them to the margin. They are the ball and not the player and their failings are not wholly their own. In an economically competitive world, they are non-competitors, instead shifting the impulse to compete into their social relationships. They may not get what they need but they take what they want. Seeing no logic in their own existence, they refuse to accept the consequences of their actions.

Yet LaBute does not homogenise them. Rich and Darrell are predators; Tim and Jenn have not yet given up, though they respond to the gravitational pull of an environment that appears to select in favour of the ostensibly strong. When Arthur Miller revisited the auto-parts warehouse in which he had worked for two years as a teenager, in *A Memory of Two Mondays*, he drew a portrait of men and women who were not violent, who treasured dreams of a different life and had a sense of the poetry of life. But what principally appalled him, in the play and in life, was that they had settled for what they had, that theirs were unexamined lives. He had moved on; they had not. And though his own youthful Marxism had made him feel guilty (the title of his first Broadway play, *The Man Who Had All the Luck* conveying a sense of his own sense of unearned success), convinced that in some way they were the by-products of a capitalist system from which he was benefitting, at the same time he felt frustrated that they had seemingly settled for half (something Eddie Carbone, in *A View from the Bridge*, working class, potentially and actually violent, did not). Like LaBute, he returned to his teenage years in part because these were the people he had left in his wake, because he had once been content to dismiss them as so much background noise to his own life, simplifying them at the time and in memory. It was not that he had an undischarged debt but that he accused himself of a certain myopia, a failure of moral vision.

On his return to the warehouse he found the same man in charge. Nothing had changed. The man failed to recognise him. It would be part of what would disillusion him with the Marxist vision of an enlightened working class leading the struggle for true equality. LaBute never embraced such a vision but in *The Distance From Here* he expresses something of the same sense of those whose lives have been evacuated of meaning, in part because of the culture into which they have been born and in part because of a failure of will on their part, a failure to acknowledge moral and social obligations. But since the characters in his other plays, who inhabit a different social environment, display a similar failure, he is not aligning himself precisely either with Miller or Bond.

Saved opens in a living room which is remarkably similar to that described in *The Distance From Here*, with a sofa, chairs and prominent television set watched in a desultory way. The play features a group of barely articulate characters who inhabit the same space but seem to share nothing but sexual desire and a tendency to violence. Just as Shari, in LaBute's play, ignores her baby's cries and abandons her baby to enjoy herself, so does Pam in Bond's play. In the former, the baby is killed when Darrell drowns it; in the latter it is stoned to death.

Bond has said that his play '*is* about sex and violence, but it is also about other things: humour, dignity, suffering, hope. Sex and violence are in the play not for the effect that they will have on the audience but for the effect they might have on the characters in the play. It is the indignity and suffering that is affected in the characters that I hope will affect the audience.'[6] The horror and revulsion, he trusted, would be transitory. What struck many was the apparent incongruity between what seemed the irremediable bleakness of the play and the word 'hope'. Indeed in the 'Author's Note' to *Saved* he spoke of what seemed to him to be the almost irresponsibly optimistic nature of the piece (a remark quoted by LaBute), this being based on the smallest of gestures, as one of the characters begins to mend a chair in the concluding moments.

LaBute's play ends on a similar note of irresponsible optimism as Tim tries to retrieve the body of the dead child: 'I know we swore not to tell nobody and shit, get us into trouble, but I don't like it much . . . that kid just down under water there'. (127) Jenn confesses to a similar feeling. What has happened is irretrievable but something is retrievable, if only a vaguely conceived sense of responsibility. When Tim remarks that 'Never actually freezes completely over again, something breaks through a sheet 'a ice', (126) something more is implied than the physical aftermath of the killing. Darrell has left but these two are drawn back, the two who throughout have been reluctant to wed themselves to Darrell's anarchic impulses.

The act of violence in Bond's play is deliberately linked to a wider concern, a point which he made with more than a hint of irony. 'The men in my play kill a baby. In the audience at any showing of the play there will no doubt be people who fought in one or more of the recent wars [*Saved* was first presented in 1965] : some of them will have killed. Probably one or two of them were war airmen. They may very well have dropped incendiary bombs that burnt a baby to death – a man who has done that may very well be present in the audience. In one respect I would claim that the men in my play are more moral than him – at least they urinate on the baby to put out the flames.' (88)

LaBute's wider concerns are made plain through his references to the Gulf War. The death of the child, presented in front of our eyes, is repellent. The narrated death of others, unseen, their humanity denied by the language with which they are described – 'ragheads', 'sandniggers' – seems insignificant. A play produced in 2002 might or might not be seen by a Gulf War veteran but audiences would still recall pictures of those who had died not by ice but by fire.

For Edward Bond, 'It is the job of the serious, moral dramatist to open the subject of violence, and make thoughts about it possible and, because of the impetus generated by drama, necessary and alluring. And naturally a serious, moral dramatist is drawn towards the most pressing problems he knows – and at present this is the problem of violence ... If the dramatist is going to pursue this aim effectively – it is not enough for him to talk about violence – he must demonstrate it,' (88) it being the essence of theatre, he suggested, to show rather than tell. The 'necessary and alluring' are distinctively Bond touches, since there is patently nothing alluring about the assault on the baby in *Saved*. The more appropriate word might be 'compelling'. As to the necessity to show rather than tell (he describes the reverse as a 'novelettish' theatre, 'essentially second-rate and trivial'), we have LaBute's *bash* to suggest otherwise, language plainly having the capacity to confront. It is true that we see Gloucester's eyes put out in *Lear* (and Bond's own version is even more gruesome than Shakespeare's) but we learn of the murder of Macbeth rather than see it, its horror hardly mitigated by this fact. In *The Distance From Here* LaBute does show but unlike *bash* this is a play in which audiences are to be required to act as witnesses to their own discomfort, provided with the body and not just a report of the crime.

For Bond, the discomfort he engendered in *Saved* was designed to stir to action. For LaBute, with seemingly no political prescription to offer, it was designed to stir to consciousness, not least in a society in which violence is endemic, thirty thousand Americans dying each year from gunfire and the images of war an increasingly familiar backdrop to daily life. Bond has spoken of the stoning of the baby as 'a typical English understatement' compared to 'the cultural and emotional deprivation of most our children'.[7] LaBute might justifiably see the death of the baby in *The Distance From Here* in similar terms.

Perhaps, though, his characters, adrift, disconnected, in search of an elusive meaning, transcend this group of individuals whose deprivations can be seen as rooted in social alienation. The issue, in other words, goes beyond a question of social dislocation, of gender differences, of the desire for dominance. For as Jonathan Franzen has said, 'the problem of consciousness mixed with nothingness never goes away. You never stop waiting for the real story to start, because the only real story, in the end, is that you die.'[8] It is, surely, the plight of many of LaBute's figures that they are in search of a story, or generate their own, for want of belief in any transcendent truth.

8   *Seconds of Pleasure*

I was living for thirty minutes at a time
With a break in the middle for adverts.
You treat me like a piece of human furniture.

I thought I knew you too well,
Now I find the man is a mystery,
And the promises you made
Are really only ancient history

Elvis Costello, 'Seconds of Pleasure'

LaBute's first collection of short stories, *Seconds of Pleasure*, has an epigraph from Ford Madox Ford which might apply to all his work: 'Who in this world knows anything of any other heart – or of his own.' His work, after all, is full of what Melville called isolatos. They join with others, in college, work, marriage but remain, like the figures in an Edward Hopper painting, together but apart. (Indeed there is a Hopper print on the wall in one of his stories, 'Time-Share', though in this case it features a solitary man. 'Lucky bastard'[1] thinks the man who sees it, as his marriage is about to collapse.) Like those Hopper figures, LaBute's characters are often caught staring blankly ahead and if they speak they do so in part to themselves. There is a loneliness at their heart that they seek to neutralise through momentary contact, seeking control over their own lives by exerting it over others. He writes of the imperial self which regards others as no more than psychological provinces to be manipulated and commanded for personal benefit. At its most extreme, in a story called 'Ravishing', this takes a literal form as a gang of men make a snuff movie, raping a woman (whose children she has abandoned in a motel room), murdering her and then watching the tape of the murder. But this is only at the extreme end of a spectrum which also includes less violent forms of betrayal, abandonment and cruelty.

His characters are game players who imagine themselves the originators of the game, in command at all times except that there is an underlying insecurity. They navigate through their lives blind to the shallows through which they move, vaguely conscious of threat but seemingly content to be guided by their own compass. Sometimes, as in 'Boo-Boo', they are gripped in a compulsion they are powerless to resist, even as they seek to rationalise their desires. In this story a man, shopping in a store, is drawn to a young girl, desperate to touch her, even as his wife is paying at the cash register. Far from feeling guilty, he is exultant. The desperation of his marriage is not explored, merely implied. In 'Wait', a man waits for a prostitute whose function is to do no more than urinate on a lonely man for whom this is the contact he craves. Sometimes, LaBute's characters wilfully break faith as if they inhabit a world in which human obligations no longer exist. In 'Spring Break' a truculent and self-confident undergraduate ends an affair with the head of his department, even as he checks out the co-eds he may already have slept with or may do in the future. She is too old for him, he explains, and besides 'I just don't dig this anymore.' (71) He is already educated, it seems, in a callousness and self-concern that will characterise the many other men who feature in this collection, as they follow their own pleasures oblivious to or disregarding of the feelings and needs of those to whom they acknowledge no loyalty and no obligation.

American males, it seems, are inducted early into a disregard of others. They are predatory. In 'Look at Her', a monologue, a man watches what he takes to be a married woman, planning his strategy, thrilled by the very idea of the hunt. In 'Grand Slam', a semi-educated young man accepts sex from a woman he despises as in 'Soft Target' a film producer contemptuously uses a would-be actress, one of a succession of such, happy to graze freely in the lush meadows of Hollywood.

Marriage, meanwhile, offers a holding pattern, pending something more interesting. It is a base from which men can securely emerge from time to time for adventures, proving to themselves that they have not settled for what they see as a kind of stasis. So, in 'Layover', a man in an airport makes advances to a young woman before retreating to his waiting family, proud that he may have aroused desire in someone else, embarrassed when that young woman sees him with them but unembarrassed at what he has done. In 'Whitecap' a stewardess has a chance encounter with the wife and child of a man with whom she has been having an affair, an encounter which gives her a curious satisfaction. In 'Open All Night' a married man spends four hours in a strip club, only to find the battery of his car flat when he emerges, concerned only that the elaborate fiction he had invented to cover his absence is about to collapse. Now on his third marriage and accustomed to slipping his wedding ring off on such occasions, he is rescued by a young woman from the club, a student at the nearby community college, whose child is being looked after by her mother while she performs nude. Such is the sexual topography of LaBute's America.

'Loose Change' also turns on a removed wedding ring. On the basis of nothing more than the pale impression of a circle on the leather of a wallet, a woman conjures up the image of her husband as someone who prefers to travel as a single man. In terms of evidence, it is scarcely convincing but it serves to unlock pre-existing doubts. Before the children came, the wallet had been kept on the chest of drawers. Then it had disappeared into his pocket, absent, as she says to herself, like a husband's love. His trips, after all, surely mean that he would 'rather be anywhere but here with you'. (147) Why else would she find herself 'looking for a clue ... At the corner of despair and desperation. Just across the tracks from damnation ... This is where the journey of her married life has led her.' (150)

The very language suggests her mounting hysteria as she imagines a world so at odds with her hopes. The story ends as she throws herself 'like a rabid dog' (153) at the family car when her husband returns. He grabs his safety belt 'for all he's worth ... Holding on for dear life.' (153) How safe he is, what he is worth, whether he will succeed in holding on to his own life is by no means clear. It is, perhaps, less important whether he was guilty as charged than that his wife should believe that he was. The mark on the wallet is a trifle. The doubt, anxiety, panic it unleashes are not.

Somehow, sex is never far from the minds of the men LaBute features. And since, as the protagonist of 'Full Service' observes, they have an 'innate and uncanny ability to misread, misinform and misunderstand ... our collective gift and curse', (136) they are constantly finding themselves exposed and embarrassed. Trying to read the signs they imagine women to be flashing at them, they have a seemingly infinite capacity to decode them erroneously. The central figure in 'Full Service' simply mistakes a pleasantry for an invitation, as the protagonist of 'Los Feliz', a married actor who has failed to seduce an actress, mistakes her brother for her lover.

Somewhere at the heart of these men is a sense of dissatisfaction, of discontent, as if they are victims of a confidence trick which proposed marriage as a destination rather than a way station en route to an endlessly deferred meaning. They are all looking for the green light across the bay, for the woman who will embody their dreams, aware that dreams cannot be possessed and hence moving on as if the solution to the mystery of life lay somewhere ahead, as if change means progress. Theirs is a discontent that can never finally be resolved so that even if their betrayals are not always literal, they are betrayals nonetheless. Somehow, life seems to have passed them by and they are trying to climb back on the moving walkway.

The twenty stories that make up this collection, some no more than a few pages long, add up to a dismaying view of human nature and human relations, particularly those between the sexes. It is like helplessly watching a series of motorway crashes as relationship after relationship impacts. The title implies momentary satisfactions but in truth there are few of these so that it seems primarily ironic. They are almost like the 'takes' in his movies, complete in themselves but part of a larger narrative, in this case to do with emotional desolation, a largely urban landscape of lost souls.

The first story, 'Perfect', owes something to Nathaniel Hawthorne's 'The Birthmark', and, indeed, the connection is made by the protagonist. The narrative voice is flat, uninflected with emotion. All feeling drains out of an account which seems to aspire to objectivity. It is a confessional without the guilt. What we learn of him is to be derived less from the story he tells than from its emotional aridity, from his apparent unawareness of what he inadvertently reveals of himself even as he lays claim to total honesty.

He is two years married, though nothing of his account suggests that he takes much satisfaction from the relationship. 'Yep, got myself hitched about two years ago,' he remarks, 'but marriage takes up a lot of time and energy if you do it right ... A solid marriage is a real commitment.' (2) He seems to derive little more satisfaction from his work. There he prefers a certain anonymity. His bachelor life consisted, he explains, of little more than a few passing affairs, a 'couple of hearts broken, no doubt, trampled and left in the ditch along the roadside of love' (3) Among those left in the ditch, however, was evidently one sufficiently moved to commit suicide, a suicide which he obligingly describes. It 'was her fault completely', (3) he explains, meaning by that that no fault attached itself to the driver of the bus which struck her. It plainly never occurs to him that he himself might bear some blame, not least because the world he inhabits requires him to accept no responsibility. They had, he conceded, quarrelled earlier that week, a quarrel continued in public and private. She had stepped into the path of the bus she would use when visiting his apartment, but it had nothing to do with him: 'It was simply her time.' (4) As far as he is concerned, this is the past and, in an echo of a phrase LaBute has used elsewhere, 'the past is called that for a reason. Because it is behind us.' (4) With no past, there is no causality. With no causality, there is no responsibility. Hence, his statement that 'I like to live in the present.' (5)

The narrator opens the story by claiming that he himself is not perfect, though the claim quickly proves suspect in so far as he disavows responsibility for anything that might be seen as marring that perfection. On the other hand he does look for perfection in others, certainly in his wife. As they are about to go out for the evening he suddenly becomes aware that she has a blemish on her shoulder, a fact which immediately becomes an obsession. What is first described as 'a skin thing' becomes a 'mound of darkened cells' and subsequently a 'wart cluster ... erupting from the deep'. He tries to persuade her to cover it with her clothes and when she becomes angry and refuses to go with him he leaves her behind, relieved that he will not be seen with her.

In the Hawthorne story a similar obsession leads to the death of the woman. Here it leads to her psychological death. The scene moves on a year or two. They are still together, though after problems they are no more than 'pretty much OK', (14) even if this is apparently sufficient for the protagonist. He no longer mentions the mark but now fantasises doing what Hawthorne's protagonist had arranged to have done, except that he, rather than have someone else excise the birthmark, roots out the growth himself, plunging a potato peeler into her shoulder and tearing it out. For a moment, the stance of objectivity, the tone of neutral disinterest, is abandoned. The prose becomes vivid. These visions, indeed, seem to give a vitality to his life that has been lacking even as they are evidence of behaviour which seems to disturb even him, no matter with what calmness he has endeavoured to tell his story.

Not all the stories have quite this force. 'Maraschino' is a none-too-plausible sketch of a sexual encounter between father and daughter, he having left the family home when she was only six. Here the casual objectivity seems less a product of character than evidence of an imposed irony, unless we are asked to believe that his desertion of the family home has so traumatised the young girl, now grown up to work in the marketing department of a major pharmaceutical company, that it has bleached out all sense of perspective and morality. If revenge is implicit in the act it is none too clear who the object of that revenge might be. If it is a desperate attempt to claim back a love betrayed then the literalness of the attempt is potentially something more than a distraction to the reader.

LaBute has a fondness for exploring the extremes of sexual and emotional situations, more often than not moments of betrayal which serve to cast a retrospective light on relationships. Accordingly, he follows 'Maraschino' with 'Time Share', a story in which a woman discovers her husband being fellated by a man, a former college friend who has temporarily moved in next door on a time share, though for the first half of the story it is not apparent that his infidelity involves a man. The title is a reference to the holiday home but also to the protagonist's brief encounter and to what is clearly now the time-limited nature of his relationship to his wife. In a post-Clinton world, there is something both embarrassing and ridiculous about his attempts to explain away his predicament, moving, as he does, from qualified denial to the suggestion that it was a natural product of past friendship, a college thing, a man thing, simply a thing. In the end language runs out for him as it did for President Clinton. The story concludes as he intones a mantra reminiscent of that which concludes Guy's encounter with Bobbi in *Some Girl(s)*: 'It's OK, it is, it's OK, this is gonna be . . . it's all right. Things'll be fine. It's . . . OK, this is all O-K.' (38) Composed, as it is, almost entirely of dialogue, 'Time Share', like the title story 'A Second of Pleasure', (which is entirely composed of dialogue), could easily have been a play, the interpolated narrative fragments being an equivalent of the ironic stage directions which appear in several of his works. The line between prose fiction and drama, it seems, is not always a sharp one.

'A Second of Pleasure' is also concerned with betrayal or, rather, multiple betrayals. A man and a woman are at a station, about to spend a weekend together. They are both married, to other people. At the last moment, though, the woman decides not to go, having, she explains, been suddenly touched by the sight of her husband eating a children's cereal for dinner and doing the puzzles on the back of the pack. The second of pleasure this occasioned recalled other such moments and hence the reason she had married him. This epiphany leads her not merely to abandon their plans but, it seems, to end the affair. On the other hand, she has evidently reached her decision only ten minutes before the train is scheduled to leave. She was, she confesses, 'on the fence here. I couldn't decide.' (87)

Her lover, meanwhile, is indignant that she has not consulted him because, as he explains, 'I'm big on sharing. On being open about stuff, whether it's painful stuff or not,' (89) this from a man who has not been open with his wife and whose comment on sharing exposes his moral ambivalence. He has, after all, been sharing rather too much. He complains that his lover seems to have little concern for his feelings even as he gives no consideration to those of his wife.

Indeed, he later confesses to a certain pleasure he derives from deceiving her: 'It warms me a bit, to look into her eyes and deceive her . . . it's become a kind of ritual between us, even if she's not really in on it. It's a form of closeness, actually. I mean, I wouldn't lie to just anybody.' (98–9) He is betraying her, he seems to suggest, the better to feel close. It is what they share, presumably all that they share.

What holds the woman to her husband, meanwhile, is not their children, not passion or real commitment, but a sentimental moment, a sense of her husband's vulnerability, the very vulnerability that had made his betrayal so easy and at least momentarily pleasurable. She, too, lays claim to honesty, who has been perpetrating a lie not merely in deceiving her husband but in living a life whose purpose seems to have eluded her. Her redemption lies in her sense of guilt, her sudden awareness of the hurt she is doing her husband, an awareness plainly beyond the man.

So, little by little, and by indirection, LaBute deconstructs the affair as he does the two marriages. The protagonists have come together looking for a sense of excitement missing from their lives. Yet there is no suggestion that they have discovered anything but that. They make no declaration of their love for one another. Indeed that seems beside the point. At the story's end, they return to their separate families, he after making use of the booking at a resort hotel, staying away from his wife and children even when there is no compensating frisson. She, presumably, will return to a man she has described only in terms of an endearing defencelessness, he to a wife whose betrayal he has convinced himself has enabled him to sustain their relationship.

The dialogue, played out in the neutrality of the station, reveals not so much their mutuality as the space that had always existed between them. Asked by the man whether she had ever felt anything for him she confesses she had not. Nor is there any suggestion that he had felt anything for her. For all their insistence on the importance of truth they have plainly lied to one another and to themselves. The story ends on a dying fall: 'I'll see you, then.' 'Yes. Sometime.' 'Bye.' 'Good-bye.'

'Opportunity' could equally have been a play, specifically one of the scenes in *autobahn*. As in that play, it is set in a car. A man is driving while his wife talks. It is, effectively, a monologue, the man's actions being identified in the equivalent of stage directions. The woman speaks of her youth and family life. She and her brothers and sisters had, she explains, been dominated by their father who would tolerate no resistance to his will. And when he saw evidence of such resistance, as he did with one of his daughters, he had set out to break her, refusing her permission to go out with boys until she was eighteen, at which age she suddenly disappeared. It was assumed that she had run away. He preferred to say that she had run off with the circus. There had, however, been rumours of something worse and the sheriff had come to call. For reasons she does not explain, except her youth or her subservient nature, the narrator had offered her father a false alibi, thereafter searching the farm for signs of what she clearly believed would be her sister's grave. Her mother, meanwhile, had 'just kept going', (57) surviving without living.

In the end, though, this is less a gothic tale about a family murder than a portrait of the woman who speaks and the man who remains silent. In reaction against her father, she had sought out a man whose nature seemed the very opposite. He had gone to work and handed over his pay packet, but there was clearly something wrong, something she attributes to herself. He was 'so quiet', (58) as he is throughout the story. She could never tell what he was thinking or feeling or quite how to please him. She could never tell whether he loved her. And though she claims to be beyond such feelings now there is nothing to suggest that anything has changed. Once or twice she puts her hand on his leg. Once he encloses her hand in his, but this seems the limit of their contact. There is evidently more than one way of being buried. Her spill of language as they head for Spokane fills a silence which might be lifelong. Like the mother who she likes to feel she takes after, she, too, is surviving without living, covering her emptiness with memories which, significantly, are of lost control, loss itself.

The car carries them both forward, towards their home. But the truth seems to be that it is also carrying her back, recalling an experience she has not escaped as the home towards which she travels has the same silences that had once oppressed her as a child. Side by side, she and the man who was to have rescued her from the past travel: he silent, unyielding, she chattering to fill the silence, reassuring herself that she is not in despair of her life. The car disappears into the night taking with it one more story of desolation, one more account of mismatched expectations, one more glimpse into the heart of a domestic darkness lit by nothing but a desperate hope.

In 'Some Do It Naturally', not one but two relationships collapse, one scarcely beginning, the other long established. Invited to concentrate on one, we discover that the primary focus is in fact on the other as the two are played against one another. On a Sunday lunchtime visit to a restaurant, a man and his wife overhear a discussion between a couple over whether or not to abort a baby. Initially, the couple appear to be debating ethics. He advances a scientific justification as she counters with religious convictions. What matters to her, she explains, is 'how we treat each other'. (179) What matters to him is clearly to disembarrass himself of an inconvenience. Slowly the cracks in their relationship begin to open. They plainly come from different backgrounds. He, a college student or graduate, plainly sees himself as an intellectual, insisting that there is no reason why 'we can't hope for some sort of synthesis between our disparate visions of life'. (180) For her part, she fails to follow, not simply because she cannot understand his language but because his reference to 'this baby situation' hardly matches her own commitment to 'human life'. (181) In the end philosophical discussion defers to an argument about whose responsibility it had been to secure contraceptives. Their discussion peters out and they leave.

Meanwhile, the fragility of the other marriage becomes increasingly apparent. The wife remains silent throughout, disgusted, it seems, that her husband should bring her to a restaurant and then spend his time eavesdropping on others rather than talk to her. So the story of their failing marriage is interleaved with the story of those others, seemingly at the beginning of a relationship. 'I can feel you looking at me,' he says, 'I don't even have to turn around to know that you're doing it. I sense the heat coming off your eyes. You're like something out of a science fiction film.' (186) He is sitting, then, with his back turned to her. For her part, rather than speak she lets out 'puffs of displeasure'. (187) She is, he insists, 'self-consumed' having 'gotten that way over the last few years'. Her good looks, he confesses, had dazzled him, 'kept me from realizing the kind of person you are'. (188) As the young couple leave, he refuses to turn round because 'you sicken me . . . piss me off.' (189)

So he is left in a restaurant, quite possibly speaking to himself as others presumably listen. He has, he says, had his 'fill of your shit and your ways . . . Your ability to hurt and mistreat me, it's like part of your makeup.' (190) He attacks her for her tan 'bought with a coupon book', the tone of his attack mirroring the superiority of the young man whose conversation he has been overhearing. Appropriately enough, he recalls their early time together when they had travelled to Venice. But that woman, he insists, 'was swallowed up long ago', by a 'two-headed beast that no longer even resembles the woman of my dreams'. (190) His only dream, now is that she should 'Go away now. Go on. Go.' (191)

Seconds of Pleasure offers a series of variations on a theme. LaBute maps a bleak moral and spiritual world, but peoples it with distinctive characters defined by their language no less than their attitudes. They share a sense of bafflement in the face of a life that has failed to come into alignment with youthful hopes, relationships which have devolved into habit, been eroded by betrayal. They share, too, a conscienceless determination to serve their own interests, discover in sex a power they largely lack in the social world. Each story, though, delineates individual sensibilities as LaBute creates vivid portraits of those who are shaped in part by public myths and in part by an upbringing that seems to have offered them little but crude cartoons of human relationships. Few if any demand the sympathy of the reader. These are exemplary tales in so far as they define the dead zone of the human sensibility and the fragility of relationships, in a culture that celebrates the family but in which family hotels provide pornography as a convenience along with the hairdryer and ironing board, a society in which one in two marriages end in divorce.

Appropriately for a book entitled *Seconds of Pleasure*, most of the stories are brief, well calculated for the magazines in which they first appeared but also perhaps for LaBute's busy career committed to his work in theatre and film. Beyond that, the pleasures they address are themselves brief, stolen moments that never seem to offer satisfaction. Indeed there is a deeper irony in that there is very little evidence of pleasure at all. What there is is a sense of desperation, as his characters search for a meaning that seems to have eluded them, reach for a transcendence they can never discover if only because they look so determinedly in the wrong place. So the men age, carrying forward adolescent attitudes which they never seem able to abandon any more than can the society in which they find themselves, dismissing the past, adrift in the present and with little hope for the future.

9   *autobahn*

So I'm sitting in my car at the same old stop light.
I keep waiting for a change, but I don't know what.
So red turns into green, turning into yellow.
But I'm just frozen here on the same old spot.
But I'm not. No I'm not.   Aimee Mann, 'It's Not Lyrics'

And you will say
That you're making headway
And put it in overdrive
But you're mistaking speed
For getting what you need
And never even noticing
You never do arrive
Cause you're
Driving sideways   Aimee Mann, 'Driving Sideways'

What else should I be,
all apologies   Kurt Cobain, 'In Utero version'

In 2004, Neil LaBute presented a staged reading of seven brief plays
in the appropriately named Little Shubert Theater in New York, appropriate because these were small-scale works, each featuring two actors. They
were not planned as a series, he explained, being inspired by a photograph
of a German production of one of his one-act plays, together with two
others adapted from his short stories. The striking fact was that they all

took place in a car. This inspired him to write the other plays, five of which were first presented as a benefit for the Manhattan Class Company.

What appealed about that German production was that it was indeed played in the constrained space of a car, and, as he explained, 'I love the infinite possibilities that a confined space offers the writer, director, performer, and audience.'[1] Just as a sonnet makes a virtue of its constraining rules so the apparent limitations imposed by the conceit of playing within the confines of a car generated its own dynamic. Indeed, he recalled his own childhood experience of being forced to witness and hear his parents' quarrels as he sat in the back seat and they in the front: 'hidden in the backseat of a late-model American sedan, I realized quickly how deep the chasm or intensely claustrophobic it was (depending on how things were going up front) inside your average family car.' (xiv) Even silences could be charged with meaning. Eugene O'Neill's characters in *Long Day's Journey Into Night* were trapped in a small and fog-bound New London house, drawn together and thrust apart but, ultimately, unable to escape a place in which they were constrained by more than a restricted space. LaBute's are discovered in a car, indiscreetly parked or travelling from one point of discord to another.

The fact of travel, though, never constitutes escape. In the words of one of the plays' epigraphs, from Horace, 'They change their climate, not their soul, who rush across the sea.' Yet a journey, it transpires, can also seem a way of deferring decisions. It can function as an apparent if not actual psychological no man's land. In the words of the plays' other epigraph, from E. B. White, 'Everything in life is somewhere else, and you get there in a car.' Action is seemingly suspended, projected forward, journeys of all kinds implying destinations. Yet in fact in these plays the drama of the lives at their centre is played out as underlying tensions break surface. The journey, it seems, is the destination. The very absence of a social context, the impossibility of walking away, the isolation, generate an unrelieved pressure. In two of the plays only one person speaks. The presence of the other, however, is vital. Both plays seem to feature a monologue but they are in fact dialogues in which one person's silence is a vital and illuminating component.

LaBute invokes what he calls 'a terrific one-hander called *The Fever*' by Wallace Shawn, to whom *autobahn* is dedicated, which the author had wished to see performed in living rooms, with an audience of a dozen people. For his own part, LaBute was attracted by the idea that actors would take his own text, memorise it, and perform it in their own cars, 'filling those intimate interiors with my words and their emotions' (xv) as they travelled through America, a depiction of whose spiritual byways emerges from works separately conceived but which cohere to offer a tessellated portrait of a society marked by loss, desperation, abandonment.

From his days at Brigham Young, LaBute had liked the idea of staging plays in any available space, as if theatre could be performed anywhere and the barrier between art and daily experience were permeable. For all his work in films, indeed, with its ample resources, he still preferred a poor theatre. As he remarked, 'the old-fashioned "Hey, kids, let's put on a show!" spirit that attracts and keeps many theatre artists going will never be snuffed out. In fact', he explained, 'the pleasure I get from setting up a couple of chairs on a bare stage and getting to work with actors and an audience will never be bested. I promise you. Peter Brook, that clever old bastard, was right on the money about the joys of an empty space.' (xv)

It was in this spirit that, having reduced seven plays to five for the New York production for reasons of time, he staged them with the minimum of rehearsal, finding virtue in necessity much as he had discovered the advantages of a constrained space for the dramas themselves:

> I ... felt that without a proper production period, which would allow us to rehearse in costume with lighting cues, we were better off following the old acting credo: 'Less is more.' In the end, each of the five pieces was presented in front of an audience with just two hours' rehearsal. The actors wore their own clothing, chosen by themselves, as appropriate to their respective characters ... This sort of seat-of-your pants production engenders a blind panic that is itself a kind of freedom.

The production was put together on a single day and that night, 'the actors were "inside" cars and driving down the "road" merely because we said so.' (xii–xiv)

LaBute was not the first playwright to realise the dramatic potential of the car. In the Pulitzer Prize-winning *How I Learned to Drive*, Paula Vogel brings together a paedophile and his victim, she being inducted into something more than the mysteries of car driving. Beside its role as metaphor, however, the car functions in that play as a place of retreat, of sexual encounter, education and forced intimacy as LaBute would recall cars as sites for covert love, battlegrounds, places of refuge. In films, scenes are regularly set in cars, not least because they are a part of everyone's experiences. In the theatre, they have appeared as props – as in Arthur Miller's *The Man Who Had All the Luck* – but have seldom constituted the stage on which the drama has been enacted.

These are plays in which seemingly inconsequential conversations slowly reveal truths which are approached obliquely. Very often it is what is not said that is crucial. Truths are avoided or alluded to rather than confronted but they slowly seep through a language that is often thrown up to conceal them. And though each play is discrete, telling its own story of personal tension, betrayal, fractured relationships, secret passions, what emerges from the whole cycle is a vision of America. In the words of the Woman, in the play called *autobahn*, and speaking of the road itself, 'Perhaps that's the way it should be . . . all of us speeding by one another, too quick to stop, too fast to care . . . just racing along on our little journeys and no sense of how dangerous or careless we're being.' (92) Inside the cars, she believes people to be safe, sheltered, protected from harm and hurt, from a feeling of damage and loss, but quite the opposite would seem to be the truth.

For LaBute, it is precisely within the cars that those anxieties are most evident. Those who in other circumstances could walk away are here forced to face who and what they are, to speak, listen or remain silent. Each option leaves the individual and, implicitly, the society exposed. So, in the course of the seven plays in the printed text he stages a series of conversations – some decidedly one-sided – which constitute an attenuated emotional world, a symphony in a minor key. Americans are forever on the move. It is a part of their mythology. Movement, however, so often equated with progress, as happiness is to be pursued rather than embraced, does nothing, finally, to kill the loneliness that sounds from these plays as dialogues devolve into

148

monologues or into parallel arias which speak of disappointment, misdirected passions, abandoned hopes.

The first play in the cycle, *funny*, was one of the two not performed in the original staged reading. It features a mother (called the Older Woman) and daughter (Young Woman), the former silent throughout. The title is ambiguous. The young woman, indeed, begins by debating the distinction between 'funny-ha-ha' and 'funny-strange'. (7) The scenery strikes her as strange, as does the fact that her father insists on driving miles to see her grandparents, one with cataracts, the other with heart trouble, when they hardly welcome his visits, when, she suggests, they may simply not 'give a shit about anybody'. (7). This, though, does not exhaust the range of meanings and as the play proceeds so another meaning begins to emerge. She has, it seems, been funny in the sense of damaged. Her 'serene' smile is not a sign that she is at peace. Indeed her spill of language, her free-associating, implies the reverse. She evidently requires no reply from her mother, who does no more than glance at her daughter.

By degrees we learn that she has been in an institution, only the most recent in what has evidently been a succession of such to which she has been sent. They are travelling from the institution to her home. She is, she insists, 'Totally all better', and knows that her parents believe this, an assertion which implies the opposite, not least when she insists that her father's remark that they are pulling for her implies their lack of confidence. Indeed, her stream of language, with its revelations and obscenities, suggests otherwise. The nature of her mother's silence thus changes as hope is presumably slowly extinguished. Her language, meanwhile, is self-cancelling, possibilities collapsing of their own weight. Thus she insists that 'I think maybe it could be really easy to fit back in at home, in a way.' (10) 'I think', 'maybe', 'in a way' hardly suggest someone confident about her future. She implies that she could get her old job back, 'or that sort of deal'. 'I could do that,' she says, 'Absolutely', uncertainty and assurance running into one another.

A picture of her former life gradually comes into focus, not so much by virtue of her statements as by indirection. The twins are off at school 'now'. Time has passed. Her former home life becomes clear when she suggests to her mother that in a car 'you can't run into the next room or slam the door in my face or throw yourself down on the bed and start crying.' This, she suggests, 'is the place to be honest'. (11) The justification for such a reaction, however, now becomes clear as her honesty, or simply a sense of recklessness or even vindictiveness, obliges her to tell her mother that she means to go back on drugs and to do anything necessary in order to obtain them. She had, she confesses, lied in order to be released from the institution. She now challenges her mother to turn the car around confident that she will not do so because 'That's what people always think is best. Get home . . . keep on driving,' (12) and because she, too, is fragile. The silent woman, who has done no more than glance across at her daughter, is herself, it now seems, an hysteric prone to call the police if the mailman opens the screen door to deliver letters, or summon her husband from work if the pool boy fails to appear. This, indeed, is one of the play's strengths as it creates a portrait of a world we never see, a woman who never speaks and a life we infer only from the sometimes oblique words of a woman who does nothing more than sit in a car and talk.

One story that the young woman tells her mother relates to a film that the inmates had watched as they smoked marijuana (a fact which says something about the institution). The film appeals to them partly because it is set in a place called Twin Oaks, which happens to be the name of the institution in which they are detained. The film is clearly *The Postman Always Rings Twice* (screenplay, incidentally, by David Mamet), which gains a certain irony when we learn of the mother's fears. This story of a passionate affair that leads to murder and the execution of one of the killers, though not, as it happens, for the crime he committed, had set all the inmates laughing, precisely because of the irony. It is, as the young woman explains, 'Not funny-ha-ha, but the other one. Strange. Or ironic. It was funny-ironic.' (13) So, in a characteristic gesture, LaBute echoes the beginning of the play. By the end all those meanings have fused together. She is funny, in the sense of strange, or odd, as is her silent mother, this being itself the source of irony as the person who had had her daughter removed from the family home is revealed as herself strange and odd. The postman does, it seems, always ring twice.

And so they drive on, trapped not only in a car for the duration of their journey but in a relationship from which there seems no escape. At the same time, and despite their enforced proximity, there is a gulf between them that is clearly unbridgeable, the mother's silence being a marker of her isolation, her resignation and perhaps dismay. In Arthur Miller's *The Last Yankee*, set in a mental hospital, one character remains silent and immobile throughout. The director employed a movement coach to help the actress express that immobility. It is not as absurd as it sounds. In the end the play ends with that silent figure whose presence thus proves crucial, providing an ironic commentary on the action. So, in *funny*, the Older Woman's presence is critical even as she is expressive of a profound absence, her instinct, as we learn, being to withdraw herself or to have her daughter removed. One expresses her desperation with a flood of words; the other with an abandonment of language. Denial is their common currency, a hopeless hope doomed, as it appears, even as it is endlessly reborn.

bench seat, the first of the plays in the staged reading, is a two-hander in which, within the confines of a car, gender, class and power are explored as a relationship drifts towards its end. The characters are identified only as Guy and Girl, she calling him 'stupid funny', (19) a term of endearment which, presumably not incidentally, offers an echo of the first play. They sit together in a parked car, she sensing that he is about to tell her that he is moving on. At first, the language is oddly staccato, a form of interrogation as she probes his motives in coming to a place where, it is rumoured, girls are brought to be told that affairs are ending. Even their perfunctory love-making is a form of interrogation as she struggles to assess the level of his commitment. She is seeking reassurance. He, it eventually transpires, is seeking release. When she moves towards him, he makes a slight move away. In the context of the confined space the smallest movement is magnified. Her suspicions intensify.

By degrees the differences between them become apparent. He cannot resist correcting her usage. Her sensitivity to this, we learn, is a product of their different backgrounds. He is a teaching assistant at college or, as he insists when she takes the word assistant to be reductive, a teaching fellow who was given a classic car when he went to university to study engineering. She, as she points out caustically, had worked at Ben and Jerry's and then Wal-Mart. Her anxiety derives from the fact that she has been in just such a relationship before. Another graduate student had taken up with her but only for the duration of his time in the area. Then he had driven her to the same spot and ended their relationship on the grounds that they were 'different people'. (26) When she confesses this and insists that a repetition, two years on, would lead her to have 'a complete seizure or whatnot', (27) the Guy 'slides back toward the driver's side a bit.'

It quickly becomes apparent that he has indeed come to this place to end their relationship, that she no more fits into his plans than she had into those of the other grad student. What he had not anticipated is that she has no intention of going quietly. She has marriage in mind, as she had before, and behind her apparent desperation is a disturbing vindictiveness verging on psychosis. She had, she confesses, 'wanted to hurt' the student who abandoned her and to that end had pursued him, sending him dead animals, attacking his dates, putting such pressure on him that he failed to graduate on time. Even now, she explains, she is sending him obscene pictures via email: 'all these pictures of horses shitting in a woman's mouth and various acts of that nature ... because, you know, that's basically what he did to me ... took a shit right on me.'(31)

In a play in which power seemed to lie with the man, she reclaims it. The brief exchanges give way to an extended aria as she effectively silences him. Describing how she had terrified a young woman, she screams at the top of her voice, the more disturbing inside a car. The casual obscenities which suddenly punctuate her speech carry with them a threat underlined by the recitation of her calculated attacks on the man who had tried to dismiss her but became her victim. He had called the police, she explains, but 'so what? Fuck him. I just kept it up.' (31) Then, as a sly reminder of the shift in power between her and the young man who had just begun to edge towards ending their relationship, she asks him what the past tense of the word 'shit' might be, an ironic indication that his pedantic intelligence will be of no utility to him now.

As he sits stunned she describes his potential fate in describing that of his predecessor: 'This Mr. Grad Student with a Trust Fund. He shat on me and sent me packing, and that is wrong. That is a bad, bad thing to do to someone, a someone who loves you, so I said to myself, I said, "Hey, little man, no! Uh-uh! I'm not through with you yet. Nope. And maybe not for a long time, either."' (32) The play ends as the girl lies back and invites him to 'relax'. She, indeed, drifts off to sleep. He is 'frozen, like a deer on the interstate'. He 'sits with his hands held wide, his eyes open, staring off into the night'. (32) What he sees is his own future. A trap has sprung shut which he thought he could escape with ease. He is now side by side in the car with a woman from whom escape suddenly seems impossible. A symbol of freedom has become a symbol of constraint. A young man who had been ready to move on, oblivious to the feelings of the girl he was abandoning, has now been brought to a halt. The silence with which the play ends floods with meaning.

bench seat has echoes of David Mamet's *Oleanna*, in which a shift in language had underscored a reversal of power. There, too, a supposedly intellectually superior man had found himself outmanoeuvred by a woman, his self-confidence destroyed by her native cunning. He was the teacher, as is the young man in LaBute's play, she his intellectual and social inferior. Mamet's two-hander takes place in an office, LaBute's in a car. The office should be the teacher's domain, as the classic car should be the young man's. In both plays that sense of security is eroded by nothing more than words. In both, the man stares ahead into a blank future. Thinking to betray, the young man is betrayed. Thinking to abandon, he now has to abandon his plans for his future. Thinking to use the woman, he is used by her. Anxious to correct her use of language, he is stunned when she lets out a primal scream and shocks him with the bluntness of her words. Suddenly, he is on a journey to nowhere.

Language is no less central to *all apologies*, a three-page monologue. A man and a woman sit in a parked car as the traffic zooms past. She is silent. He defends himself against an unspoken accusation, though it quickly becomes clear that his immediate offence has been linguistic. He has, it turns, out, called his wife a cunt, and done so in company, a fact which, he acknowledges, is 'inappropriate', a word which he holds at arm's length as a form of 'Oprah lingo'. (38) It is, he seems to assume, no more than a problem of language as he endeavours to defend himself without causing further offence, despite a tendency towards obscenity. He complains about the imprecision of language, its inadequacy to experience, its decay – anything, indeed, but confront the central problem which is his violence. His linguistic aggression, his speculations about language, are merely correlatives of his physical violence and his desire to deny it. He is ready, he says, to apologise 'if that's what it's gonna take to wash away all the running around and drinking and putting my fist through your windshield that time and me chasing you down at the mall and screaming at you outside Penney's store'. (37)

He is, he says, 'indignant' at being required to apologise but ready to do so if it means they can resume where they left off, except that where they left off seems to have been nowhere in terms of their relationship. Even now what worries him most is that the neighbours, neighbours he despises, will see them arguing in their parked car. The more desperate he becomes, the more his language deteriorates. In the process of declaring his love for his wife he exposes its vacuity: 'I'm sorry and I love you. Honestly. Now can we please just go, for chrissakes?' (38)

The play ends as he sits back and waits for a gesture: 'Anything. She continues,' the stage direction indicates, 'to stare at him.' (38) Their relationship is no less stationary than the car. There is, effectively, nowhere for them to go. The traffic streams past. He is what he denies. They sit, together and apart, a marriage in which there is no communication, only his voice, dominating, justifying, pleading.

In the course of his one-sided argument with his wife, the protagonist, perhaps significantly simply identified by his gender, observes to his wife that, 'You win the damn prize and maybe that Dr. John Gray guy will forge you a medal over on Mars or whatever planet he's living on these days.' (38) Dr John Gray is the author of *Men Are from Venus, Women are from Mars*, a book which suggests that men and women do, indeed, occupy different psychological planets and it seems clear that in LaBute's world, or, indeed, Mamet's or Shepard's, this appears to be true. It is certainly true in the next play in the sequence.

merge, which in the original production starred Kevin Bacon and Susan Sarandon, features a man and a woman in an expensive car. The only stage directions indicate that he is driving and that she is wearing sunglasses. In the course of their journey through city streets, she issues directions as he probes her about an event that had apparently occurred at an exhibition she had attended, careful to control his anger, evidently an issue between them. Indeed, LaBute interweaves the traffic directions, issued largely by the woman, with the unfolding story she tells, the one commenting ironically on the other as in Vogel's *How I Learned to Drive*. At first, the conversation seems no more than a petty disagreement over the meaning of words. Referring to an encounter with two men she uses the word 'all'. What seems like a familiar marital dispute over trivia, however, slowly becomes critical.

As they drive so she recounts what may or may not have been an assault she suffered at an exposition she had been attending. Every statement is tentative, partially withdrawn. She is unsure of the men's age, their precise number, whether she had encountered them before, what happened when they entered her room whose door she later confesses she may have left ajar, 'Or something.' At that moment she instructs her husband, 'Careful, it's a yellow,' a warning about the approaching traffic lights but also, it seems, about approaching danger of another kind.

She believes, she explains, that she may have fainted, but is uncertain given the darkness of the room, though she refines her description to 'darkish' (even as she suggests that they should take a route through the city with 'fewer lights') as she had equivocated between 'two' and 'all'. It had certainly '*felt* like blacking out'. (46) That, she insists, is 'How it happened', (47) except that it becomes apparent that she has not yet concluded her amendments, the refinements to her story which suggest that this is not in fact how it happened.

Then she recalls coming to, not, though, it seems, from a faint, since it is noon. She wakes, as she recalls, in a leisurely way. She was, apparently, 'undressed', 'naked', 'nude', not quite, of course synonyms, each word moving away from innocence, each word edging towards agency as if she were leading her husband away from secure ground, along a ledge. As disturbingly, she awoke to find herself on the carpet, though she herself relates this as no more than an interesting detail, a puzzle, perhaps, but hardly one that seems to have caused her concern then or now. And since she had gone on to order room service, some coffee, Sanka, as she explains, plus possibly a bran muffin, perhaps nothing untoward had happened.

At this point, she explains, she had telephoned him. When he observes, 'I'm totally lost here,' she apparently takes this as a reference to their whereabouts in the city, though since by this stage he is shouting – evidently a long-standing issue between them – it is clear that she is aware of his real concern. Indeed, as if to turn the screw a little further, she now confesses to feeling sore, as she says 'down there'. When he asks her if they had forced her to have sex she replies, 'No.' Asked if she is sure she replies, 'Not one hundred per cent, but yeah, I think so, no,' (51) a self-liquidating assurance which leaves him bemused, not least because his satisfaction that she has perhaps not been forced leaves him with a still worse scenario.

By this stage the audience is several steps ahead of the man, though his growing alarm implies something familiar about the story, an inevitability that he resists. Even as they discuss the best route to the freeway, so the story advances towards an inevitable destination. Why, after all, had she been so relaxed if she had been assaulted? Had she not telephoned the police? – 'I don't think so, no ... not specifically.' (54) And what, above all, had been implied by her use of the word 'all'? 'Maybe', he tells her, 'I don't totally believe this.' (45) Why, she asks, would she lie to him?

By degrees, though, and under his questioning, she admits that she had met the men in the hotel lobby – which she then refines to the 'lobby-slash-lounge,' and then to the 'bar' – that, indeed, she may have taken the initiative, even inviting them upstairs to her room. She had, then, been drinking. She did not, as she now remembers, faint so much as black out 'at some point along the way', since, as she says to her husband, 'I shouldn't have liquor.' (55) At this moment, ostensibly with regard to their car journey, she says, 'We can jump on the freeway right up here. We're probably past the clog now.' (55) The remark applies with equal force to their conversation. The truth is almost out. As she confesses, 'I thought the story of them breaking in or whatever might be easier, ease you into something, but in the end, it's better to just . . .' (56) Now, she suggests, they can 'start afresh . . . start again, from here. Clean the slate.' Thus, when she says, 'This lane ends in, like, a block or so,' (56) this remark about street directions applies with equal force to the story she is telling. And there is one more block to go, one more piece of information for her to deliver as it becomes apparent that the word 'all' was the accurate one. There had, it seems, not been two men involved, or so he now infers. 'You weren't up there with a bunch of, not like a *whole* group . . . some line running out your door?' he asks, with an air of desperation, though since he adds, 'you wouldn't do that again?' it is clear that this is part of a familiar ritual. The play concludes with her offering further street directions whose implication for their relationship seems clear: 'This lane ends. You need to merge.' (57) The man drives on in silence, stealing glances at the woman who now goes to sleep, like the young woman in *bench seat*.

What emerges from their conversation is apparently a strange marriage in which an alcoholic, nymphomaniac is married to a man who has learned to live with humiliation (echoes, perhaps, of *Who's Afraid of Virginia Woolf*?). The implication is that they have accustomed themselves to their flawed characters. She, at least, is relaxed, used to being in charge, to confessing her lapses while sustaining their relationship. She sleeps at the end almost as if his probing and her response were a substitute for a sexual relationship which depends on such stories. Indeed, it is never clear that this is anything more than a fantasy, a game they play. They do merge, in that they evidently accept one another's flaws. Indeed, it seems possible that, since this has happened before, their conversation is part of a recurring ritual.

In *long division* two men sit in a car. The man at the wheel does most of the talking. What is at stake, ostensibly, is the recovery of a game system from his companion's former girlfriend/wife (which, is never clear), a companion whose sole contribution to the conversation is 'Go Down Division,' itself an ironic instruction given that the play turns on division. For the Man the recovery of the Nintendo 64 becomes a matter of principle, he being a man, as he explains, in a Mamet-like construction, 'who stands up for what's right ... whether it is or not.' (63) It becomes a matter of 'justice', of 'gravity'. He would, he explains, 'stand up in front of Judge Judy', she being a no-nonsense television judge who mediates between embittered friends and family members in a programme which for all her lucid common sense offers a depressing vision of personal relationships in America. It is a programme which precisely turns on the return of property (often computers, MP3s, CDs), small sums of money, restitution for supposed slights. What is at stake in these programmes is trivial. What is revealed is profound as the litigants emerge from court to assure the camera that they have learned not to trust friends or family members, never again to make a commitment.

In *long division* the issue is a piece of electronic equipment. This is the urgent issue to be settled. Meanwhile, the children of the relationship are a secondary matter: 'The kids, I mean, you can't deal with that now.' (63) Yet, when he recalls a couple in a cinema who asked for their money back because of a minor problem with the film's projector, he accuses them of failing to get things in proportion, a complaint he puts down to the man being gay. Yet the loss of the Nintendo (as opposed to the children) is 'about principle and fair play and that type of consideration,' (65) the bathetic last words undermining the elevated tone of the first. He is not, he assures his listener, advocating that 'you just grab-and-run' (65) having advocated precisely that only moments before – 'you run in ... untwist a couple wires and you're outta there.' (62) He is serving '*Truth*' even as he is 'dying to play a little Mortal Kombat' (65) on the liberated console.

The Other Man now calls out to 'Go Down Division,' having decided to go along with the plan. The man executes the turn, calling out, 'Oh my. Oh my, my, my, oh my. Yes, yes, yes ... Some lady with a new boyfriend and who's feeling no pain ... she had better take heed.' (66) What is at stake is plainly not the games console, still less the needs or otherwise of the Other Man, oddly unconcerned for his children. What is at stake is the Man's desire for action. The 'readiness is all', he says, unknowingly quoting from *Hamlet*, who accused himself of substituting words for action.

road trip features a man and a girl, who are driving across country (in the original production the text was modified to take account of the fact that the role written for a girl was actually performed by Kieran Culkin, with Brian Dennehy as the man). Though we are not given their ages, the relationship which gradually unfolds is revealed as being that between a teacher and his pupil. They have been on the road for almost twenty hours. At first, the nature of the relationship is not clear. If she is missing her friends, that, he explains, is natural since 'Anybody in their right mind would miss their parents when they go off somewhere for a while. Camp, or travelling, or whatever. Boarding school.' (70) So, presumably none of these reasons applies, though he recalls his own distress when, at the age of seven, he had been sent to a military boarding school for four years, but that, he says, in a formulation used by other LaBute characters, is the past, 'That's why they call it that, "the past," because that's what it is. Past ... It's not just some made-up word, convenient for journalists and scholars or whatnot ... It means what it is. It's the perfect word for it. "Past."' (71) (In *Fat Pig* a character insists that 'We've all got work ... that's why they call it that. "Work." Because that's what we do here' – language once again chasing its own tail, though here for the comic effect which comes from slamming a linguistic door in the face of an antagonist.) (19) This linguistic Moebius strip is a denial of communication, a verbal cul-de-sac which nonetheless reveals an anxiety that floats over the subsequent conversation. Not merely does it hint at trauma in his own youth, it quickly becomes clear that he has a motive for wishing to persuade his young companion that she should draw a line across the past.

The young girl was, he suggests, understandably scared to be driving across the country, a casual remark which becomes more pointed when she admits that she had hit him. He speaks as if this were no more than a child's tantrum, except that he then confesses to having been angry when she had hung onto the bathroom door at a rest stop and kicked out at him, crying. The grand adventure, it seems, is not quite what it appears. He had, he confesses, shouted at her, as he had seen her mother do, and threatened to hurt her. She is clearly afraid that he might still do so.

Their trip to a remote cabin is, he explains, 'our little thing. A secret', (79) a place, he suggests, where she can swim without clothes, an idea which clearly disturbs her ('our little secret' being a familiar formulation of paedophiles anxious to secure the silence of their victims). On the other hand there is a suggestion that she had originally been complicit, even bringing her Game Boy with her (only one of the echoes which reverberate through the play cycle, establishing a connection between what are otherwise discrete stories). As in *How I Learned to Drive*, he had been her driving instructor and, as in that play, there is a suggestion that he has taught her far more than driving skills. Again as in that play some of the remarks about driving constitute ironic comments on the relationship between the man and the girl. So, he speaks of the need to keep to 'the speed limit ... Following the rules', (80) he who is conspicuously not following the rules, maintaining limits. The play ends as the man fingers the hair of a girl who drifts off to sleep.

Hemingway spoke of his prose style being like that of an iceberg, only one eighth of which is above water. The force of his stories in particular derived from what was not said but only implied. LaBute works in a similar way. Here, a girl, whose mother has, as far as she can recall, never stroked her hair but who had frequently shouted at her in public, and whose father is never mentioned, travels with a man whose memory is of an absence of love in his own life. Some kind of pact seems to have been arrived at between what emerges as a teacher and his pupil. They had left suddenly, only for her to have second thoughts when they stopped briefly. Hence her desperation and hence his threats, now regretted but suggestive of his true nature. He seems to have no plans for anything but the immediate future. Indeed, he appears to have planned nothing but the site of their retreat. What lies in store for her there is ominous. They could, he suggests, 'play house and do whatever you want to. Anything at all ... swim. Don't even have to wear a suit,' because 'there's no one around there. It's very secluded ... Hidden. Off the beaten track,' no other people, no telephone, 'Just you and me.' (79) The language is of a romantic tryst. The reality, only partly understood by the young girl, is something quite other as she drives across country with a man who has threatened to hurt her and who now plans to isolate the two of them where no one will find them.

The title play, *autobahn*, features a man and a woman in the front seat of a car. The man, who is driving, and who in the original production was played by Philip Seymour Hoffman, remains silent throughout, while in many ways turning out to be the crucial figure. In a cycle of plays about problematic relationships and betrayed hopes, this is in some ways paradigmatic, as the speaker circles around a subject which she forebears at first to address before edging towards truths which she lays down like the playing cards in a losing hand. Acutely aware of her own dilemma, she sees this as part of a wider collapse of values. 'We just keep doing lousy things,' she observes, ' I think it's just the way it is these days, the whole country is living with this now ... A sickness. Yeah, a sick sort of feeling in your gut that says, "Hey, hello there, what's going on? I got a real ache in here that tells me we're up to no good."' (85) In part, she is generalising the better to exorcise her sense of personal failure, but in part she is acknowledging a genuine shared condition, the shared condition expressed in the play cycle.

They have, she confesses, failed, but the nature of that failure takes time to emerge. Indeed, she seems unsure as to what exactly it consists of. They have, it slowly transpires, adopted a child who has grown up to commit crimes, taking their car and joyriding, stealing their money, verbally abusing them, carrying a gun to school. Their first failure, then, is as adoptive parents. As she says, in a revealing slip of the tongue, 'I'm a working adult and I don't have time to do that. Be someone's mom. No, I don't mean that. I was his mom, I am.' (88) Her very equivocation suggests something about the nature of her commitment, or lack of it. Their second failure is that they had handed him over to the authorities, washing their hands of him even as they accepted the final cheque from the adoption agency. Beyond that, though, is something altogether more serious for a relationship which itself has seemed anything but secure: 'It is "we," right?' (86) she had asked the man as if seeking assurance of a mutuality which is in doubt in a play in which the man is not described as her husband but her 'companion' and in which, she confesses, he tells her that she overdoes her use of the word 'love'.

His silence throughout becomes ever more ominous as we learn that, perhaps as an act of revenge, the boy had accused him of sexually abusing him. His denial is not voiced, not here, in the car, in the immediate privacy of their relationship. The alternative interpretation hangs in the air, not least because he seems to avoid direct eye contact with her. There are, perhaps, hints that she, too, might have been a victim as she recalls an uncle who was 'always taking pictures of me'. (90) Her assurances of support are less than fulsome, her confidence not finally convincing: 'at least none of this has touched us. Right?' she insists, '... our union is not sullied by the experience. Am I using the word correctly? Sullied? ... we remain untouched by this nonsense. Without sin, really.' (91) The question marks, the linguistic query, the word 'really' all undermine the assertions. When she remarks that 'it'll go away and then we'll be right back where we were. All fine and good. Fine and good because we are that ourselves ... fine and good people who enjoy a place in the community,' the statements are self-negating, anxiety-generating assertions, much as Ronald Reagan had spoken of Americans as 'a good and worthy people', and George W. Bush had remarked, 'I know how good we are.' And perhaps it is not fanciful to see the plays in the cycle as a comment on America as, more broadly, on human relationships.

The Woman notes that we spend an eighth of our lives in cars and that we largely spend that time speeding past one another with 'no sense of how dangerous or careless we're being', (92) blanking out an awareness of pain and betrayal quite as if it were possible to escape who we are and what we do. What is apparent from these plays, and their ruling metaphor, is that though we travel together there is always a gap of understanding, a misalignment of needs, usually, though not invariably, between the genders. Nor is that a divide that can be bridged by language since that itself is evidence of the divide.

There is a sense that for much of the time the characters in these plays address themselves rather than their companions and that the most articulate moments are those in which silent characters stare blankly ahead or snatch a glance at those who claim an intimacy almost invariably resisted or seen as a threat. This America is on the move but there is no sense that it is going anywhere in particular.

autobahn

What emerges from *autobahn* is a sense of ache, of bruised individuals travelling sometimes in hope but more often in a kind of despair that masquerades as its opposite. But then America has never had a destination, only a fate, which is why it announces with such assurance its own perfection even as it is confronted day by day with evidence of the reverse. These are its citizens, asking themselves where it went wrong even as they insist on the need to move on.

In *autobahn* character is action. The plays are necessarily static. That fact, though, gives added significance to the smallest gesture, even to the blank stare ahead through the windshield which is the commonest response to what is often a nervous flow of language. These are not radio plays for the stage. They turn precisely on the co-presence of individuals who frequently seem to share little beyond their temporary location. They journey side by side, their stories barely intersecting, shaping what meaning they can out of the frustrations, disappointments, betrayals which seem to characterise their lives.

10

Fat Pig and *This Is How It Goes*

> And how am I different?
> How am I different?
> How am I different? ...
> Just one question before I buy
> When you fuck it up later,
> Do I get my money back?
>
> Aimee Mann, 'How Am I Different?'

LaBute, frequently challenged for his supposed misanthropy, insists that he is not misanthropic but sceptical. That scepticism, he has explained, is a product of the fact that 'it is very hard in this society today to take the time to be caring, to worry about other people. Relationships take work, and that's not just love relationships but work and friends. You have to give of yourself and I think that people do a lot of just getting by. I think that is a pretty real and cruel thing that people do. They just slide by with enough effort to get to the next day.' It is, he has said, 'easier to go under the radar', something he detected in himself, preferring, perhaps like most people, to avoid conflict and the anguish which comes with a fight or even with the social embarrassment of going against received opinion.[1] His next play, *Fat Pig*, explores precisely this failure of nerve, the small betrayals which infiltrate daily experience and which make greater betrayals possible. *Fat Pig* is a bitter comedy.

Whatever other issues it addressed, *the shape of things* responded to what seemed to LaBute an American obsession with appearance. A society which had mythicised the self-made man, with winning friends and influencing people, had become increasingly concerned with the reshaping of the self in such a way as to assure that happiness. The physical and spiritual being was to be sculpted, renewed. Religious cults (often suitably adjusted so as not to offend the wealthy, indeed sometimes, as with Scientology, actually charging the faithful), offered a state of spiritual grace. Psychotherapy could adjust the psyche to an assumed norm. The plastic-surgery supermarket offered a range of desirable noses and breasts, usually modelled on those of Hollywood stars, themselves often precision-engineered to match a paradigm of the desirable. And in a society that had taken the idea of conspicuous consumption altogether too literally (advertising food by its weight, providing doggy bags for animals supposedly with a taste for haute cuisine), there were those who offered colonic irrigation, exercise videos, health clubs, diets or stomach stapling. Each summer is liable to be greeted with horror by those for whom the winter had offered an opportunity to turn surplus income into surplus fat, sexuality being assumed to be the province of those with well-toned, tanned bodies, super-white smiles and hair that glows in the sun of conditioners enhanced with products of the Amazon rain forest. This is touted as a route to the kind of power which comes with conforming to a template of desirability. For those with longer-term plans there were sperm banks and the prospect of genetic manipulation, breeding for the perfection that America had always implicitly claimed as its ultimate objective.

LaBute has confessed to being somewhat on the ample side himself. Indeed, in his preface to *Fat Pig* he describes his own attempts at self-improvement. Like Adam, in *the shape of things*, a character not wholly remote from his creator, he set himself to trim some of his excess weight though not, he insists, at the behest of a woman. He simply 'didn't feel so hot ... looked like shit' and 'was tired of wearing the same pants'.[2] He lost sixty pounds in eight months, which is nearly two pounds a week. The result was that he felt a great deal better, became narcissistic and obsessive and wrote less. A 'few personal and professional mishaps' sent him back to food as, he recalled, a crisis had sent Adam to eating in part as a sign of tension but in part, surely, also as a gesture that he wanted his life back as it had been before he allowed someone else to dictate his notion of the desirable.

In *A Moon for the Misbegotten* Eugene O'Neill created the figure of a woman weighing a hundred and eighty pounds, who he describes as 'freakish,' and initiates a bitter-sweet relationship between her and a figure plainly based on his own brother, Jamie. Both are afraid to reveal their feelings. It was a kind of benediction on the part of O'Neill, as he reached out to his doomed brother. In the same play Jamie describes another woman as a 'fat pig'.[3] A hundred and eighty pounds, and five feet eleven, no longer seems quite so freakish. LaBute never tells us Helen's weight (Ashley Atkinson who played the part in the Broadway production was five feet eight and two hundred pounds, but even then was required to wear a 'fat suit') but describes her as the 'overweight, sensible, and perfectly lovely heroine of *Fat Pig* who disdains fiction for reality'. (xi)

Earlier in his career he would have disdained such a description but it is an indication that this is a play in which he largely forsakes irony, even as his characters deploy it as weapon or protection. He remains as interested as ever in human cruelty but explores it in the context of a play which does indeed seem to have an unequivocally good character at its heart: vulnerable, the victim of other people's assumptions, of cultural presumptions, but resilient and honest. She is someone who has lived as she wished, who retains a sense of humour and proportion, despite or because of her own proportions, though she is also someone who registers the pressures that would make her something else, insist that she conform. In the end, love seems on the verge of accomplishing what social pressure cannot, but, perhaps not unsurprisingly in LaButeland, that moment coincides with betrayal.

Fat Pig had its world premiere at the Manhattan Class Theater in New York City in November 2004. It takes place in a 'big city near the ocean' and opens in a crowded restaurant where a character at first identified only as Woman encounters a Man. They gain names – Tom and Helen – only as they come to know one another, the speech indicators reflecting their growing intimacy as the first scene edges towards its end, she giving him her telephone number. She is described as 'a plus size. Very',[4] so that his first words, 'pretty big' seem to be a comment on her appearance rather than the restaurant. What follows is a wry conversation during which it becomes clear that they share a good deal, not least a sense of humour.

In the original production, Jo Bonney, the director, had Helen already on stage as the audience came into the theatre, an idea not indicated in the stage directions. She was eating and, necessarily, at length. LaBute approved because of the sense of discomfort it inspired and also because the audience are placed in the same position as Tom as he first encounters her. His reaction can thus be judged against their own. They are already implicated in the aesthetic, moral questions raised by the relationship which now unfolds.

She is a librarian or, as he guesses, a 'printed-word specialist'. (9) This is a world in which nothing must be called what it is. He complains that he can no longer speak of girls, rather than women, for fear of 'getting hit by a *lawsuit*', (9) though as he points out being a '"refuse technician"' (9) still means 'picking *shit* up off the street'. (9) It is a conversation which bears directly on her situation and their developing relationship. She confesses to not being bad at 'the truth'. (7) The question is whether he will be able to show the same facility, not least when it comes to explaining the nature of their relationship to others.

At one moment the Woman recalls a wig commercial, only to suggest that 'people should just go with it . . . whatever they look like.' (8) In effect, it is a statement of intent, seemingly a declaration of her own position as she and the Man begin what she already seems to see as a possible relationship – or why stake out her territory with such care? Yet she is plainly looking for confirmation of her statement. Beneath the assurance is not only doubt about the man she has just met but self-doubt concealed by her self-deprecating jokes. When she identifies herself as Helen, he replies by invoking Helen of Troy, apologising for the obviousness of the reference. For her part, however, she suggests that it would take a thousand ships to carry her. It is a linguistic pre-emptive strike but as such it reveals a vulnerability she is otherwise inclined to deny.

The play, despite its title, is not, finally, about the problem of being fat. As LaBute has explained, 'the story really deals with human weakness and the difficulty many people face when trying to stand up for, live up to, or come out for something they believe in.' (Preface,

xii) This is an issue, he suggests, 'that's pretty much me in a nutshell –
well meaning as can be, but surprisingly lame when push really comes
to shove. Heroism, it would seem, is a tough gig.' (xii)

According to the woman, the Man, who we later come to know
as Tom, is good-looking, though in his own mind lacking in special
qualities. He is, he suggests, a 'Faithful friend and co-worker, depend-
able, takes directions well', (12) though later it becomes apparent that
his life has been one of temporary relationships from which he has
extricated himself with a lack of grace. It seems they may have discovered a mutually satisfying relationship though, in contrast to her,
he is plainly on a diet, checking the calorie count of food 'like some
Bible scholar'. (11) When she makes a self-deprecating joke about her
own weight, he admonishes her. That he should be embarrassed on her
behalf says something about his growing feeling for her. For her part,
and below the apparent assurance, though, there is plainly a nervous-
ness as she asks that he should not mind what people think if they
should go out together.

Part of the play's power, of course, comes from the degree to
which the audience itself will see the relationship as being as awkward
as we soon learn his workmates do. LaBute specialises in making
audiences unsettled, in confronting them with their own prejudices
and impulses and Tom battles for much of the play to face his
own growing unease at a relationship which leaves him vulnerable
to ridicule.

Each scene carries a title. 'That First Meeting with Her' is
followed by 'The Work Friends Figure it Out', and, indeed, a workmate
does quiz him on his private life. Carter seems a distant relative of
Chad in *in the company of men*, witty, callous. He has been in therapy
but has abandoned it because 'she was a total bitch,' (22) though the
fact of the therapy suggests something about a man who otherwise
seems so assured, so confident of himself. Having heard rumours of
Tom's new relationship he deliberately leaks the news to a character
first identified as a Co-worker and then as Jeannie, a woman with
whom Tom had previously had a relationship. For Carter, women are
to be judged by their appearances. Jeannie is looking 'a bit sloppy ... In
her ass ... her arms have gotten chunkier.' (21) It is, he insists, not 'like

some derogatory thing I'm saying about her – not the therapist cunt, but Jeannie – it's just an idle thought. She seems to be packing it on some. That's the problem with winter: chicks don't get out much and they bloat up.' (22)

Tom's relationship with Jeannie had been tentative, unsure. For her part, she had been desperate. He is uncommitted; she craves commitment. Indeed, Tom seems by nature equivocal. His relationship with Carter is more a product of habit than a natural affinity. Even his growing involvement with Helen is characterised by uncertainty, a distancing irony. Their joking banter simultaneously brings them together and maintains a space between them.

The next scene finds them once again in a restaurant, as if food were their point of contact. Having explained to Tom that he was meeting out-of-town colleagues, he is nervous lest he be discovered. His embarrassment, though, goes beyond this. When he holds her hand, he glances around the restaurant. Despite his assurances, to her and to himself, he is plainly not yet immune to the embarrassment of dating a fat woman. His private relationship is subject to public pressure.

And she has a history of rejection. Her penchant for war movies derives, she explains, from the fact that she grew up in a family of men, trapped indoors by the fact that no boys came to date her. In a way she is no less desperate than Jeannie. If she had been looking for early commitment, however, it is not yet what he is willing to offer. When Carter appears to check up on his story and finds them together Tom is afraid to admit to the truth, continuing to maintain his story. Within a minute of Helen insisting that 'I just want you to be truthful,' (32) he is lying out of embarrassment, first to Carter and then to her. As Jeannie remarks, when she confronts him with the fact that there had been no out-of-town colleagues, 'You are, like, the worst liar ever. I mean it. In *history.*' (45)

When Tom is caught out in his lie, Carter, despite his instinct for revelling in other people's problems, offers the information that his own mother had been fat, his account combining callousness with what is evidently a sense of guilt if also resentment. He describes the embarrassment this had caused him as a teenager: 'I'm fifteen and worried about every little thing, and I've got this fucking *sumo wres-tler* in a housecoat trailing around behind me ... And the thing was, I blamed her for it ... she just shovelled shit into her mouth all the time, had a few kids, and, bang, she's up there at 350, maybe more.' But 'the thing was, I blamed her for it.' (48) In retrospect, it seems to him that his father had absented himself from the family home precisely because of his wife's appearance.

What he primarily recalls, though, was the moment, in a super-market, when he had snapped, 'screaming in her face ... "Don't look at the package, take a look in the fucking *mirror*, you cow!! PUT 'EM DOWN!"' (49) She had said nothing but as they drove home, in the light of a stoplight he saw a tear in her eye but though he acknowledges that he should not have shouted at her, he still insists that 'there's a pretty easy remedy, most times. Do-not-jam-as-much-food-in-your-fucking-gullet.' (49) For Chad, in *in the company of men*, this story would merely have been a tactic, a web spun the more easily to capture his prey, but there is a dimension to Carter missing from Chad and he is given a line that in many ways sums up a key theme of the play: 'Very rare is the dude who stands up for the shit he believes in.' (49) Indeed, as he points out, Tom is very like him: 'you get bored or cornered or feel a touch nervous, and you drop 'em like they were *old produce*.' The question is, will he do as much with Helen? Will his social embarrassment infect his relationship with her? Meanwhile, the detritus from his last relationship is still evident as a hostile email from Jeannie arrives and he is seen pounding a reply on the keyboard before stopping, exhausted, having run out of words.

As he and Helen grow ever more intimate, so she becomes increas-ingly aware of his reluctance to introduce her to his friends or to meet her own. Intimacy, indeed, seems a form of escape as she senses his desire to sit at the back of cafés or enter movies after the lights have gone down. Yet the very intimacy she craves is not without its ambivalence as she opts for making love while a war movie plays on the television, an echo of the time when such films had constituted the soundtrack of her early life, when she had dealt with rejection by denying her sexuality. Beyond that, though, a bedroom scene between the two of them confronts audience members with their own embarrassment at seeing a partly dressed, over-weight woman embracing a not unattractive man.

The disturbing fact is that Carter is more honest than Tom, that he confronts what Tom shies away from, and not merely the opinions of others. Nor is this only a play about attitudes towards the fat. Tom's fears tap into something altogether more disturbing and Carter is the person who provides a wormhole from the unconscious to the conscious. Not infrequently, LaBute's more obnoxious characters display an honesty lacking in those who seem less brutal. As he has said, 'while Carter can come off as a bit of an ass, he's someone that also says a lot of things that we take to be true ... They may not be put in a fashionable way but often they're worth saying.'[5] They are worth saying in the sense that they reflect feelings often kept under cover, the cover of language. He does not deal in euphemisms or liberal sentiments. For him, the world is as it is. Tom shies away from his own fears as he does from exposing himself to ridicule. Carter, however, is, he acknowledges, 'not talking about what people deserve, I'm saying what they *get* ... Truth. People are not comfortable with difference. You know? Fags, retards, cripples. Fat people. Old folks, even. They scare us or something.' (71) He punches the words out not so much with relish as with an acknowledgement that whatever the current orthodoxies, below the surface is a fear that disturbs our equanimity. 'The thing they represent that's so scary is what we *could* be, how vulnerable we all are ... We're all just one step away from being what frightens us. What we despise. So ... we despise it when we see it in anybody else.' (71–2) For all his treachery, meanwhile, he genuinely seems motivated by a bizarre sense of camaraderie. He simply cannot understand why a man who is 'good-looking ... successful, a bit of a player in the industry' is 'taking God's good gifts and pissing on 'em'. (70)

Tom seems to believe that if feelings do not make their way into words they can be denied. He is intimidated. In America, Ashlie Atkinson observed, 'There's a lot of people that would rather risk death than disapproval.' (chinadaily) What Tom suffers is what Alexis de Tocqueville identified as a defining characteristic of America: the tyranny of the majority. He retreats behind shared interests, an affected diffidence or humour. But what had at first seemed a charming aspect of his character slowly begins to alarm a woman who had begun to allow hope to triumph over experience. 'I don't need you to be clever here! No jokes. Or *film quotes* . . . Just be very clear . . . and honest.' (60) Honesty, though, is precisely what is beyond him, not simply because of social pressure but because commitment itself frightens him. His response to her is revealing in its rambling imprecisions: 'I don't know how to deal with this. To say exactly what I'm feeling because, you know, I'm a guy, and we're taught how to *kick stuff* and tear the wings off shit, but, look . . . I can see that we've got something here, I'm not stupid right – do not answer that – and I need you to know. That I know. I'm really just so damn . . . *overcome* by this. Here. Us.' (60)

The play ends as Tom and Helen are seen at the company beach picnic, though Jo Bonney, in part for technical reasons to do with scene changes, introduced a brief scene, not included in the script, in which Helen is seen trying on different costumes, trying to decide which would be best for what she clearly sees as a vital moment in their relationship. As LaBute admitted, it was heartbreaking.

If he was moved by the plight of Helen, he was equally concerned with that of Jeannie. As a result, after the initial production, he decided to give her more to say because, 'I wasn't unfair to her but I put her in a difficult position. She is very single-minded in her pursuit and anger throughout the show because she has been thrown this curveball that Tom is going out with somebody else. So I wanted to see her back at the top of her cycle of dating and feeling good about herself, where she could honestly say how she felt about the time she spent with Tom.'[6] This is not the Neil LaBute of the early plays who was seldom to be caught mitigating the pain his characters cause and suffer, but the mood and tone of *Fat Pig* is different. These, for the most part, are characters who are struggling to sustain an integrity which is nonetheless real for being compromised. Their commitments are real, even if they, and especially Tom, lack the courage to sustain them.

Tom has arranged that they should sit away from his colleagues and though for a while he struggles to find some justification for this he finally admits to being paranoid about what other people think. He confesses that he is unable to fight it. He wants nothing more than to keep his head above water. Whatever feelings he has for her he lacks the courage to go through with their relationship, even when her desperation becomes apparent as she offers to have an operation to stop her eating. In the end, they sit side by side, in tears, staring out to sea.

Fat Pig differs, then, from LaBute's earlier plays. It is, in effect, a love story, the story of a relationship in which neither party is manipulative. There is never any suggestion that their feelings are anything other than genuine. Their problem is that they exist in a world in which she fails to match the prevailing paradigm of the desirable and he lacks the courage to swim against the stream. It happens that she is fat. She could be any one of a number of other things judged unacceptable or simply unfashionable. Beyond that, though, Tom has evidently had a series of unsatisfactory relationships, as has Jeannie who ends up as a partner of the seemingly cynical Carter. There is an air of desperation around. Jeannie and Helen alike feel that time is running out for them while the men's relationship smacks of the adolescent. They are American boy-men, able to deal with women, it seems, only as temporary diversions or inhibited by a fear of stepping outside the protective circle of male camaraderie.

The irony is that Tom defers to the views of those for whom he has no respect. He may be unhappy with aspects of the locker-room mentality but it provides protection of a sort. Just as Sinclair Lewis's George F. Babbitt had scuttled back to the protection of an adolescent brotherhood which in his heart he despised, so Tom sacrifices something of value for something with none. And there is an element of Babbitt about him. His rebellion against contemporary norms is momentary, a fantasy he indulges even as he knows he cannot sustain it. He lacks the courage of his own lack of convictions, prefers comfort to passion, acceptance to resistance. Somewhere beneath the confident assurance of American society, a cold current is running, a world of personal ads, singles bars, momentary alliances, in which those who feel excluded from whatever it is they seek look for relationships which they simultaneously desire and fear, not least because they involve a degree of commitment they find difficult to sustain. Men and women are drawn together out of mutual needs only to discover that mutuality can be an illusion. Tom's affection for Helen is real enough. It is simply not strong enough to resist his contrary desire to avoid embarrassment, ridicule, exclusion from the dubious embrace of social values to which he subscribes even as he distrusts them.

The titles which introduce each scene – 'That First Meeting with Her', 'One of Those Blustery Beach Days' – suggest nothing so much as a Harlequin Romance. That there is a wind blowing in the opposite direction creates the irony within which Tom in particular is prepared to exist. LaBute might be accused of sentimentality in the final scene, with the shattered pair sitting side by side but not together, but they are the victims of nothing but Tom's own failure of moral courage or simply imagination. The emotion is not unearned. Their relationship has ended precisely because of his inability to sustain it. That he would choose to trade something of considerable value for something of no value at all is an indication that this attractive, witty, humane man is as capable of betrayal as the most cynical. So, we are left with a Beckett-like stasis as, anxious to move forward, they do not move, united now only in their sense of abandonment.

LaBute constantly metamorphoses as a writer. One minute he is David Mamet, the next Sherwood Anderson. He is a poet of the spiritually dispossessed, of those never quite able to grasp the principles of the world they inhabit. They fall among strangers, sometimes struggling to protect themselves from intrusion, sometimes contriving to seek advantage but sometimes looking for a sense of completion. Their needs are real enough. Their problem is that few of his characters are willing to pay the price for the protection they seek, the mutuality for which they yearn but which they equally fear. In *Fat Pig* Tom denies himself the very thing he craves but only because he craves something more – an untroubled life in which he need never acknowledge his vulnerability or the pain he causes others not out of intent but as a consequence of his own dereliction, his failure of will and purpose which in the end adds up to his failure of humanity.

LaBute's loyalty is, he insists, finally to those characters on the page

> and that's what sometimes leads to the plays ending in what I think of as relatively realistic but sometimes unfulfilling ways for an audience. Things do not always end happily or in the ways

they wished. In *Fat Pig* that is certainly the case. In many ways, even though I find the ending of *Fat Pig* sad, I find it quite truthful and honest, which is the very thing that Tom is asked to be throughout the play by two very different women . . . He finds that within himself but through his honesty he hurts somebody but also realises that he is not a very strong person. And this is a terribly sobering thing to find out about yourself. It is not that you are a bad person. It is just that you are not a strong person, that you can't stand up for yourself. Particularly for a man, it is a hard thing to admit. But that's where I saw Tom was. It is not the end of Tom's life. I rarely ever write characters who die. I don't think of it as hopeless. These people could change. Who knows? But I write about a very specific portion of their lives.[7]

This is how it goes
One more failure to connect
Aimee Mann, 'This Is How It Goes'

In Thornton Wilder's *Our Town* a Stage Manager summons characters onto the stage, underscoring the factitious nature of what follows as Pirandello, in *Six Characters in Search of an Author*, presents characters who struggle against the text which entraps them even as it grants them a paradoxical immunity. Both writers draw attention to the theatricality not only of what confronts the audience but also of the lives they stage. Pirandello remarked on the fact that, 'We believe ourselves one person, but it is true to say that we are many persons, many according to the possibilities of being which exist within us. We are one for this and another for that person – always diverse and yet filled with the illusion that our personality is always the same for all.'[8] In his preface to *This Is How It Goes*, LaBute speaks of the many versions of truth 'that we offer up to different people',[9] while one of his characters assures us that 'people are so many things, faces, in a given day.'[10]

Secure notions of reality, in other words, are illusory. Iris Murdoch, in *The Sea, The Sea*, has a character observe that, 'the theatre, even at its most "realistic", is connected with the level at which, and the methods by which, we tell ourselves everyday lies,'[11] as Wilder insisted that 'Out of the lie, the pretence, of the theatre proceeds a truth,'[12] a truth which is the more compelling for its root in an acknowledged theatricality.

In February 2001, Edward Albee's *The Play About the Baby* opened in New York. It featured a character called Man who moved in and out of the action, commenting on it. As a narrator, he engaged the audience, speaking to them familiarly, welcoming them back from the intermission, remarking on the unfolding action. He summoned the characters onto the stage as if bringing them into existence, as if he were in some degree the writer whose imagination generated the action. Yet he also seemed to be involved in a conspiracy, though its objective remained unclear. It was in some ways a play that explored the problematic status of the real, that asked whether 'that which we *feel* we have experienced is the same as we have,' whether reality 'is determined by our experience of it. Or our *sense* of experiencing it?'[13]

The Play About the Baby, with its intertextual references, its prevailing writer/stage director, seems in part an exploration of play-making itself and its paradoxical relationship to reality, fictions which nonetheless offer to edge towards truth. As the Man remarks, 'Pay attention to this, what's true and what isn't is a tricky business.' (10) In *This is How It Goes*, LaBute's 2004 play, a character also called Man similarly invites the audience to 'pay attention' (37), even as he is confessing to the unreliability of what is about to be acted out, quite as if this were an act of homage to a writer he has acknowledged as an influence.

Indeed, *This Is How It Goes* seems to do rather more than tip its hat in Albee's direction. The figure called Man in LaBute's play, like the similarly named figure in Albee's play, steps in and out of the action. He, too, establishes a familiar bond with the audience and summons the characters into being. This, too, is a play in which the problematic nature of reality is not so much debated as staged, and in which there is a conspiracy. LaBute's play, however, goes places that Albee's does not. Though both explore male–female relationships and have a concern for power, LaBute makes race a part of his enquiry, though even here a game is being played whose terms are, perhaps, not entirely clear. Meanwhile, his acknowledged debt to Mamet surfaces in his fascination with confidence tricksters, masquerades, legerdemain, sudden changes of direction.

The character designated simply as Man is both a narrator and a character in *This Is How It Goes*. He begins with what turns out to be a suitably equivocal speech: 'This is how it goes. I meant, went. This is the way it all played out, or is going to. Or is . . . right now. Doesn't matter, you'll figure it out. I think . . .. You know what I'm saying! Sort of. And which is okay, because I only sort of know, too, at this point. Geeze, I think I might end up being an unreliable narrator here.'(5) As it happens, this was an accurate statement of LaBute's own position as he wrote those words, unaware, as yet, how things would develop or who his characters were. It is also an accurate statement in that the narrator invites an intimacy with the audience, a trust, that will, as he hints, later be betrayed.

LaBute has explained that his writing method often has to do with disturbing audiences' expectations. He has a liking for turning the action through a hundred and eighty degrees. In *This Is How It Goes*, he makes a point of performing a number of such manoeuvres. In his earlier plays, his characters have a habit of blindsiding one another, manipulating their desires, reversing their own direction. They are frequently actors, performing in scenarios of their own devising, to the point at which their own identities seem problematic as they become lost in their own inventions. Sometimes, as in *in the company of men* and *the shape of things*, this is a conscious tactic in the service of power, ambition, the self. Here, as in a crime story, whose processes he mimics, there are suppressed facts, suppositions. What seems certain at one moment is cast in doubt the next as the author makes a writer the apparent generator of his text. His fondness for abstract designations – Man, Woman – which mirrors Albee's, suggests the extent to which his are morality plays, albeit plays in which moral clarity is undermined by his sense of the relativity of truth.

This Is How It Goes began, LaBute has explained, with its title, derived from a song by Aimee Mann. And though it was the title rather than the lyrics which attracted his attention, one line in Mann's song – 'One more failure to connect' – would seem relevant to more than this play. It is a title that implies a truth to be revealed, a story to be told. As it turns out, there is more than one story and the truth is hard to discern. Indeed, in some ways this is a play about the composition of a play which mimics the process of its own creation. As LaBute confesses, he put two characters together, located them in a neutral setting, and waited for a story to be generated. Since his central character describes himself as a playwright, and steps out of the action to comment on it, this meta-theatrical dimension is underscored from the beginning. *This is*, the audience comes to realise, in fact not necessarily *how it goes*, not only because stories have the capacity to move in unlikely directions but because the real is not to be captured with total assurance. It depends who is telling the story.

To the original two characters, he added a third and, as he explained, with this came 'a meditation on truth' and, since, apparently to his surprise, the third character was black, 'some notion about how racism still affects all of us on a simple, daily level'. (ix) That latter notion, though, itself proves problematic in a work in which the real proves increasingly difficult to validate. Indeed, since the narrator himself warns of his unreliability even the racial attitudes adopted or implied by the characters are something more than a matter of perspective. They are generated by a suspect text. LaBute confesses to having 'utilized everything I could get my hands on to help tell the truth or at least one side of it – the shifting sands of a narrator's voice, the repetition of scenes from different perspectives, a set of stage directions that has more asides than a borsht belt comedian'. (xi)

Betrayed trust has always lain at the heart of his plays. Here, it simply extends to the process of the narration, to the scenes enacted and then re-enacted, to the characters arbitrarily invented and then invited to explain their existence and their relationship to a world no less contingent than themselves.

The dramatis personae of *This Is How It Goes* lists four characters but in effect there is another in so far as in the published version LaBute maintains an ironic commentary by way of the stage directions. 'Let's give him a little light,' the directions read, as a man walks onstage. 'There, that's better. Now what? Wait – I think he's going to say something. Yes, he is. Good.' (5) When a woman appears, the stage directions again intervene to indicate that another light is needed. These whimsical and ironic comments serve to underline the contingent nature of what follows, for the reader if not the viewer. There is a series of Chinese boxes as the stage directions comment on a character who himself, at times standing outside the action, comments on other characters who themselves present shifting versions of the truth.

The Man now crosses to the Woman (though we are later given her name) and says 'hello' before immediately returning to the light spot, which designates his place as narrator, and offering further information. He and the Woman, he explains, had known one another at school and are meeting, it appears, for the first time in many years, though even now he casts doubt on 'whether this is happening or, umm, has happened, is all in my head – *however* that works out'. (6)

Initially the play seems the story of one-time high school acquaintances who meet a dozen years later. One, Belinda, is a former cheerleader who grew up to marry Cody, an African American and one-time track star who is now a rich member of the community. She, we are later told, married him to stand out from the crowd, to counter her sense of her own insignificance. He married her because he was in search of a trophy wife. By chance, as it seems, the narrator now meets her outside a Sears store in a small and anonymous Midwestern town. He seems scarcely more identifiable, being defined in part by what he is not. He is no longer in the army, no longer a lawyer, no longer married. Indeed, he proves remarkably resistant to offering any positive information about his life, beyond their shared memories, though in truth Belinda scarcely remembers him, even though he had been in her English class, not least because even in high school he barely registered except as an overweight boy who compensated for his unattractiveness by being a jokester.

In the course of their conversation, it quickly emerges that her marriage is not a happy one (indeed we later learn that she is hated not only by her husband but also by her six-year-old child) and that she, too, has turned her back on possibilities. Her husband, she confesses, no longer communicates with any ease while she has evidently settled for what she has got. Even with a near-stranger she is unable to conceal her sense of disappointment. Indeed, after only a few minutes they arrange to meet one another again.

The problem for the audience lies in the fact that we are offered a running commentary on events by the Man who steps out of the action in order to feed us what later turns out to be erroneous information. Their meeting, he tells us, had been fortuitous. He had known nothing of her life since school, had been unaware, indeed, he assures us, that she was married. When he invites the audience to meet the previously absent Cody, to 'take a second and get acquainted', he does so, he explains, because 'I think it'd start to help pull this thing all together for you.'(18) In a sense, though, the play finally makes complete sense only at second viewing, though the deceptions are integral to its meaning, in the sense that it is precisely concerned with the difficulty of reading experience, with pulling it all together. Belinda's insistence that 'People should be honest with each other' (15) and Cody's question, 'What's the matter with the truth?' (20) derive their irony only from what follows as it becomes apparent that almost nothing is what it seems, that this is not in fact how it goes. In particular, and most crucially, this was not, we later discover, the protagonist's first meeting with Cody nor was his encounter with Belinda fortuitous. There is a master story only gradually to be revealed.

The Man, as narrator, invites a feeling of intimacy with the audience, a suspect intimacy as he shares his thoughts about Cody, a man, we are told, who was always ready to play the race card, what he and his friends, he explains, used to call the 'Ace 'a Spades'. 'Just gotta call a spade a spade,' he adds, recalling a joke they had shared. As he says this, so the stage direction indicates that 'The MAN looks to us for validation' and asks, 'does he get any?' adding 'Well, we'll have to see. For now let's imagine that it remains silent out there. He nods, then turns back to the table.' (27) Whether the response is confederacy, embarrassment or distaste, the audience becomes a part of the play and his nod confirmation that he has registered that response, that the line between audience and performer has been eroded. This is, after all, a play in which the audience's expectations and assumptions become part of the games played by the characters.

Shortly after this, the Man, now stepping back into the restaurant scene, suggests that Cody should consider returning to Africa, another dubious joke which turns on a reference to Alex Haley's novel turned television mini-series, *Roots*. Do the audience laugh? If so, they become complicit, albeit only in a joke.

By now, the narrator has begun to sound remarkably like the similar figure in *The Play About the Baby*, promising to speed up the action because 'Most of you'll need to get on home after this, right? I'm sure you do. Even if you have no one to get home to, you still need to get there.' (36) Even the apparent folksiness has an edge to it. He will, he explains, not 'be in this next bit, except in *spirit* or whatever, because I'll be talked about, things like that, but I won't actually be there'. (36) Who, then, is recalling it? What in fact follows is a scene in which Cody beats Belinda only for the narrator to say, 'okay, so maybe it wasn't *exactly* like that. I dunno. Hey, look, I'm a writer – would-be writer, anyway – so, what can I tell ya? I've got a hell of an imagination, and I just go with it sometimes.' (42)

Having invited the audience to 'pay attention' he confesses that 'I wasn't there, so I didn't see it – but *you* get to see it. If you pay attention. All I know is later, when Cody's out of the office, she comes in, and I see it and freak out a bit, but she never actually tells me about what happened. Not really. So this is how it goes.' (36) The logic, of course, is that, once again, this is not how it goes and that paying attention will ostensibly tell us more about his imagination than any supposed reality. We are then offered the same scene, this time replayed to match what we are told was Belinda's own description of the event. She had, she explained, banged her eye on an open cupboard door. The scene which now unfolds pictures a Cody who is solicitous at first even though they argue and she ends in tears. In the first scene she is beaten; in the second she is browbeaten. Perhaps the essential truth remains the same and in the words of Albee's character, 'that which we *feel* we have experienced is the same as we have'.[14]

The narrator not only invents scenes, he puts words into the mouths of his characters. When Belinda remarks that she had been attracted to Cody 'because I like a nice, thick black cock' (56) he immediately confesses that she would have been incapable of saying such a thing: 'obviously she didn't say it like that. I mean, it's *obvious*, right? She's not that way, would never say a thing like that ... God, can you picture *her* saying that?' except, of course, that, at his behest, she has, a character obeying her creator. It is, he confesses, 'what *I'm* thinking right now. Or ... what I've had in my head since the first time I heard about her and Cody. Or anytime you see a white girl and a ... well, you know.' (57) Again, the audience is invited to become confederate, to provide the missing word because, he insists, 'a cliché is just a thing that's true, usually. Some true thing that gets said over and over.' (57)

Is he, then, a racist? Certainly it would seem so from a story he tells. Under pressure from Cody he admits to having been fired from his law firm for a remark he had made on board an aircraft. As an African American had filed past him towards the back of the plane he had said, 'Well, at least they still sit in the back of the bus.' (66) When she had remonstrated, he 'grabbed her by both her shoulders ... shook her and said, "Hey, Carol, stop it! Stop acting like some *blue-gummed chimp*, just fell outta the tree!"' (67) Unsurprisingly, Cody responds by asking him to leave.

Since he puts words in other people's mouths, however, are his own remarks reliable? What, for example, are we to make of his assurance that he and Belinda had kissed, or will kiss (time is one of the uncertainties in the play). At one moment this was 'Not a big deal ... very nice', at the next it is 'like there's a respirator between us and our lips are the only thing keeping the other person going'. (70) As the stage direction notes wryly, 'We probably should've shown it before, but too late now. Or is it?' (70) Accordingly, he and Belinda obligingly play the missing scene and this, in turn, prompts another missing scene. This one, however, sends the play in another direction.

Man and Cody meet and we learn that they have been in a conspiracy from the beginning. The encounter between Man and Belinda had not been accidental. He had effectively been hired by Cody to seduce his wife and justify his leaving her without having to pay the full price, his own affections having transferred to a young co-ed. He wanted to rid himself of an impediment, in the words of Man to 'do a *Mayor of Casterbridge* thing', (74) the Mayor, in Hardy's novel, having sold his wife at a fair. Somewhat oddly, he recites the history of their agreement, remarking that 'I'm only saying this to help remind you,' as if he would need such a reminder. However, his injunction, 'do not forget the truth here. The truth is always of some importance,' (75) is itself a reminder that in the context of this play little is to be taken at face value.

The story of Man's racial outburst on the plane had, it now transpires, been calculated precisely to provoke his ejection from Cody's home and speed up the realisation of their plan. He had not, he explains, been fired, instead abandoning his career to become a writer. His marriage had ended because he 'was a liar', (78) an odd remark given his insistence on the truth. And that, of course, is the dilemma for the audience. It is the Cretan paradox. Is the person who tells you he is a liar telling the truth? The man who had been so solicitous of Belinda now explains that he does not see his own child because she is a girl and 'I'm just not into that.' (78) Cody and Man, it seems, as the stage direction indicates, 'may just be more alike than we first suspected.' (80)

The racist stories, he now explains, were simply part of his strategy. Yet, at the same time, they are based, he insists, on fact and in his conversation with Cody he exhibits precisely the racism he ostensibly disavows. As a result, the two fight, but, in his role as narrator, Man explains the scene as 'just a shameless attempt at a bit of action ... little treat for the "gun and knife" crowd', invoking Elizabethan drama for its mix of intellectualism and violence. When Cody walks away, Man suggests that the audience 'need to take a good look at the last few moments, decide for yourselves what happened there. I mean, how much is real.' (85) Their meeting, he insists, was real enough, 'But the rest? Well, hey, that stuff's for you to decipher ... But you guys had to be expecting at least one exchange like what you just saw ... some swearing, the digs at women. A crazy plot twist.' (86) Why else would an audience be expecting this, however, unless this were a play by Neil LaBute whose reputation is for just such elements? And this seems scarcely less so when Man goes on to draw out what he suggests is the essential theme, in doing so reflecting a familiar LaBute conviction: 'People, they tire of each other, give up on what they've got instead of fixing it ... We're weak ... We are lazy and pushy and we want it all today ... who really gives a fuck what happens to anybody else?' (86)

Did any of this happen? He raises the possibility that 'this *might* just all be going through my head when I'm standing there at Sears,

staring at Belinda again for the first time ... I mean, don't look at me ...
I dunno where this damn thing is going, either ... I've started work on a
play – it's *this* story, *technically*, but I've changed some of the situations
around so that it's not.' (86–7) That being so, what are we to make of the
information he now offers – that Belinda had moved in with him while
Cody was revelling in the success of his plan? Was there even an agreement or was the whole plot devised by Man as a way of winning a girl he
had always wanted at school, with Cody doing no more than watch
something which simply served his own interests?

In the concluding scene Man wonders whether to tell her the
truth, appealing to the audience for help. The problem, though, is that
'the truth is just so damn ... elusive, isn't it. I mean, *unknowable*. In the
end. The second you start telling somebody what the truth is – how it
goes – it all starts to slip away. Not, like, some lie, exactly, but close.
This half-remembered version of one side 'a things.' (91) And one aspect
of his own truth and, he implies, other people's truth, seems to be that
beneath the civilised veneer there is a latent racism ready to break
surface, as it does again now as he dismisses Cody as 'a nigger', a 'lazy,
mean-spirited coon' who he accuses of spouting 'that sort-of post-Civil
War, Malcolm X, heavy-lidded bullshit that guys like him've been
trading on for years ... Well, hey, man, forgive us for dragging your
sorry asses over here, 'cause-it-wasn't-fuckin'-worth-it!!'" (93)

In the final scene he sits together with Belinda. They kiss. They
are, the stage direction indicates, 'together now, but lost in their own
thoughts. Alone.' (96) But since throughout Man has explained that if
these events happen at all he is uncertain whether they are past
actions or future possibilities, what we are witnessing may be no
more than two characters in the mind of the playwright waiting, in
silence, to be animated rather than reanimated, summoned into existence from the darkness to which the stage now returns as they look
straight out at an audience invited to resolve the status of these
characters and the legitimacy of their own reactions.

On one level the play seems to be about betrayal, prejudice, the
attenuation of relationships, deception, the blunting of emotions, a failure to grasp life in its essentials. On another it is concerned with the
near-impossibility of reaching an agreement as to the substance of

reality, the truth of individual feelings, the nature of a social world in which private desires shape perception. As Thornton Wilder said of *Our Town*, 'Each individual's assertion to an absolute reality can only be inner, very inner. And here the method of staging finds its justification.' LaBute's play, like Wilder's, has very little scenery. For Wilder, the reason for this was that 'Our claim, our hope, our despair are in the mind – not in things.'[15] On still another level, *This Is How It Goes* is about the process of writing, of improvising alternative worlds from fragments of experience, the spontaneous inventions of the imagination, an associational logic which is only partly available for interrogation. Beyond that, perhaps, in a play in which creation is a central motif, lies the question of how meaning is to be fashioned from past events or future potential by individuals adrift in their own stories, looking for some kind of shape that will satisfy them that life has a spine, a form, a purpose beyond immediate experience. His are, in effect, characters in search of an author reflecting individuals who are doing no less.

Nurse Betty, Possession
and The Wicker Man

Arthur Miller's resistance to cinema stemmed not only from his sense that it reduced the significance of the writer and that it was likely to be un-amenable to his social and political views (an opinion strengthened when the film version of *Death of a Salesman* presented Willy Loman as a victim less of American myths than of psychosis), but also from what he saw as its aesthetic limitations. It seemed to him that in moving from the page to the screen, screenplays became 'brittle'. The forward momentum of a film lasting ninety minutes meant that shadings of meanings were liable to be lost. Beyond that, though, a 'description in words tends to inflate, expand, and inflame the imagination, so that in the end the thing or person described is amplified into a larger-than-life figment. But something photographed is lifted out of the imagination and becomes simply what it really is, or less ... Words, unable to imitate reality, must serve it up in meta-phoric guise, but film gives us the appearance of reality directly.'[1] Film may require a writer's sense of form, but it rejects his love of words. With luck, he confesses, what is lost in terms of verbal language is replaced by a visual language, though he was inclined to believe that 'the quality of the final work is rougher and cruder, more brutally telegraphic, than when it was action described in words.' (vi)

The irony is that this essay appeared as a preface to a film, *Every-body Wins*, related to one of his stage plays ('Some Kind of Love Story', part of *Two Way Mirror*), and for which he had written the screenplay (though the experience was not a happy one). It might seem odd, therefore, that he insists that 'Among "real" writers – novelists, playwrights, poets – screen-writing, when it is not regarded as a cousin of engineering, is seen as an art on a par with clothing design; the product has no life of its own until it is occupied by the wearer,' a view, he insisted, that was 'truer than one would wish'. This was not, he explained, an attack on film but an acknowledgement that the best screenplays (and he accepted the fact that there had been more significant films than plays or novels in the previous twenty-five years) 'tend by the nature of the art to be self-effacing', disappearing into the total impression of the film. Drama existed as literature, independent of performance; the screenplay had little significance outside the finished work in which, anyway, it became invisible (though he was inclined to grant a special status to Pinter's unproduced work for the screen). A play was a thing in itself, a screenplay 'a libretto for the screen'. In the theatre everyone and everything serves the play, which is to say the text. In the cinema, the screenplay is only one element. The screenplay, he suggested, was the equivalent of the titles given to photographs or paintings or even 'the words in a cartoon balloon'. (vii)

In the cinema, the actor has primacy and to the extent that this is true the screenwriter recedes because, 'in effect, the actor has eaten him,' while beyond the actor lies the director. There could never, he insisted, 'be a Eugene O'Neill of the movies'. (viii) Film may have been an offshoot of theatre but the most effective film actors were those to whom one could attribute 'attitudes and feelings – usually simple ones like anger or sexual desire, indignation or aggression'. The director's first instinct when confronted with words was to ask, '"Why do we need this?"' The purpose of words in movies was 'to justify the silences that are the picture's main business ... Language tends to get in the way of images, and the brighter the language, the more it draws attention to itself, the more it interferes.' (ix) Dialogue 'is the musculature of the gestalt, the combination of images whose interactions create meaning'. (x) The closest analogy was to the dream, with its compelling images. In film, the brain can coast along in neutral, simply registering without the power to intervene or mediate. In the theatre we are active collaborators, sharing a time and place with performers. At the movies 'we decide nothing, our treasured infantile inertia is barely nudged.' (xii) We merely submit.

For the above reasons, he explains, screenwriters are often disinvited, his word, from film sets, 'like a guilty conscience'. (xiii) And lest we might be in doubt, he concludes by stating that without 'in the least belittling screenwriting, I would say that it does not require one to write very well'. (xiii) Nonetheless, he adds that the condensation required of screenwriting is reminiscent of poetry, as opposed to the prose of the stage, an odd remark given the poetry of his own plays but one that would perhaps explain something of the power of *The Misfits* and of his final film, Nicholas Hytner's impressive version of *The Crucible*, an achievement which perhaps ended what had been virtually a lifelong disenchantment with film. But by then his reputation was such that his screenplay, based very closely on the play and with its language foregrounded, was highly resistant to interference.

David Mamet, for all his enthusiasm for film, is scarcely less wary of the marginal role of the screenwriter: 'Working as a screenwriter I always thought that "Film is a collaborative business" only constituted half of the actual phrase. From a screenwriter's point of view, the correct rendering should be, "Film is a collaborative business: bend over."'[2] Told that the job was analogous to being a carpenter for hire by a homeowner, he discovered that instead of being in the employ of the eventual consumer he was in the hands of a producer concerned only to maximise profits. He recalled a producer's remark when he had made a suggestion: '"The great respect that I have for your talent doesn't permit me to sit here and listen to you spout such bullshit."' (141) The writer's recourse in such circumstances is 'to deal with it by becoming enraged, leaving the business, or, by suiting up and joining in the game by exploiting the *producer* for as much money as possible'. (135) Hollywood, he explained, with something of the young Arthur Miller's distaste, 'is the city of the modern gold rush, and money calls the tune. This is the first and last rule, as we know, of Hollywood – we permit ourselves to be treated like commodities in the hope that we may, one day, be treated like *valuable* commodities.' Scripts, in his experience, got worse with each new draft. The alternative was to be both writer and director. The first result was *House of Games*, his experience of which he contrasted with working on *The Untouchables*: 'Our budget was modest and theirs was large; *Untouchables* has big-name stars, and our does not; and *Untouchables* was made by an ad hoc group, while *House of*

Games was made up of a group of friends and colleagues of long standing.' (139)

LaBute's good luck was to begin where it took Mamet several years to arrive. He did not suffer Miller's fate of seeing (as he believed) his plays traduced on film. LaBute's first films were exactly as Mamet describes, made for low budgets, with no stars and working with established friends, people, as Mamet said of his own friends, who 'had no need to prove themselves to me, and, more important, I had no need to prove myself to them'. (140) Miller's sense of a clear distinction between theatre and film was negated by the fact that LaBute carried across the aesthetic of the one to the other. The very restrictions on which he had thrived as a young playwright at Brigham Young proved equally liberating in the cinema. And though with *the shape of things* he was dealing with bankable stars, this was a stage production transferred to film with the minimum of changes. He had the chance, therefore, to edge his way into film on his own terms. The bottom line was never a primary consideration. His subsequent decision to make a different kind of film, therefore, on which he was not the screenwriter (though with influence on the script), came as a shock to some, as if it were the equivalent of Bob Dylan abandoning his acoustic guitar. But by then he had found his feet in the cinema.

Nonetheless, for those familiar with what the writer himself called LaButeville – a cold human environment of isolated individuals, self-concerned, manipulative, cruel, presented, on stage and on film, in an uncomplicated and even spare style – his next films, beginning with *Nurse Betty*, were something of a surprise. What had seemed a quintessentially independent film maker, who directed his own scripts with largely unknown actors, and for whom the camera essentially framed the action as an equivalent of the proscenium arch, was suddenly commissioned to direct a Hollywood film written by someone else with major stars and multiple locations (it was filmed in Durango, Colorado, in the Grand Canyon National Park, Lakewood, California and Rome). The $25,000 budget for *in the company of men* was exchanged for a budget of $24 million (it made almost precisely that at the US box office), a script with ten scenes for one with 154, while a director who was sparing in his use of music directed a film which credits sixteen tracks. For an action sequence, he found himself shooting with seven cameras and all the paraphernalia required for staging a car crash and a shoot-out between a gangster and police. This was decidedly not the Neil LaBute of his own early films. Perhaps that was part of the attraction. He also seems not to have suffered the kind of problems experienced by Mamet. His relationship with producers proved anything but fraught.

The film began with Steve Golin, who had worked on *Your Friends & Neighbors*. His company, Propaganda, which produced that film, was already working on *Nurse Betty*. It was written by John C. Richards and James Flamberg, the screenplay winning the Best Screenplay Award at the Cannes Film Festival. LaBute later explained that he had been drawn to it precisely because he had not written it. The principal question was, 'could you do it? Bring someone else's vision to life, juggle the tone, deal with a female protagonist, get paid more than ever before?'[3] From the point of view of James Flamberg, one of LaBute's virtues as a director lay in the fact that he was 'not scared of the rough edges in the script! . . . He thrived on the "uncomfortable moments", and, in the shooting, made them even more authentic.'[4]

For LaBute, *Nurse Betty* was not, in fact, as remote from his own thematic interests as it appeared. 'Was I trying to say anything with the film?' he asked, 'Make a comment about the way reality and fantasy can so easily bend to our will, or bend us to its will? Point out that sometimes we have to go a little crazy to find ourselves? Probably.' ('Introduction', p. ix) He did the film, he explained, 'because I liked it . . . it's clever and fun and sweet and romantic and madcap and frightening and provocative'. (x) The words 'sweet' and 'madcap' sit uneasily beside 'frightening and provocative', which seem closer to his usual territory. It is this blend, though, that gives the film its particular tone.

The film centres on thirty-year-old Betty, a woman 'with a wholesome attractiveness', who is married to a womanising and none-too-successful second-hand car dealer with a sideline in stealing cars and, in a new twist, selling drugs. She maintains a bright optimism, though her life is plainly sinking into the sand, as she fills her low-rent house with romance novels and fixates on a television soap opera set in a California hospital: *A Reason to Love*. Indeed, she is desperate to train as a nurse (an ambition thwarted by her husband) in an effort to live out her fantasy, instead working as a waitress in a coffee shop. She is an innocent insulated from what might otherwise seem the banality of her life by her essential goodness.

That life is now transformed when two gangsters arrive, searching for the drugs concealed in one of the cars her husband has bought from a trucker, the car which, unbeknown to her husband, Betty herself has borrowed. Unseen by the killers, she watches as her husband is first scalped and then shot dead. The trauma sends her spinning into her own fantasy. Not registering, on a conscious level, that her husband is dead, for the first time she shows sufficient resolution to leave and sets off from Kansas in search of the soap-opera doctor who she believes is her true love, not merely thinking him real but believing that the two of them had once been engaged.

Arriving in Los Angeles, she masquerades as a nurse feeling sure that she can track her fantasy lover down in the fictional hospital which she believes to be real. Presenting herself as a nurse, she is rejected by a hospital administrator until her apparent coolness in the face of a sudden spasm of violence (a gangster drives up to the hospital, throws a man out of the car and then has a shoot-out when he crashes into another vehicle), and her ability to carry out an emergency procedure which in truth she has learned from watching the soap opera, makes her a temporary heroine, albeit having to exchange her bloodstained nurse's uniform for her waitress outfit, a reminder of her former life.

Life, in other words, for a moment, is a reflection of art. This was not, though, the kind of action scene that LaBute had ever shot. Indeed in some ways it was antithetical to his aesthetic. When he did shoot it he discovered that, with multiple cameras and all the paraphernalia of safety requirements, he felt marginalised: 'I felt completely out of place there. I did a quick study of how you are supposed to do this but I felt completely out of water.'[5]

Betty does, eventually, run into the man she seeks, who takes her for a would-be actress whose insistence on a relationship with him is simply an act she stages to convince him of her skills. An amused producer duly asks her, 'Do you have a headshot?'[6] meaning by that a publicity photograph except that in the context of a film in which the principal hitman advises his son on the need to go for headshots, it is hard not to see the Hollywood machine as another means to killing off the individual. Finding herself on the hospital set in a television studio, she is finally shocked out of her illusions, able at last to distinguish actor from role.

Meanwhile, the father-and-son hit-men set out in pursuit. Vaguely Pinteresque characters, one, Charlie with 'the suburban father look' (19) is, seemingly, an intellectual on the eve of retirement (looking forward to relaxing on his boat with a glass of port), a man who combines a respect for morality with the etiquette of murder. Even as he systematically kills people, he laments the state of his society and in particular, the '"make a statement," do an end zone dance, shake your ass and sue everybody in sight attitude that's dragging this whole country down the drain'. (77) He sees himself as the last of the professionals, living according to some agreed contract. He is, in Morgan Freeman's words, 'settled. He knows what he's doing, knows what he is about.' In the course of the film, however, he reveals 'an extraordinary vulnerability. It just needed the right key to open it up: Betty.' (Director's Commentary)

For all his apparent wisdom, Charlie misreads the woman they are hunting. In a film in which misreading is a central trope, appearances rarely coincide with reality. Indeed, he turns Betty into precisely the kind of fantasy figure she herself is pursuing. Charlie is a mentor to his son, Wesley, a man in his late twenties, 'the kid who used to mow your parents' lawn', but who is simultaneously anarchic, streetwise, violent (though also, ironically, a fan of the same soap opera as the woman they are pursuing).

LaBute chose to make the two hit men black (Charlie is played by Morgan Freeman, who had himself appeared in a soap opera – *Another World* – for eighteen months, and Wesley by Chris Rock, better known as a comedian) and has them confront and kill an inveterate and unapologetic southern racist as earlier they had scalped and killed Betty's husband, in part out of a sense of affront at his attitude to

Native Americans (his house has a wooden Indian on the porch). By a calculated irony, Charlie seems more dedicated to genuine American values than anyone else in the film.

Charlie and Wesley eventually catch up with Betty only to be killed themselves as her hometown sheriff and a local newspaperman stumble into her apartment, though not before Wesley, apparently also unsure where fiction ends and reality begins, has sat watching the latest episode of *A Reason to Love*, appalled that the character to whom he is plainly attracted turns out to be a lesbian. For his part, just before he dies, Charlie proposes to Betty. While confessing to being 'a garbageman of the human condition' who deals with 'people willing to trade any part of themselves for a few more minutes of their rotten lives', he nonetheless stakes his claim as if he were devising a lonely hearts ad, insisting that 'I like the symphony, walks in the rain, sunsets, animals and children. I read passionately, and I like to discuss things. I'm basically conservative, but flexible.' (134) He has, he confesses, killed thirty-two people (in fact thirty-three but he omits Betty's husband out of a sense of tact). When she objects, ironically given the action, that 'I'm not really who you think I am,' he replies, not unreasonably, 'No one is, honey.' (135) His final piece of advice before he shoots himself is that 'You don't need that doctor. You don't need that actor. You don't need any man ... You don't need anybody. You've got yourself ... and that's more than most people can say.' (141)

The film ends as Betty's sudden fame, as a result of the shoot-out, makes her so marketable that the producer of the soap opera hires her and she becomes the love interest of her fantasy doctor in *A Reason To Love*, stepping into the world which had drawn her to Hollywood. In the final shot she is seen alone in an Italian café, following in the footsteps of another waitress who had told her that her own trip to Italy (inspired by watching Audrey Hepburn in *Roman Holiday*) had been the best thing she had ever done, 'because I DID IT'. (57) There is a double irony, of course, in that she is replicating a trip made by another person who had in turn been drawn there by a work of fiction. The logic of the film seems to imply that she, at least, has been liberated from fantasy, but in a world in which fantasy and reality are so intermingled it seems almost impossible to be clear which is which, and what it is that constitutes the self that Charlie had invited her to embrace.

Until *Nurse Betty*, LaBute noted, there had been no guns in his plays or films. Now he directed a film in which not only were there guns but a number of people were messily shot. Indeed the question was how graphic to make the violence. 'Key for me', LaBute explained, was the fact that

> just the idea that a scalping takes place was enough to make people react ... it was certainly more graphic when shot, as the end was, the shoot-out before the end of the film ... but for this section I felt it was really important, if we were to believe what happened [to Betty], and that [she] stays in this state for two-thirds of the movie ... We tried an almost Hitchcock approach where as Chris [Rock, who played Wesley] began to attack Del we cut to just [Betty's] face, watching it through the door. It never felt as if the audience would believe that ... If they didn't find it repulsive they would be less apt to believe that [Betty] was so frightened by what [she] saw that [she] slipped into this state.

Even so, the scene on screen was considerably less violent than several versions that were shot.

This was true, too, of a later scene in which a man is burned to death and the scene in which Wesley is shot in the face. A version in which his head was virtually blown apart was rejected ('this is so sanitised from what we shot. We shot the most extraordinarily awful shots of [Wesley] getting his head blown off. It was the kind of thing that when audiences first saw it they stopped watching. I understood that. They just tuned out when his face literally came off.') (Director's Commentary) Thus, a writer who had eschewed genre writing, defining his own territory, now found himself directing a film which seemed to include a virtual bran-tub of genres, from soap opera, road movie and crime drama to comic satire and romance.

Nurse Betty is a dark comedy which plays with the very genres it deploys. This is a Hollywood film which not only satirises Hollywood and television (a conventional enough subject) and Hollywood's products, but which proposes a version of America in which virtually all the characters prefer a dream to reality, reality being by turns banal and brutal.

LaBute's own mother had been a fan of soap opera and he was aware of the degree to which it constitutes an ironic meeting point, a shared set of images for those who perhaps share little else. He has spoken, too, of the degree to which celebrity has moved to the centre of social concern, and fame become a kind of human currency. *Nurse Betty* is a film which takes pleasure in satirising its own premise as its characters go on a journey less towards understanding than a fantasy resolution. And that irony extends to the music in which the songs carry such titles as 'I Won't Be Home No More', 'Just a Touch of Love', 'Lovey Dovey', 'Double Cross', 'Don't You Know', 'Poor Little Fool' and 'Whatever Will Be Will Be'. Love songs and western music evoke precisely what has been evacuated from the world that Betty can only embrace at the level of fantasy.

There is more than a touch of the Coen brothers about the film, that same mix of small town desperation, humour and violence as can be found in *Fargo*. Indeed, LaBute has confessed that hitmen 'are a staple of US indie cinema. I like the impulse', he explained, 'but it's dangerous ground because it's material that has been done a lot lately and done really well by a number of people, most famously, of course, by Tarantino'.[7] *Nurse Betty*, indeed, is full of references to other films just as in LaBute's own work the characters are constantly referring to plays, films and television shows, though usually in the process revealing how little they share with one another.

For a director who had previously shot in sequence and, faced with budgetary and time constraints, of necessity restricted the amount of stock he used, making a Hollywood film represented an aesthetic revolution. The first edited assembly of *Nurse Betty* ran to just under four hours, for a film that would end up with a running time of ninety-six minutes. 'It's amazing', he remarked, 'that you cut out more than you have on screen and that you can still tell the story. You start to find some arc that makes sense.' (Director's Commentary)

His own contribution in terms of the script included work on the dialogue. It is hard to believe, for example, that Charlie's observation, 'I had to shoot him! It was the only decent thing to do,' (30) was not LaBute's contribution, given Cary's defence of the indefensible in *Your Friends & Neighbors* in precisely the same terms. It was LaBute who introduced a scene, set at the Grand Canyon, in which Charlie fantasises a romance with Betty, the woman who is to be his next victim, reconstructing her as a character in his own sentimental drama. It is a scene that echoes an earlier one in which Betty herself visits the same site, a familiar LaBute touch as he uses repetition for ironic effect.

For LaBute, part of the challenge was to avoid accommodating the film to his own vision. It is not hard, though, to see connections. These are, after all, characters who barely relate to one another, who stare at life through a single window, using language to reshape experience in such a way as to make it understandable to them. As he himself remarked, 'you can still tell it's one my films ... There's a woman running for her life from bad men. That's a pretty big red flag.'[8] 'I can see my hand in it. There is a woman in peril. The male characters throughout are not particularly great guys. The implicit sense of danger and violence, the idea of illusion versus reality, which is very theatrical.' (SBS)

Few people in the industry knew quite what to make of the film until it was taken to the Cannes Film Festival where it won the prize for best screenplay. For a first foray into something approaching a mainstream film, *Nurse Betty* was an impressive achievement.

A. S. Byatt's novel *Possession* (1990) won the Booker Prize for fiction and the *Irish Times* International Fiction Prize. It was inspired by her memory of attending F. R. Leavis's seminars at Cambridge on the subject of Robert Browning. *Possession* is a literary detective story and a double love story. Like John Fowles's *The French Lieutenant's Woman*, it operates in two time periods. Roland Michell and Maud Bailey are conducting research into the lives of two Victorian poets – Randolph Henry Ash and Christabel LaMotte. Gradually, they uncover a liaison between their two subjects, in the process forging a romantic alliance between themselves. Ambition, power, sexuality intertwine in a book which debates all aspects of possession, including the rights claimed by a biographer over his or her subject. In one sense, it is surprising that

LaBute should be drawn to adapting and directing such a work but, given a number of its central concerns, perhaps this was not quite so surprising after all.

It took twelve years for *Possession* to reach the screen. A succession of writers and directors worked on the project before LaBute became involved some two years before shooting began. He wrote the adaptation with the American playwright Henry David Hwang and Australian screenwriter Laura Jones.

His first choice, in terms of casting, was a controversial one. For the part of Roland Michell, he cast his old friend, Aaron Eckhart, an American. As he explained,

> we made a decision to change the character's nationality not as a means to reach a broader American audience or accommodating Aaron ... the most interesting thing to us was to create sparks between Maud and Roland and one of the ways we thought that the modern-day audience might create more friction between them is to have a number of differences. We made him not only American but a brash academic who jumps from A to Z rather than do all the work in between.[9]

The process of adaptation inevitably required significant changes. As he explained,

> a number of key characters and episodes get taken out entirely or refigured when one is writing an adaptation of a book. One of the most difficult things I've done is to adapt a novel because I went into it such a big fan ... but knowing that I would never be able to put everything on the screen. It is very difficult to make some of these choices. Key figures, like Roland's girlfriend Val, and Beatrice Nest, were just two of the characters I was sorry not to find their way into the film. Lenora Stern, a feminist professor, even made it into the screenplay but eventually we cut that part out because we just didn't find that it helped propel the story in a significant way. It is a difficult job to say that this five-hundred-page novel can be pared down to two hours or less of screen time. (Director's Commentary)

He had never previously worked on a period film, or what in many ways is a love story, *Fat Pig* aside. The challenge, as in the book, was to interweave the two stories while maintaining the integrity of each. As he explained, the Victorian scenes were 'lit by lightning'. They were, in essence, melodramatic in that they dealt with an illicit romance, a child born out of wedlock, a suicide. It was 'almost operatic'. In contrast, 'you have two people' in the modern story, 'who don't really want to fall in love and spend their time reading'. The question was 'how to make that as interesting as the Victorian' story (Director's Commentary).

The two periods were differentiated by style, a mode of acting, music, and lighting. Most of the night-time shots in the Victorian period were lit by candles. His own fondness for a painterly approach, for tableaux, gave the nineteenth-century scenes a quality which echoed the artistic concerns of Christabel's lesbian lover, herself a painter.

In one sense, there was a clear distinction between this film and his earlier work. In the end, though, he was inclined to recognise similarities. To be sure, in contrast to the figures in his previous plays and films, these were characters with genuine commitments to one another. Nor, in either period, did they inhabit an alienating environment. In *Possession* he luxuriates in the beauty of the English countryside while even the contemporary scenes take place in a world which respects and frames the past. On the other hand, as he himself recognised, the human concerns remained a constant. 'It's a really difficult concept', he explained, 'to show that someone is genuinely conflicted by what they do, and the cost of those decisions on a human being. But it's always an exciting thing to investigate. I am', he confessed, 'constantly drawn back to that in my writing – the morality of a situation, what makes a person good or bad or make questionable choices. That's really what this film and most of my work is about.'

The relationship between Roland and Maud focused 'a lot of our thoughts about men and women ... We are very selfish people who are motivated by our own needs. And because of that we find it hard to give to other people. That's often one of our great problems with another person, i.e. that we are not as selfless as we would like to be.

And it creates great strife between men and women and men and men, friends, whatever it is. We find it hard to be as giving as we want to be and we end up being takers rather than givers.' (Director's Commentary)

In *Possession* misunderstandings recur. Love proves redemptive and destructive in equal proportions. Selflessness does battle with desire, possessiveness with relinquishment. A love story that can only be reconstructed through the fragmentary evidence handed down through the years ends in division and a degree of despair. People are damaged because emotions assert presumptive rights. Yet out of lives that never found true purpose comes purpose as a story is shaped from a disregarded past, as a living link is established, as a kind of vicarious completion remains possible through two people who began looking at the dead letters of dead people, in the dust of an archive, yet in the process animate not only the past but themselves.

Was LaBute revealing a sentimental streak in choosing to adapt Byatt's novel or was he hearing echoes of his own concerns? He was certainly resisting categorisation much as the characters in *Possession* themselves resist being possessed by others and few people would have predicted his next move as far as cinema was concerned as he undertook a remake of a decidedly idiosyncratic British film of the 1970s.

Labute first saw *The Wicker Man* as a teenager in Spokane. He was working in the local movie theatre. Written by Anthony Shaffer (who was paid £11,000), with first-time director Robin Hardy (paid £4,500), and starring Edward Woodward and Christopher Lee, it is one of the more unlikely cult movies. A low-budget British film (it cost £448,300), shot on the west coast of Scotland, it told the story of a policeman's search for a supposedly missing girl, following an anonymous letter from an offshore island called Summerisle. He arrives on the eve of midsummer's day only to discover that everyone denies the existence of such a girl, including her mother. A strait-laced narrow-minded Christian, he is shocked by the sexual licence he sees in a community presided over by the Lord Summerisle who explains that theirs is a society which practices pagan rites. A young woman, who dances nude in the room next to Sergeant Howie's, tries to seduce him. Unbeknown to him, he is the victim of a plot which requires a human sacrifice to return a lost fertility to the island. The story of the lost child was no more than a lure. The film ends as he is burned alive inside a giant man made from wicker, a conceit derived from Caesar's account of his war against the Gauls. As he dies, so he shouts out his faith in God. The head of the wicker man slumps forward to reveal the setting sun.

Filmed not in May but November, it was a difficult shoot. No one seems to have been quite sure what the end product would be and almost immediately it ran into trouble, with the company's owner declaring it to be one of the ten worst films ever made. It was shown, in a cut-down version, only as a B feature and sold to an American distributor which went bankrupt four days later. It briefly fell into the hands of Roger Corman before Warner Brothers tested it in a number of Florida drive-ins. In Britain, the British Film Institute's *Monthly Film Bulletin* praised its script but called it 'Absolute nonsense'. Because of the nudity, featuring Britt Ekland and, to her disgust, a body double, it earned the soubriquet of 'sex film' in the *London Evening News*. In America, it received favourable mention in *Variety* and then faded from the scene. Something, however, indicated that it might have another life.

In 1977, five years after it was made, *Cinefantastique* magazine devoted virtually the whole of its winter issue to *The Wicker Man*, describing it as the *Citizen Kane* of horror movies, not a phrase that pleased Christopher Lee, who had made the film precisely to escape the horror films with which he had become associated. But the magazine's publication was an indication of the changed status of the film. Over the years it became more and more highly regarded, even though the original cut was almost impossible to locate.

Various plans were made to shoot a remake and a sequel back to back. But in 2006, Neil LaBute, an admirer of the original, was approached by Nicolas Cage and agreed to direct a remake, with the action moved from Scotland to Washington state, where he had been raised, though it was to be filmed in Vancouver. This was never going to be acceptable to the aficionados of the original film, the more so since along with a radical change of location went other significant alterations. Out went the nudity and the folk songs which had provided such a distinctive counterpoint to the action. As he remarked, 'there's a lot that I find goofy. The songs . . . you're like, "What is this?" If you want to make a movie that is less scary, put that song on there. And yet by the end you're going, "What a weird fucking movie this is."' Out, too, went the key figure of Lord Summerisle, the Magus figure. In his place came a matriarchy, ruled over by a woman who functions as a queen bee with such men as are permitted playing the role of drones. Indeed, the metaphor is in some degree made literal as the community dedicates itself to bee-keeping.

Nonetheless, LaBute wished, in his words, to remain 'true to the dynamic of the original'. The central character, albeit now a highway patrolman, would still end up trapped as much by his own beliefs as by those into whose hands he falls. It was, he said, 'more important to me to be true to the story than the audience's expectations'. He was aware that he was dealing with a mainstream audience who, on the whole, preferred not to see their stars killed off – in this case Nicolas Cage – but was determined not to make any compromises with respect to the ending.

In place of the dour Presbyterian Scottish policeman, narrow-minded, intellectually constrained, we are offered a California highway patrolman, sensitive, traumatised by witnessing the apparent death of a child and her mother in an accident as their car is hit by a passing truck. Given leave from work, he is struggling to recover with the help of antidepressant drugs when he receives a letter from a woman with whom he had once planned marriage but who had abandoned him. She pleads with him to help locate her missing daughter. She lives on a private island in Puget Sound. He is drawn to travel to the island less by his role as a policeman – indeed he has no jurisdiction there – than by a sense of duty, loyalty to a woman who had offered him none, loyalty to his own earlier feelings. Indeed when he finds the woman he is seeking she reveals that the missing child is his own daughter. In a nod to the original film, the policeman's name is Edward and the missing girl's last name is Woodward (another inside joke is the fleeting appearance, in a bit part, of Aaron Eckart, by this stage a virtually talismanic presence in LaBute works).

The protagonist's vulnerability is foreshadowed by the fact that on an island of bee-keepers he is allergic to bee stings, carrying hypodermics loaded with adrenaline to save him from anaphylactic shock, though when he is stung it is the island's physician who revives him. The film ends almost as in the original, indeed it is even more violent as the patrolman's legs are both broken before he is hauled, upside down, into the wicker man and burnt alive. The difference lies in a final scene, set six months later, in which two island girls set out to seduce two men in a bar as they look for those who might impregnate them, thus keeping the community alive, and who, in case of need, might prove suitable sacrifices to appease the spirits.

While he remained faithful to the original story – and full credit is given to the originators – LaBute's version differs in significant ways. In the original, the island was populated by those who were strange only by virtue of their beliefs and rituals. LaBute's island is peopled with grotesques, with elderly, witch-like twins, with women prone to chanting in unison, with bee-keepers wearing hoods reminiscent of *Star Wars*. The few men on the island are decidedly odd, emotionally and socially inert, much given to blank stares. The protagonist, meanwhile, is prone to distorted flashbacks, induced by drugs or trauma. LaBute, in other words, opts for a surrealistic style. In the original, Sergeant Howie died as a sacrifice, in his own mind, to his Presbyterian God, a virgin whose very purity makes him an ideal sacrifice. Nicolas Cage's highway patrolman is no virgin, believes in nothing but challenging disorder and is betrayed by his former lover and his own child.

In contrast to a Scottish law officer, for whom everything must be done by the book, his American counterpart is happy to punch women in the face and smash the doors of houses as he searches for the lost child, though he also carries a lock-picking kit with him – not, presumably, standard issue for highway patrolmen in California. And these island women are not only prepared to kill him, a sacrifice, after all, rather than random violence, they are also prepared to murder the man who flew him to the island and destroy his plane, oblivious, as it seems, to the FAA investigation this will necessarily provoke.

The folk music which had served as an historical bridge and source of irony in the original is here abandoned in favour of a more functional but perhaps less thematically relevant score. The songs in the original drew on folk music and the lyrics of Robbie Burns. Anthony Shaffer's brother Peter rewrote some of the Scottish folk songs, many of which derived from the collection of the Victorian Cecil Sharp. The songs, appropriately enough in a community rooted in sex, were sexually suggestive. That they were also earthed in place and time gave them an additional resonance.

The score of LaBute's film is by Angelo Badalamenti, known for his work with David Lynch and that connection hints at something of the mood of this remake. In the original, the strange community of Summerisle was held together by a disturbing sexuality. In a scene omitted for reasons of length rather than propriety, a young boy was sent up to be initiated by the sexually voracious character played by Britt Ekland, while the strait-laced Sergeant is always stumbling on naked young women as well as copulating couples. 1970s Britain seems to have taken this in its stride, or those few who saw it on its original release did. Between then and 2006, however, paedophilia had become a major issue and though LaBute could address it in his plays, it was an unlikely subject for a mass-market Hollywood movie.

What, then, holds this Summerisle together? Sex is only reluctantly engaged in to maintain a continuing supply of young girls (the fate of the boys being a secret they are ominously not obliged to explain). It is not, though, at the heart of their ceremonies, which are pagan rites surviving only in this secluded island on the outer edge of a country in which cults have always exerted an appeal, some of them a deal more lethal than one which only sacrifices an occasional man. What holds Summerisle together is a story that its inhabitants have embraced as a truth. A myth has become a dogma and true believers have seldom shrunk from sacrificing others to bolster their own faith. *The Wicker Man* came after 9/11 and though America is scarcely threatened by female terrorists, it has been reminded that ancient myths can pose a real enough threat to those who believe that rationality and reactive force are sufficient to preserve a presumed state of innocence.

What the new take adds to the original is the fact that women no less than men evidently have the ability to deceive, betray and kill. So they had in the original, but there the central figure was a man, albeit one who could disturbingly cavort in women's clothes, one of the more risible elements in a film which always trod a difficult path between horror and self-parody. In LaBute's film, by contrast, power resides with a woman who has that disturbing serenity to be found in those prepared to sacrifice others in the name of their own certainties. But, despite her recitation of the pre-history of the group – driven out of seventeenth-century England to settle near Salem, with its handy aura of witchcraft, then on to the very edge of the continent – she and her community seem less grounded in a set of coherent beliefs than Lord Summerisle and his community had been in the original film, not least because Scotland was a more likely site of pagan rituals, having once been such. But, then, LaBute was rather more interested in the tension between the needs and sensibilities of men and women which the various rites merely formalise and which reach out beyond the limits of Summerisle. As he explained, 'while I'd been interested in religions ... I've also been interested in this loose clash between men and women.' The film would, he thought, be 'an interesting study in politics and dynamics'[10] in the context of a community in which men are subordinate (indeed no men speak after the first fifteen minutes, with the exception of the protagonist).

The Wicker Man, then, for all its distinctive qualities, and rather like aspects of *Nurse Betty* and *Possession*, is not quite as remote from LaBute's familiar concerns as perhaps it appears. It turns on an act of betrayal and is a study of power. At its centre is a well-meaning man whose fate is shaped by a woman. Here, as in his earlier work, the human capacity for cruelty is highlighted – the pagan ceremonies, indeed, recalling the longevity of such impulses. Sergeant Howie, in the original film, had been a dogged logician and a blinkered zealot, a combination which lies at the heart of his vulnerability. The protagonist of LaBute's film is altogether more American. He places his faith in action, confident that mysteries have solutions and that the hidden will be revealed.

To LaBute, the idea of a remake presented no problem. Coming from theatre in which every production is in effect a remake, he was used to the idea that no production is definitive. If Shakespeare plays could be transposed in time and space why should the same not be true of a movie? There certainly seemed to him to be no point in remaking the film if it was not reinvented. 'It's not a big deal', he explained, 'for me to say, "I'm taking this thing and I'm going to re-imagine it in my own way." I find it more difficult to figure out why someone would want to remake something really closely. If it made money I understand why, but artistically why would you say, "I just want to make exactly the same movie?"'

He was drawn to the genre because, as he explained, 'it pushes people to extremes' and he was interested 'in how people respond to power', acknowledging that some of his earlier films had been called horror movies because of the nature of the relationships they staged. In his view *The Wicker Man* engaged with concerns which had always been part of his work. It was 'about how men and women interact'. It also offered the opportunity to explore the idea that 'if women were in control things would be so much better'.

What was he aiming for? He hoped, he explained, that audiences would feel '"That's unlike any movie I have seen in a long time." That's what you hope for, I guess – some new take on existing material.'[11] Asked what he would say to those who might have thought this a strange film for him to make he remarked, 'I'd tell them to take another look at my earliest films – they're pretty scary! I guess you're never an obvious choice until you do something and, hopefully, do it well. It's an easy position to get pigeon-holed in ... I feel capable of a great many things that people might not expect.'[12]

12 *Some Girl(s)*, *Wrecks* and *In a Dark Dark House*

It's one of my faults that I can't quell my past
I ought to have gotten it gone . . .
Oh, baby, I wonder if when you are older
Someday
You'll wake up
And say, 'My God, I should have told her
What would it take
But, now here I am and the world's gotten colder
And she's got the river down which I sold her'

Aimee Mann, 'Fourth of July'

Oh you can write the play
And every word I say
But I don't have to stay
To see the credits

'Cause it's all over now
Yes it's all over now
And I'm free

Aimee Mann, 'All Over Now'

This is for the one who was false
Who taught me about building walls
One who could always turn it around
To leave me here on shaky ground
This is for the one who made good
In someone else's neighborhood

One who was never anything but
The shifty eye of sheer bad luck
One I thought that I would never forget
And I have not quite done that yet

But I could hurt you now
I could hurt you now

Aimee Mann, 'I Could Hurt You Now'

In September 2005 a new comedy series from NBC began its successful run. It was called *My Name is Earl* and featured a character who drew up a list of all those he felt he had harmed and then revisited them to set things right. LaBute anticipated him by four months. *Some Girl(s)* opened in May 2005 at the Gielgud Theatre in London. Its protagonist, on the verge of marriage to a twenty-two-year-old nursing student, decides to draw up a list of those women he has loved and left. Aware that he has left a trail of damaged relationships, he sets out, ostensibly, to pay old debts, ironically describing his journey as a Pilgrim's Progress, though this pilgrim seems to have made very little progress in terms of his emotional relationships or moral perception.

The fact that his name is Guy suggests that he is something of a representative figure in LaBute's continuing exploration of the nature of male–female relationships. Indeed, whatever the names of the characters they are referred to in the stage directions as 'the man' and 'the women'. When a critic described Guy as a serial monogamist, LaBute suggested that this was relatively close to a serial killer. It was a gloss which underscored the calculated cruelty which turns out to lie behind his mask of well-meaning disingenuousness. The play sprang, LaBute explained, from a desire to write 'a series of duets that features a hearty number of women's roles and follows the journey of a modern-day Candide as he stumbles through a landscape familiar to most men – the mess he's made of his romantic life on his way to manhood'.[1] That may have been the impetus but there is more at stake, it turns out, than the confusions and mistakes of an innocent abroad.

The actress Fran Drescher, who played in the 2006 New York production, was initially dubious about appearing in a LaBute play: 'A few years ago, I would have said he was like the Francis Bacon of cinema ... so twisted and so disturbed ... But with this, I think he's really tapped into the female characters. I think he allows them to emote their feelings about the relationship and the man. I was really impressed. I said to him, "it shows you are evolving as a man – good for you."' Perhaps oddly, she adds 'he had an estranged relationship with his father ... I think therein is where the root of it all is for him ... After reading this play, I think *he* is the woman in his scripts,'[2] and interestingly, all the women in *Some Girl(s)* – Sam, Tyler, Lindsay, Bobbi, Billi, Reggie – have names that could equally well be those of men.

Though the scenes are set in different cities, they all take place in the anonymous surroundings of hotel rooms which differ from one another only in terms of minor details of décor much, perhaps, as LaBute seems to imply, male–female relationships offer variations on a familiar theme. Whatever it is that the women characters are looking for it is not the same thing as Guy. Not only does he fly from city to city and woman to woman, he is in flight from consequence. The hotel room is his natural environment. It is a place for passing through. You pay the bill and walk away except that now, he insists, he wishes to confirm that there were no small items missing from his bill. On the verge, he explains, of a final commitment he wishes to leave no wreckage in his wake, except that his description of his bride-to-be as 'some girl is all' (44) hardly suggests that he has changed his ways, since this is a phrase that he applies to others on his list. The impending marriage, which has supposedly stirred his conscience and initiated his belated desire to do penance, itself seems a contract he is liable to break.

In the initial productions there were four scenes, though LaBute later wrote a fifth. Each one is discrete, the nature of each relationship differing. Taken together, though, they build a portrait of a man whose commitment is largely to himself and who remains curiously blind to the betrayals he practises. On the other hand are the women, different in their backgrounds and ages but similar in being drawn to a man whose protestations of loyalty have proved so untrustworthy. *Some Girl(s)* is in part a story of desertion, abandonment, loss, all familiar LaBute tropes. It is also a story of the bafflement that characterises those who look for a solution to their needs in other people whom they seem fated never to understand. What had once seemed intimacy had, it turns out, been nothing more than momentary contact. They simply inhabited different stories.

LaBute's conception of Guy as a Candide figure, and Guy's own description of his trip as windmill tilting, is surely ironic (Quixote would surface again in his version of *The Wicker Man*). Far from being an innocent, quixotic, idealistic, struggling to make sense of a reality at odds with his expectations, he is calculating and callous even as he denies being such, denial being a primary aspect of his character. Indeed, from the extra scene, written during the London run but used neither there nor in New York, we learn that there is another aspect to this man which forces a radical re-evaluation. This is true of each new scene, but the additional one edges the play in a wholly different direction.

The opening scene takes place in a hotel room in Guy's home town of Seattle, though he only comes back to visit his family, he explains, 'every couple of years', a passing remark but one that gains an edge when later we are told of his mother's complaints at his lack of contact. The women he pursues, it seems, are not the only ones he abandons. It is here he has arranged to meet Sam, like Guy in her early thirties. Fifteen years earlier, they had been high-school sweethearts, planning marriage, but he had abandoned her, as he now explains, because he wanted to go elsewhere to college and had an ambition to be a writer. She had seemed to him, at the time, someone without ambition, whose future was implicit in her present. She appeared content to stay where she was and content that he should end up managing a Safeway store, as her husband in fact does. For her part, she had believed that he had left her for another girl, 'some girl'. (16) Indeed, she recalls hearing his mother talking of his taking such a girl to the prom in a nearby school, the memory of this betrayal stirring her to slap him across the face, an action which suggests that, married or not, she still feels the pain of her abandonment, has kept alive the fact of her hopes as she has resentment at her desertion.

When she leaves the room, he drops her coffee cup into the trash, picks up a can of nuts, switches on the television and begins to open a drawer as if his mission had been accomplished. Nothing seems to have registered. He has merely ticked a box, accomplished whatever he had set out to do. When she returns, briefly, he tries to explain away the television, caught out, it seems, for a second time. She has returned to ask for the name of the girl with whom he had betrayed her, and why else if she is not still troubled by events now a decade and a half behind her, why if she is so content with her present marriage?

The scene has all the characteristic marks of a LaBute play. Social embarrassment, personal misunderstandings, mismatched intentions combine to generate humour and desolation in equal amounts. Almost by indirection, and with the minimum of deft touches, he creates a portrait of a disappointed woman whose hopes have been crushed and who has been damaged by a man wholly insensitive to her feelings. In a sense, as she confesses, their break-up had been 'just a teenage thing and you dated somebody else right after me'. (18) But it was plainly much more to her because, as she explains, 'You want to believe that, at some point in your life, you mattered to someone ... *Really* mattered.' (18) Even now, with a husband and children, she had called Guy's mother only a year before, simply to hear her voice and through her to feel some sense of contact with the person who had walked out on her. When she received Guy's message to meet her, she confesses to having thought that he might be about to ask her to run off with him. The implication of this scarcely seems to register. His response is to thank her and then tell her of his impending marriage.

Sam is stranded with her memories. Her life is not what she had imagined for herself. Seeing Guy look at her face, she apologises for the blemishes she is afraid he will detect, as if, even now, she treasures some hopeless hope. The pain of this scene lies, though, not primarily in the fact of Guy's callousness, though that is a first intimation of something that will be elaborated in the remaining scenes. It resides in its familiarity, in the knowledge that, for whatever motives, love affairs do break up, teenage relationships are brought to an end and often with an unfeeling abruptness, as one person moves on to other people, other experiences, what Jonathan Franzen calls the 'adolescent stew of love-and-reconsider, of commit-and-keep-your-options-open'.[3] What for one person is a matter of indifference or sentimental regret, for the other may be traumatic, damaging in a way that is nonetheless real for being concealed. And the hope born in youth may never entirely be extinguished, the tenuous thought that a lifetime of settling for second best might be wished away with the return of a lost love. In *in the company of men* a woman was the victim of calculated cruelty. Sam is the victim of indifference.

This first scene of *Some Girl(s)* begins the process of exposing the truth about the protagonist but it is also a subtle and painful exploration of human needs. There is a difference between the ironies which infect the lives of Guy and Sam. For the former, it is, seemingly, a matter of momentary embarrassment, of being caught in contradictions; in the case of Sam it is a product of the mismatch between her dreams and the reality of her life. Yet, despite her continuing vulnerability she seems to reach a level of understanding of herself that is beyond Guy, who for all his talk of setting out on a mission to heal old wounds is as much concerned to serve his own needs and desires as he had ever been. In this 'duet' it is by no means clear that one voice dominates. In terms of their relationship, Guy seems to hold all the cards. His power comes from his detachment. At the same time, he is left alone in the hotel room again, a can of nuts in his hand, the television blaring, as she returns to the world for which she had settled and which she now seems to accept as her fate.

The second scene moves the action to Chicago. This time the woman, Tyler, is slightly younger than him and wholly different from Sam. She holds no torch for Guy, is happy he is getting married and impressed that he has had a short story published in the *New Yorker*, a fact that had also been known to Sam but which had not impressed her unduly except that she thought it revealed a knowledge of women, ironic enough from a man who plainly understands nothing about them.

Nor, under her questioning, does he seem overly enthusiastic about the prospect of marriage or about his fiancée. In response to Tyler's observation that marriage is 'cool', he replies, 'it should be,' while when she suggests that his wife-to-be must be attractive he says, 'Umm, yeah, you know . . . yes. A very attractive woman. I mean . . . quite pretty . . . like you.' (20) He had, it turns out, promised her the same future that he had Sam. As Tyler says, '"Always". Now there's a word you used to throw around a lot.' (20) He had, she recalled, 'made a bunch of promises back whenever'. (27)

If his relationship with Sam had been sexually innocent, the same can hardly be said of that with Tyler, a fact, she notes, which seems to have fed into his *New Yorker* story, though she hardly resents this. Indeed, she tries to renew their former relationship, his impending marriage seemingly irrelevant to her. She appears wholly at ease with the idea of temporary relationships: 'It's easy to fall out of favor, or just off somebody's radar ... I've known a few men that way – I'm mad about 'em for a couple months, then, bam! Totally gone, just these tiny green blips on my screen ... guys are like that sometimes. And women, too, I'm sure.' (28) Their break-up had been reminiscent of that in *autobahn*: 'you finished your master's and, I dunno, felt the need to go off and become some big *citizen* or what have you, a member of society.' (29)

For his part he justifies using other people's pain for his own purpose. 'That's the deal when you're a writer, I guess. Doesn't matter how much it stings or how *painful* it is for the other people in your life ... you just can't let shit go! You gotta turn it over and study it and poke it ... at times some *scrap* of life will find its way into a story, and that may get sold.' (30–1)

But this is not the only betrayal. While he was going out with her, he confesses, he had been anxious about the woman, 'some girl' as he characterises her, who had preceded her. This was not, though, he now finds out, a secret and the apparently free-thinking, free-loving Tyler admits to the pain she otherwise conceals: 'It is never cool to be second, you know. In a relationship. It's not. And I was a *distant* second there for a bit! ... I was not always your big number one priority during our time together. Not by a long shot ... and I'd tell myself, "Hey, no problem, we are not that kind of couple"; I mean, you can talk yourself into *anything* if you say it enough. But it's not really true. That shit hurts.' (33) A tear comes to her eye. The scene ends as she breathes smoke from her cigarette into his mouth and they negotiate the conditions of a kiss. He stands balanced on the edge of another betrayal.

Through little more than shared memories and partial confessions LaBute offers an oblique picture of a disappointed woman. Presenting herself as happy to indulge the moment, to renew a relationship that was never anything more than a series of sexual encounters, she nonetheless exposes a sense of disappointment at a life not lived, at a relationship that was never what it seemed and a man who was always moving on, trading one woman for another.

In the third scene, set in Boston, the woman is older than Guy. The hotel room is virtually identical and, we learn, had once been the site of their assignations. Lindsay has read his short story – 'The Calculus of Desire' – and recognised herself in it, a fact which she resents. She has not joined him to reminisce.

Their affair had followed his time at college, when he had just begun to teach and when she was already married to the man who hired him. The web of betrayal was clearly a tangled one. They had been seen and, despite his declarations of love, he had immediately left town, leaving her to face the consequences. Having promised her the future, he abandoned her to the past. He had left partly through fear, through a desire to avoid the consequences of his actions, and in part, as she finally persuades him to admit, because she was older than him. Now, she is a teacher of gender studies and has decided to respond to his invitation by telling her husband who, she explains, is waiting outside in their car. Together, they have devised a means of revenge. Since he is about to marry, Lindsay proposes that he should betray his wife-to-be sexually as they had once betrayed her husband. Unlike Sam and Tyler, she is not so much disappointed as angry.

Accordingly, she undresses and instructs him to do likewise or she will telephone his fiancée. When he has done so and when, on her instruction, he closes his eyes, she slips away, his humiliation and preparedness to betray his fiancée now clear. The scene ends as he goes to the window and waves down to Lindsay and her husband in an apparent acknowledgement of defeat, except, of course, that he now has more material for his fiction.

The final part is set in Los Angeles. This is evidently the woman he had abandoned for Tyler and who he now refers to as 'some girl'. Her name is Bobbi and she and Guy had come close to engagement in their three years together, though he now admits that he had been drawn to her twin sister who, once again, has what might as easily be a man's name – Billi. Asked why he has sought her out, he explains to Tyler that he had wanted to meet those who had been, 'instrumental. To me and where I am now. As a person.' (56) Seeking absolution, it seems, takes second place to meeting those who had helped shape him into his present self.

Bobbi feels no angst about their break-up but she does suspect his motives in revisiting the women he has abandoned. To her, his primary reason is that before marrying he wishes to make sure that there is nothing better on the market, that he did not make a mistake in passing on his earlier conquests. When he insists on his good intentions she replies: 'Oppenheimer meant well. Pol Pot *meant* well. It's not about the meaning, it's about the doing. Guys always *mean well* – right before they fuck somebody over.' And here, perhaps, is a wider meaning for as he says, 'You think it's okay as long as it's just one person, rather than a dozen? Or a million? When is *hurting* okay? When *you* say so, or is it just open season, all of us going at it in any way we see fit.' (63)

When Arthur Miller was accused of a sense of disproportion, in *After the Fall*, in equating betrayal in personal relationships with the human betrayal implicit in the House Un-American Activities Committee or, still more, the Holocaust, he replied that it had to start somewhere: 'So it's all one thing to me and the attempt, in *After the Fall*, was to unify both worlds, to make them one, to make an embrace that would touch the concentration camp, the Un-American Activities Committee, a sexual relationship, a marital relationship, all in one embrace, because that's really the way it is ... There is, of course, a disproportion. No question about it. But the underlying principle of taking up a commitment and betraying it, if not the same, is pretty close.'[4]

In the context of *Some Girl(s)*, perhaps the leap seems all the greater, not least because of the comic thrust of much of the play. On the other hand, Bobbi's comments suggest the extent to which here, and elsewhere in his work, LaBute is concerned to do rather more than offer an ironic comment on human foibles and the gulf which exists between those who might seem joined by a common predicament if nothing else. When Guy objects that 'you *cannot* equate like, some *war* with me not calling you,' she replies, 'Why not? Who says I can't ... because when you do what you do, what it sounds like you've done – a lot – people get hurt. Injured. A bit of them, some piece ... it dies ... you didn't care. You did not even look back, and *that* ... that one little brutal gesture ... makes you more than just some ex-boyfriend. You are like a killer. An assassin. Some emotional *terrorist.'* (63) LaBute and Miller, it seems, are not so far apart.

LaBute, however, had one more card to play, one more, that is, until he wrote the scene not included in either the original British or American productions. As Guy suggests that even now he cares for Bobbi, that his feelings for his fiancée are no more than displaced feelings for a woman he now realises he had foolishly abandoned, so she inadvertently backs into a lamp, knocking it over and revealing what until then had been a concealed microphone. He has been recording his encounters with a view to writing a piece for *Esquire.* Suddenly, what had seemed spontaneous encounters stand revealed as dramas he has staged, conscious improvisations, at least on his part. And here, too, there is a link to Miller whose *The Archbishop's Ceiling* also involved microphones which are (or may be) concealed in the ceiling and whose assumed presence changes the characters, or those aware of it, into actors.

Guy's defence is the writer's defence, that all experience is grist to the mill, that art has a higher morality. He boasts that he has been called a 'cartographer of the human soul', a familiar enough phrase (used by a reviewer to describe Thomas Moore's *Soul of Sex: Cultivating Life as an Act of Love*), and one that could not implausibly be attached to LaBute himself. But he acknowledges that such spiritual intent is wedded to a material motivation which, as he confesses, 'makes me an American', (68) and this play, criss-crossing America, is surely offered in part as an account of an America in which ambition and self-interest frequently cloak themselves with spiritual justifications, God and Mammon having seemingly negotiated a mutually profitable deal. So it is that Guy claims to be engaged in a search with spiritual overtones. He wishes, he explains, to 'reach out for my happiness on a profoundly human level,' (68) embracing an American injunction even as he elides this with a claim to the significance of his work on the grounds that 'this is *Esquire!'* an up-market magazine justifying what might otherwise seem suspect. Thus he insists that the fact that he is an author 'doesn't mean I'm not able to have human . . . *stuff*', (68) his reaching for a word suggesting precisely what he lacks. 'Stuff' goes along with 'some girl', as a marker of more than linguistic incapacity. It is the equivalent of 'whatever' in LaBute's earlier plays, a shrug of indifference, a dismissal of significance even as he lays claim to it.

Guy acknowledges the bleakness of contemporary life, the existence of those who 'sit up until *four* in the morning searching for sex on the Internet while a loved one is sleeping fifty feet away . . . or some guy *text-messages* to his wife to say "I'm leaving you,"' (68) though this is a suspiciously precise description and hypocritical from a man who has specialised in walking away from relationships without even that suspect courtesy. Indeed, as if to underline this he now declares his love for Bobbi, in doing so betraying the woman he is about to marry who he now characterises as 'this girl', (69) a girl who, after Bobbi has left, now telephones him. He promises to fly back to see her that night, effortlessly switching his allegiance back.

Meanwhile, he has taken the concealed tape-recorder from a drawer and begun to pull the tape out, as if he regrets what he has done. As the play ends, however, he winds it back into the cassette, as he does so intoning, 'And love you, too. Yes! Love you so much, I do. I love you very much. Very, very much . . . and always will. Yes. I promise. Uh-huh. Will always and always and always . . . yes, and always more. *Always* . . .' (70) – always being the word that Tyler had said he 'used to throw around a lot'. It is unclear who this incantation is addressed to since the word 'love' had not formed part of his telephone conversation. Is it simply a way of fending off doubts, of assuring himself of a commitment which his own past would seem to deny? Or, since it is only a moment since he had declared his love for Bobbi, is he affirming a rediscovered feeling which will leave him a victim of his own equivocations and betrayals? Or, is this a self-love as, like Cary in *Your Friends & Neighbors*, he rehearses what he clearly takes as one of his best lines, while he re-dedicates himself to his vision of his own future as a writer, processing other people's pain for his own benefit? Whichever it is, he is still making the promises he made to so many and on which he had so consistently reneged.

And there the play ended, until LaBute decided to add a fifth scene which took it in a wholly different direction. The text had, he conceded, already undergone a number of changes during its London run. Those changes had served to alter the thrust of the play: 'What played onstage … was a more streamlined and somewhat simpler tale of a man who travels back into his life to honestly try to find something of worth in the wreckage of his past relationships. The original text, though, had a parallel story of journalistic opportunism running alongside the more romantic elements, which we ultimately trimmed out of that first production.' (Afterword(s): 'Deleted Scene', p. 71) The latter element subsequently began to seem more timely as revelations about journalistic fraud and bad faith emerged in the American media. This, in turn, raised questions about the limits of literary freedom. Accordingly, LaBute and his American director, Jo Bonney, decided to reinstate the omitted material. The challenge was 'to help a character negotiate the difficult waters of actually caring for the very people he's about to knowingly hurt'. The result was that the 'first version of *Some Girl(s)* shows a man making casual blunders in his relationships; this edition tracks a more ruthless romantic terrorist'. (72)

To this, however, he now added a further scene played in neither London nor New York. It was not, he insisted, prompted by a feeling that the play as performed was unfinished. It did, though, seem to him to round the action off, returning the protagonist to his home city and the start of his odyssey – Seattle. It is also full of cross-references to the other scenes, pulling together seemingly disparate events. The scene could, he conceded, stand alone and, indeed, be performed as a one-act play. But since he also refers to it as a 'movement', this would seem to imply that he does see it as an integral part of *Some Girl(s)*, even though it ends the play on a distinctly discordant note.

This time the girl – Reggie – is twenty-five years old. Like Sam in the first scene, she enters carrying a Seattle icon, a Starbucks' coffee cup. What differs this time is that Guy's relationship had been with her brother, Kelly (equally a girl's name), then his schoolmate with whom he had severed his relationship as abruptly as he had with the girls in his life. Why, then, return, especially since he has not responded to an approach from Kelly who had been intrigued by his *New Yorker* story? The answer is what turns the play around.

As it happens, Reggie explains, she had been about to approach Guy and, she imagines, for much the same reason that he had called her. The fact is that when she knew him initially she had not been a young woman but a girl. Her memory of him was of someone who used to run home when he and her brother were accused of anything, even then choosing flight over responsibility. There is a hint, too, that this was a tactic he had learned at home in the face of family arguments. For the first time, in other words, we are offered a reason for his behaviour, for his inability or unwillingness to commit or even stay around.

For her part, she is now a journalist and, noting that he has used his own experiences with others to build a reputation, feels she might do the same. The issue which connects them relates to an occasion on which he had made a sexual approach to her at the age of eleven when he was eighteen. LaBute's tactic here is akin to that used by Paula Vogel in *How I Learned to Drive* in which we first see an eighteen-year-old woman, L'il Bit, with a man in his thirties with whom she plainly has a sexual relationship. Then, Vogel regresses the age of the woman until she is a young girl, a victim of the man who was plainly a paedophile. Whatever we have learned of Guy has suggested nothing more than a disregard for others, an emotional cruelty. Now we are offered something else. The event was, he objects, nothing more than a kiss, albeit a passionate one. She recalls something else: 'Do you remember touching my ass? ... Your hand was there, slipping into my panties.' He had, she insists, then whispered, '"I'm gonna marry you someday."' (88)

At first, she seems to threaten him, but she has no intention either of retaliating or being a victim: 'we're basically to blame for our own shit.' As she leaves, however, she thrusts him against the wall and kisses him. 'There', she says, '*That's* what a woman kisses like ... see the difference?' (91) Guy watches her go and sits on the bed, breathing heavily.

Offered a series of lessons by his encounters, Guy is confronted by a version of himself at odds with that which he projects in his fiction. In that, he had apparently been no more than a well-meaning young man recounting a series of amusing experiences. The impending marriage that had supposedly led him to revisit those he had damaged on the assumption that he could heal or at least placate them, has left him exposed. That marriage seems increasingly implausible. He is a permanent adolescent with a seemingly infinite capacity to deny the real significance of his actions, in a country in which past crimes can be neutralised by a language of honest repentance and 'closure' is a desirable objective available to those willing to discuss their faults, the better to deny their lasting effects. He appears to accept the accusations levelled at him, to acknowledge his faults, but there is little sense that this is anything more than a convenient tactic. Words, for him, are in some way detached from their meaning. He takes pride in correcting other people's grammar while showing little interest in correcting his own behaviour. What matters is not to change but to purge himself of any inconvenient intimations of guilt.

His list could have been longer, indeed was. It is simply that some of the women he contacted never bothered to show up, plainly not affording him the significance he affords himself. The parenthesis within the title – *Some Girl(s)* – suggests that to Guy there is an equivalence in his disregard. To him, the women he encounters are rather like the hotel rooms in which he chooses to hold his confrontations. They are similar, with only minor differences. He is the common factor. It is his peace of mind he seeks, not theirs and even then this project is compromised by its utility as source material for his career. He is a teacher with a disturbing capacity to learn nothing except the American conviction that in every disaster there is an opportunity, that every moral failure can be retooled in the service of celebrity. He ends, as seems appropriate, alone in a hotel room, having abandoned all those who might have rescued him from an isolation he confuses with self-sufficiency.

There is, perhaps, a confessional element to *Some Girl(s)*. It is not that LaBute is testifying to his own relationships. What he does seem to be acknowledging is the amorality of the writer, the potential price of transmuting experience into art, a price not paid by the writer but by those whose lives become no more than raw material. In that sense, it picks up from *the shape of things*. Betrayal, which is so frequently a major theme of his plays, is also, it seems, a defining quality of the author for whom art or, more simply success, may be constructed out of other people's pain.

Robert Browning's 'My Last Duchess' is, effectively, a dramatic monologue, a poem addressed to an invisible person in which he seems to praise his former wife, now dead but captured in a painting. Little by little, praise turns to something else and we begin to suspect a secret he is tempted to reveal. In 'Porphyria's Love', another Browning soliloquy, a woman's beauty and goodness prompt a perverse response. The effectiveness of these poems lies in the light in which they cast the speaker rather than their apparent subject. The urge to confession does battle with something else. Motives are tangled. Self-justification displaces celebration or even simple justice.

LaBute's *Wrecks* works in a similar fashion, in a similar fashion indeed, to his own first plays in *bash*. It opened at the Everyman Theatre in Cork, in November 2005, and had its American premiere at the Public Theatre, New York, almost a year later, in October 2006, its text slightly modified but with the same actor, Ed Harris. Despite LaBute's assurance that 'There's none of the kind of cruelty that some of the male characters have perpetrated in other pieces,'[5] it is reminiscent not only of his earlier plays but also of Browning's poisoned encomiums as love turns out to be the source of more than consolation and transcendence.

The play takes place in a room 'shrouded in shadows'.[6] At the centre is a casket, covered in flowers. There are photographs of a woman on a nearby table. At the back is an archway through which light spills, along with sound from those evidently gathered there. They have, it seems, come together to mark the passing of this woman. Among their number, we learn, is her husband, Edward Carr. Yet the same Edward Carr is discovered in this shrouded room, lighting a cigarette, the first of many, as he begins to speak. Who does he address, since there is no one present but the body of the woman to whom he was married? To whom does he confess, since what follows has something of the air of a confessional, but himself? On the other hand, confession hardly seems his natural mode. Even justification implies something altogether too defensive. There is, it seems, a pride in his account. As Ed Harris remarked (he played in both the Irish and US productions), 'He has a certain code of ethics. He's out there, though – he doesn't give a fuck. He's, you know, his own animal.'[7]

Tomorrow, Edward explains, he is to deliver a eulogy, a celebration of his wife's life (Ed Harris actually wrote that eulogy as a means of understanding his character). As he assures us, 'this isn't about me,' only to acknowledge that 'it is, I mean a *bit*.' For the truth seems to be that he is an admirer of his own performance, that he is an audience to his own evasions. Her death, it increasingly seems, was the last act of a drama of his own devising with her unaware until the last moment of the part she was fated to play, fated, that is, in so far as he has scripted the last lines of her life's play.

In *Wrecks*, the living are so many ghosts, out of sight, present only through the distant sound of conversation. Even he is haunting his own past and preparing, as we later learn, for his own death, smoking cigarette after cigarette because, as he explains, 'When you're hooked you're hooked . . . once you give yourself over to something, it's, well . . . it's a devil of a deal to beat it.' Nor, it turns out, does this refer only to his habitual smoking, implicated, as he knows it is, in his impending death as each cigarette speeds up his progress toward extinction, as it had sped his wife to her death by secondary smoking. There is another compulsion that has driven him and brought him to this place where he stands before the casket of a woman whose life he recapitulates because his own is so deeply invested in it and because there is a secret he has guarded from others if not himself.

In the face of death, hers and his, he feels, he explains, the need 'to be honest here'. He is 'Just trying to be honest here', a reiteration which carries its own whisper of doubt. Honesty, we slowly learn, has not only not been a priority but has been guarded against lest a strategy should be disabled. It takes him most of the play to reach the point at which honesty is not so much embraced as flourished with a sense of guarded triumph. Truth is too precious to be squandered. It is a last card to be played. So, we eventually learn, it has taken most of their lives together for him to utter the single truth that explains his relationship to the woman he mourns, a truth even then only breathed into her ear as she dies, or perhaps not even then since he is the sole source of our knowledge.

He had been taught by her, he explains, to 'be open. Vulnerable', in touch with his emotions and 'all that other crap', the last a throwaway line which serves to neutralise the essence of his claim. Indeed, we slowly discover that openness has not been his intent or practice and that the vulnerability to which he refers was not his but that of his teacher, the woman who now lies dead in a casket covered with flowers whose vividness mocks the truth of what lies within. This is his Mary Josephine, his Mary Jo, his Jo or Jo-Jo, a linguistic intimacy which has overtones of a regression toward a child-like language and not, it transpires, without good reason.

He is, he suggests, old-fashioned when it comes to sex, reticent, disgusted by its degradation, especially here, in the funeral parlour where his wife lies dead, except that we will discover that his repugnance has its limits, limits which turn out to be more generous than others might allow. But he is a practised actor and even admires his own performance as he hears people crying in the room beyond, taking their cue, he believes, from himself so that 'I must be doing something right,' though he suspects they behave as they do because they have 'an audience'. The tears prompt a confused memory of Shirley Temple who he seems to recall was 'like some orphan kid that gets passed around from family to family', an observation whose suppressed bitterness makes more sense when we discover that he, too, is an orphan. A memory, it seems, morphs easily into an accusation. He had, he insisted, cried like a child at the passing of a woman who had been 'the lady in my life for over thirty years'.

Nor are those gathered together for this occasion the only actors. He listens to himself in the other room, admiring the obligatory catch in his voice: 'It's expected, what can I tell you. And I do feel it, *absolutely* do, but it's manufactured. You know? *After* the fact.' He is aware, too, of a momentary power afforded by the fact of loss as others make allowances, seek to offer something by way of consolation, an echo, perhaps, of *The Mercy Seat* and of those for whom 9/11 was an opportunity as well as a disaster. Whatever the Edward in the adjoining room may say or do, however calculated or guarded he is, this Edward feels no inhibitions in revealing his thoughts, opinions, prejudices.

He and his wife, we learn, had been business partners, with seventeen car-rental stores across five states, but theirs, he insists, had been a love affair despite an age difference of fifteen years, he twenty-five and she forty and already married, with two children, when they came together. He had not, he says, broken a marriage. It had already been in disarray, though he confesses to feeling 'a little bad', though evidently not in any profound sense since at first he affects not to be able to recall the man's name (though it would also have been his wife's). What he principally remembers is that the man was a first-generation immigrant for whom he had briefly worked, before being beaten on his orders when he suspected him of interest in his wife, though Edward's account of their encounter – which, he explains, was the first time he had met Jo-Jo – is, he confesses, 'not completely clear'. It was not a break-up without its material advantages, however, since she received a substantial settlement which enabled them to set up their business.

There is, though, more than a hint of discord, his nights sleeping on a couch aside. In contrast to what he calls 'his daughters', Mary Jo's sons, he suggests, will 'start tearing into each other' when he has died, families being the 'most unloving creatures that the good Lord ever collected together in one place'. There is, in other words, a rift in the marriage, a fault line between the children. He confesses to 'leaving a lot out here' but adds that 'you'll just have to believe me on this.' It is 'private'. Such silences invite filling. He had pursued his wife-to-be out of love. She was his obsession and, as he explains, 'When I had a goal, I stuck with it – stick with it for *years* until I'd reach it! Like a pit bull or something, one of those snapping turtles, hanging onto a stick long after it was dead,' something he ascribes to being an orphan. And, indeed, as the play edges towards its end so it becomes apparent that his obsession had been more firmly rooted in his status as orphan than he had been prepared to admit.

They had both, he insists, been missing something and had clung to one another as you would to wreckage from a downed aircraft in the sea. He had, he now admits, been looking for her all his life and when they met it was in an age of innocence where men and women were chaste until marriage. He had, indeed, been looking for her all his life, but sexual innocence was hardly at the centre of their relationship and in the last minutes of the play we discover why. She, he explains, whispered something to him, while he whispered something to her. The truth she shared with him was the existence of an abandoned child, a product, he speculates, of 'a visiting uncle'. The truth he presumably shared with her (he refuses to divulge it) was that he is in fact that child and hence that their marriage had been incestuous, carrying on the family tradition: 'I figured if she didn't want me in one way, in that way . . . as her kid . . . then maybe it'd be able to work out for us in some different life. A life like we've had together.' He had set himself to find her and, his encomiums to truth notwithstanding, had been prepared to use any means to do so, including becoming engaged to a girl who possessed a vital piece of information (dropping her immediately thereafter).

He signs off his confession by insisting that no one has suffered as a result of his actions, that love has triumphed and elsewhere, as we have seen, LaBute explores the question of whether love stands validated, no matter what its object. Edward is convinced that the expression he saw on his mother's face as he revealed his relationship to her had been one of relief and freedom. It has, he announces, been 'worth it to me', love being its own justification. He had, in other words, knowing the anguish his mother had felt throughout her life, chosen to withhold the truth which might once have set her free only to reveal it when it had become contaminated, revenge clothing itself in the garments of human concern. Regretting America's predilection for ignoring the past, he shapes that past into a weapon while insisting that he does no more than celebrate truth and the triumph of love, edging towards his own death as though vindicated. Twenty-five years of abandonment and anguish have been followed by thirty years of, we are assured, contentment, though even Edward confesses often to seeing an expression in her face which spoke of continued pain. Now, a last-second revelation sends her on her way with a shock which, presumably, would have been sufficient in itself to end her life but which he prefers to regard as reconciliation and acknowledgement. And the last word will lie with him as he plans his eulogy, in which he will write the definitive account of a woman now lying in a casket, before she and her truth are laid, if not to rest, then in her grave where that truth, as opposed to his, will be inviolable.

Why is the play called *Wrecks*? In one sense it would seem apt enough. One life is over, another running down. Entropy is having its way. Form and purpose have come into collision with the ineluctable. One life lies in pieces, not least because of what seems to have been a last-minute revelation. Another is now in freefall. Beyond that, however, beneath a surface equanimity and the semblance of contentment, a cold current has been running which itself had the power to stop the heart, a secret knowledge which was a denial of all that seemed to shape itself into an emotional logic secure in its own structure. And this had its model further back than this account of a Midwestern love affair. The title is also a homophone for *Rex*, which summons up memories of *Oedipus Rex*, in which a son and a mother became lovers, evidence of a tragic fate, except that *Wrecks* can offer nothing but an ironic parallel in that fate has had no hand in this mating which is calculated, knowing. LaBute's characters are not victims or protagonists of some cosmic drama. They are the wilful authors of their own actions with a predilection for testing the limits of those around them, observing one another with a detachment which if not cruel is at least at odds with commitments claimed, emotions asserted, declarations made.

Was the love Edward declares no more than cover for vengeance? Discovering her secret, he has one of his own which more than neutralises hers. While insisting that he has dedicated himself to making her happy, he has withheld a truth which might have been the source of true happiness to her had he not wished to corrupt that truth, to turn it into a dagger pointing at her heart. Forbearing to present himself as her child, he had infiltrated her life as a lover and thus the restored order for which she had yearned was become pure anarchy.

He refuses to disclose what he whispered to her at the end but the suspicion is that he has told her the truth, less out of a respect for honesty than an impulse to wound or at least a self-deception as profound as it is damaging. What else would he have whispered to a dying woman except this as he sought to balance the scales, exact a price for abandonment? She had once laid love aside, been the cause of anguish. Now he does no less in return. The greater their past happiness, the greater the anguish. He is not, surely, interested in anything so inconsequential as irony. What he is after is payback, even if he is convinced that it might be otherwise. This has been his addiction, and not the cigarettes that are merely the objective correlative of his capacity to kill. His life's work done, he can, in turn, die. 'What do you do?' people ask one another, much to his annoyance. In his case what he does is to pursue a logic to its ultimate end. He embraces the woman who once thrust him away. He closes a circle. A product of incest, he perpetrates incest. The first act had nothing to do with love. Did the second?

At the heart of the play, as of so many of LaBute's plays and stories, is the question of power. Beyond the fact that power in a relationship is unequal – the deeper the love the more vulnerable the individual – there is a special power which derives from knowledge withheld as there is from knowledge revealed. It is a game the protagonist plays with his wife/mother and a game he plays with whomever he addresses. It is also, though, a game that LaBute plays with his audience, here and elsewhere taking a special pleasure not merely in discommoding those who watch his plays but in manipulating expectations. It is the power that goes with storytelling.

Throughout his work, LaBute has shown a fondness for that twist in the tale that we associate with an O. Henry or Ambrose Bierce, that moment in which we are invited to reassess what we have been told or shown as if that very fact were a warning not to take the world as it appears or people for what they offer themselves as being. For Tennessee Williams, there are no lies but those thrust down the throat by the hard-knuckled hand of need. For Eugene O'Neill, pipe dreams are a means to enable us to function, if also the root of a particular absurdity. For Albee, such apparent consolations are the source of a suspect relief. The real has to be retrieved if there is to be any foundation for personal or social action. LaBute, though, is less concerned with counterposing reality and illusion as if what were at stake were a life strategy or the root of a moral dilemma. What interests him is the extent to which dissembling is instinctual, the degree to which we are a lying animal for whom deceit is a game which can seem synonymous with life: a strategy, to be sure, the source of a power which substitutes for meaning, but also evidence of an imagination with the power to degrade, manipulate and harm, or lift us beyond the prosaic circumstances of the given.

In *Wrecks*, the speaker deceives himself no less than others. He writes his life in such a way as to emerge its hero. Speaking of the woman he insists he loves, he discloses how little he loves her. Celebrating truth, he has dedicated himself to a lie. Regretting a disregard for the past, he conspires against it until it serves his purposes no longer to do so. He embraces the family but has set himself to destroy it. Himself abandoned, he abandons others. Is he, then, a hypocrite or simply someone who interprets experience in such a way as to emerge intact from the bruising business of living? Did others wreck his life or did he dedicate himself to doing such? LaBute is not in the business of mediating, merely setting in motion the conflicts which generate his drama and, beyond that, the private and public life of a nation.

Similar issues are raised by *In a Dark Dark House* (2007), originally to have been entitled *Swallowing Bicycles*. The play concerns two brothers. One, the thirty-five-year-old Drew, is a once successful lawyer now disbarred for unethical behaviour and currently charged with drug and driving offences. The other, Terry, is a security guard, a man, it seems, who lacks his brother's amoral drive for success.

The play opens as Terry visits Drew in the addiction unit where he is confined as a result of a court order. He is summoned, as he believes, as an element of the family therapy which is part of the treatment. There is an obvious tension between the two men, who seem barely to inhabit the same linguistic world. They clearly have a history, though the nature of that history is only gradually revealed.

In fact, Drew wants his brother to corroborate memories that he claims to have recovered, memories of abuse at the hands of a man called Todd Astin who they had both known as children. Terry is shocked by the revelations, though not quite, it later transpires, for the obvious reason. For the moment, though, all that Drew requires is corroboration of Astin's existence, not least because evidence of abuse may well be accepted as mitigating his own offences.

The brothers circle one another warily, the one a seeming success if moral failure, the other a material failure but apparently long since his younger brother's protector against bullies, primary among whom had been their father. Drew makes little pretence that he is after anything from Terry beyond immediate help. There is a perfunctory offer of food, followed by a suggestion that they could both watch *On the Waterfront*, this being movie night in the institution. LaBute's choice of movie, though, is hardly incidental, concerned as it is with criminality, lies, confessions, betrayals, and Drew duly urges his brother to a criminal act, goading him to seek out and do violence to the man who he alleges had once corrupted him. Terry, meanwhile, is anxious to get to a junior league baseball match he is scheduled to umpire.

In the second act, Terry encounters Jennifer, the sixteen-year-old daughter of the abuser whom he has tracked down. She presides over a mini-golf game. What follows is a seduction. Verbal sparring turns into sexual banter. The two play a one-hole game, itself described in deliberately sexualised terms. 'We did it all the time ... Him and me,' she remarks, 'get it in the hole.' It is clear that what is at stake is her submission. Is this a calculated act of revenge or is there something more to a scene in which, as in Vogel's *How I Learned to Drive*, a lonely, disaffected teenager is drawn to someone prepared to listen to her? The language is certainly that of abuse ('It'll be our little thing ... A secret') but the girl, largely abandoned by her father, who seems to be continuing with his predatory ways, appears a willing collaborator.

In the final scene, Terry and Drew confront one another again, the latter's story of abuse having secured his release. He is having a celebratory party, complete with champagne. Terry was uninvited until Drew's wife thought to include him. Even now he is relegated to the margin, having once again performed his function as protector. Now, however, they do briefly come together and truths begin to spill out. They are united by memories of their parents. Their mother has,

Terry insists, been 'a fucking ghost for as long as I can remember', while their father was 'a piece of shit', himself violently abusive until Terry had rebelled and beaten him so severely that he had been confined to a hospital for two months.

The principal revelation, however, is that Terry had been abused by the same man but that he had not seen it as abuse. Todd Astin, whatever his own motivations, had been the one bright light in a dark world for a desperate and alienated teenager. And here LaBute returns to a concern touched on in *Your Friends & Neighbors*, *The Distance From Here*, *Fat Pig* and *Wrecks*. Love is to be found in unlikely places and to be defined and experienced in strange ways. Terry's abuser offered him an understanding he had never received from his parents, a consolation not otherwise on offer. Hopelessly mismatched, they had nevertheless met in the mutuality of need, even if the nature of that need was profoundly suspect. At the same time, the impact was traumatic. It was in the name of that love that Terry had stolen a car, to get back to the person he had then believed central to his existence, and beaten his father when he mocked his feelings for the man. Now he is adrift and uncertain. His stalled career itself seems a product of shock. He is afraid that he might be gay – otherwise how could he have submitted to a man? He is equally concerned that he might be dangerous to young women, and his accomplished seduction of Jennifer is evidence of the reality of that fear. The abused has become the abuser. He is scared of,

> who I am now, what I want or might be capable of . . . So I keep myself to myself alone, and work hard at not going where I really don't belong. I'm afraid of, like, relationships, scared maybe I'm a *fag* because of what happened and not hating it . . . Know why I'm working that baseball deal this season? Huh? To try and prove to myself that I would never do that to some kid. What happened to me . . . I keep trying to figure out, in little ways, if I'm normal or not and so far I'll tell you what . . . I just don't know. (typescript)

On the other hand, LaBute raises other concerns. Was their father's calculated indifference and physical brutality not the first cause? And what are we to make of Drew, who Terry suddenly realises had faked the story of his own abuse simply to escape responsibility for his actions, and had in the process been perfectly happy to manipulate his brother, unconcerned about the damage he would precipitate? Drew's amorality may also in part have been a consequence of his upbringing but it extends out into the world, contaminating everything from private to public relationships. He moves in a world in which a disregard for others, a studied amorality, may bring its own rewards. Abuse takes many forms, the sexual being merely one.

Terry spent three years in juvenile detention for beating his father and later served in the military in the first Gulf War trying to prove something to himself and incidentally removing himself from temptation. Now his brother's abuse of their relationship has pitched him back into the dark house he seems doomed to inhabit. The play ends as the two men embrace and Drew returns to his party leaving Terry 'in the gathering shadows'. Once again, the final stage direction is something more than LaBute's habitual indicator: 'Silence. Darkness'.

Plainly LaBute has no interest in justifying paedophiles. He is, however, fascinated by the nature of love, independent of the object of that love. He is concerned with the shifting patterns of power between individuals. The play consists of three encounters in which power shifts, in which what is revealed and what is withheld become part of a strategy of living. He is struck by a callous indifference to the needs and sensibilities of others which may itself be seen as the root of psychological, social and even political dominance. Drew is a trickster whose lies define the world which he invites others to inhabit. But how else do we define the world, except in the terms we are offered by others or which we ourselves devise to protect us from knowledge of our own most profound failures?

Ten years on from his first appearance at Sundance, Neil LaBute has established himself as a major playwright and screen writer, directing with equal facility for the stage and screen. He has created a world as distinctive as Mamet's or Shepard's. Growing up in what Tom Wolf called 'the me-decade' of the 1970s and the 1980s decade of greed, in which self-interest was elevated as a value, in a period, too, in which the relationship between the sexes was being radically renegotiated, he has written about an America which seems to have lost its communal spirit. His plays shock not by their physical violence, of which there is little, but by virtue of the violence that people do to the idea of mutuality.

His are characters, for the most part, who acknowledge no moral necessities. If they come together, it is out of a need they scarcely understand, just as they are driven apart by instincts they cannot articulate. They live much of their lives as if actions had no consequences, relieved of all responsibility, free to act out fantasies which take no account of human sensibilities. If contact is made, if need is momentarily acknowledged, this tends to be a prelude to betrayal. His characters are on the move, in search of satisfactions they can hardly name, taking their cue from the images their society offers them, images to do with production and consumption, the body as negotiable currency, sex as consumer product, relationships as means to an end.

Asked whether he shared Thomas Hobbes's view that life was essentially nasty, brutish and short, he replied, 'I think we're stuck in a Hobbesian world if we let ourselves be. The world is as awful or as wonderful as we allow it to be . . . I think humans find it so easy to slide by, to take the road that's slightly easier, to make the choice that's just a bit more selfish or self-serving, that we end up creating our own Hobbesian universe.'[8] The distinctions he makes are crucial. In part these alternatives are structured into the human animal; in part, he suggests, they are a product of contemporary life. A certain moral logic seems to be in abeyance: the 'ability to have it all can create this daunting sense that we don't know what we want', the 'more permissive the society, the more people become more confused'.[9] Given such confusion, self-interest and self-concern become the lodestone.

The Mormon Church was clearly wrong in seeing his work as a threat. He is a moralist and his plays and films morality tales that in registering what has been evacuated from contemporary existence recall why such a loss is to be regretted. The fact that audiences retain their capacity for shock in the face of his work is perhaps a guarantee that all is not lost. If this seems like clutching at straws, we have Edward Bond's assurance that, 'Clutching at straws is the only realistic thing to do. The alternative, apart from the self-indulgence of pessimism, is a fatuous optimism based on superficiality of both feeling and observation.' As Bond says of Len, one of his characters in *Saved*, 'He lives with people at their worst and most helpless ... and does not turn away from them. I cannot imagine an optimism more tenacious, disciplined or honest.'[10] At the same time, LaBute has an unnerving capacity to implicate his audiences in the moral equivocations of his characters, their laughter all too often allying them with views and values they might be expected to reject.

His work is disturbing and compelling in so far as he acutely registers the cruelties and deceits of which all are capable, the self-concern that can determine the terms on which relationships are conducted. And what is true on a private level seems true on a wider scale. The dereliction pictured in *The Distance From Here*, the ash which drifts down in *The Mercy Seat*, are something more than the given of modern life; they are a projection of a disregard which begins in the self but which becomes social and political fact. The anonymous hotel rooms, airport lounges, offices, fashionable apartments he features are peopled with those who fail to connect with one another out of fear, contempt, distrust, ready at any moment to betray, abandon, abuse, because they lack any reason to do otherwise, a sense that they are in pursuit of anything more than seconds of pleasure. They serve nothing beyond themselves but seldom pause to consider their own lives.

While it is clear that the men and women in his plays operate on different sets of assumptions, see the world differently, there is a level on which they share something more than a predicament. Speaking of his own work, Richard Ford once remarked that, 'My assumption as a person who writes about moral issues is that women and men are alike. And in terms of their consequential acts, they have to be responsible for what they do in pretty much the same way, and the differences that are perhaps inspired by gender are subterior to what is more important to me – how men and women treat other people, how they act in ways that bring about consequences in others' lives.'[11] Whatever his interest in identifying those forces which drive his characters apart, much the same conviction is embraced by Neil LaBute. Ford recalls Emerson's remark about the infinite remoteness between people. It is felt with equal acuteness by LaBute. Why else write if not conscious of the tragedy implicit in that fact; why else write if not believing that art, for all its potential for bad faith, has the capacity to close that space. As Frank Kermode insisted, in *The Sense of an Ending*, 'It is not that we are connoisseurs of chaos, but that we are surrounded by it, and equipped for coexistence with it only by our fictive powers.'[12]

In the end, the shock of LaBute's work does not derive from the cruelties he identifies, the language some of his characters deploy, his vision of an alienated world. What disturbs beyond anything is the shock of recognition, the realisation that LaButeland is our land, that these plays and stories all carry our own DNA. As Proust once remarked of the novel, 'Every reader, as he reads, is actually the reader of himself. The writer's work is only a kind of optical instrument he provides the reader so he can discern what he might never have seen in himself without this book. The reader's recognition in himself of what the book says is the proof of the book's truth.'[13]

'I'm a realist,' LaBute has insisted,

> I am definitely sceptical of how we live our lives, of how we treat each other. I think that we so often take the slightly easier route which is filled with self-interest and that is usually at the cost of somebody else. So I am aware of the great good and the great bad that we can find ourselves doing. To be honest, it is much more interesting to write the bad. I have to pitch characters into conflict to create drama, so I am often looking for the bad where it may not even exist yet ... I am far more upset by reading the newspaper than I am by the writing that I do ... These are real people who are doing things that are so much more breathtaking than what I am coming up with.[14]

Explaining his predilection for characters who inhabit a dark emotional world, he asked, 'Do we find our way to bliss only through the extremes of illness, death, tragedy?' replying, 'I think so, very often, anyway. Most of the time we plod through life so wretchedly removed from our feelings that we miss everything going on around us ... Not that things can't conspire to bring us down, but we're so good at doing it ourselves that we usually don't have to.'[15]

Asked whether he would ever write about 'the good days', he replied,

> Those stories are all there. You can check them out of the
> library. There is so much of the other available all the time, from
> Hollywood, from the theatre, the kind of well-structured play,
> the well-intentioned, good-natured. My interests happen to be
> elsewhere. Will I ever write a children's story, will I ever write a
> story that ends happily? No doubt. Just because I think it will be a
> surprise. It'll be as much that I wanted to write about a good thing
> but that I also saw it as a good left hook that the audience didn't
> expect. No doubt there will always be that combination of
> punches. I want an audience to consistently be ready [for the fact]
> that I'm going to do something that they don't expect. (SBS)

13   An interview with Neil LaBute

This interview was recorded in London on 25 January 2007.

CB: Where does your family name come from?

NL: It is French Canadian. My ancestors went from France into French Canada and were there for a few years and then migrated down into Michigan, although just recently I have learned that LaBute translates into swan in Czech!

CB: And on the other side of the family?

NL: My mother's father was born in London and moved to the States when he was eight or ten. My mother's side were Irish, I believe.

CB: You were born in Detroit. How old were you when you left?

NL: Oh, probably three or four.

CB: So you then went to Liberty Lake, near Spokane in Washington state, which is a tiny community. Even today it has less than six thousand inhabitants. What was it like as a place in which to grow up?

NL: It was a great place. It was relatively isolated but it had everything. The lake was there, the woods were there. I grew up working a lot on a farm. I didn't care for that experience so much, though it created a good work ethic in me. People often say of something that 'at least it's not like digging a ditch.' Well, I have dug a ditch. I know exactly what that is like so, whether I liked it or not – and my brother still has a farm and loves it – and I found little pleasure in it, it formed the way in which I work and I think my work attests to that. I usually roll up my sleeves and do something when I say I will. It was a place that also allowed my father's naturally bad temper to flare up because we were often working with inferior equipment, or around stupid animals like cows which don't listen to you. So that would frustrate him. Being a truck driver he was in and out of town but when he was home for stretches, and working like that, you were more prone to being at the mercy of his moods.

CB: You were frightened of him.

NL: Yes, probably. I don't think you could help but be. He was unpredictable. He was occasionally a violent person. You could see that was in his nature. He would occasionally be violent to myself, or my brother, or even my mother, but not consistently. There is something even more terrifying about that because you never know when it is going to happen and what is going to set it off. He was probably – and now that he has passed away I can say he was – a classic case of bipolar, the sort who would never go to a doctor or take medication or anything like that. His moods could shift greatly and he could be on quite a high or an extreme low. Who knows what medication might have done for the guy?

CB: How far is that imminent violence and the difficult relationships it engendered reflected in your work?

NL: Now that I have enough distance from *Swallowing Bicycles*, which I think is going to end up being called *In A Dark Dark House*, the references to the father are pretty negative. I have always been harder on male characters than I have on the females even though the females may be victims at the hands of the men. I think I have been fairer to the women than I have to the men. I have probably grown up with a certain suspicion about men because the key male figure was one worth being suspicious of. He created a great deal of doubt in the other members of the family with respect to the behaviour when he was gone and the behaviour when he was at home. So I think I ultimately have a kind of general sense of worry about mankind.

CB: And your real ally was your mother. She had similar interests. Did she help spark your interest in film, in writing?

NL: I think pedestrian is the wrong word but she was a very lay person. She just loved movies. She wasn't particularly drawn to the theatre because I don't think she was exposed to it very much. The love of the theatre that I have ended up having is self-generated and it is one of those things where you never quite know where it came from. If it didn't come from one person dragging you to the theatre, what was it about the few plays that I did see that spoke to me and said that is the form of expression I would like to be part of? I am not sure. It quite immediately said that that was a world in which I thought I could find a way to create.

CB: Of the movies you have mentioned seeing when you were a teenager, none was American. They were post-war Italian and French films.

NL: Yes. There was a good series on television that allowed you to see a lot of those films and that sparked a life-long interest in international cinema. I am extremely comfortable watching Italian and French films, and kitchen sink dramas from Britain. That said, I was also sucking down movies from all walks of life as well. On television, or when we would go to the movies, I was seeing the more popular things as well. But my desire was always to see something else.

CB: I presume your father had never been to university.

NL: No.

CB: Your mother?

NL: No.

CB: Was there any problem about your deciding that you wanted to go?

NL: No, the one good thing about my father's profession is that he was not trying to pass it on to anyone. He was working to keep the family. I think his mother left the family when he was young and took up with someone else so there was always a desire to hold it together in some way. As badly as he did it, he still felt this need to provide, to keep the ideal of a family in place. But he was doing a job that he really didn't care for, that he really didn't want to do, so it wasn't a craft or skill that he wanted to pass on to me.

There was no real sense of accomplishment that led him to expect me to do the same. At times there would be a kind of ridicule about what I was doing which wasn't much of a job, especially when there wasn't much to show for it. In those years when I was trying to make it I did feel like this perpetual out-of-work person. But I think he had always wanted to do something else with his own life and simply didn't get that chance, so he never stood in my way. Going to university, whatever I excelled in, was OK. Not that he took an active interest in it, but it was alright. There was never any push to be something other than what I wanted to be.

CB: America is full of good theatre programmes. What drew you to Brigham Young University, a Mormon university?

NL: At the time I think I was young and open, susceptible to something different from the experience I had grown up with. So it seemed like a different experience, and the Mormons that I had been exposed to I liked very much. It also happened that I got a scholarship as a non-Mormon and that was one of the best offers I had. It was also far away, a few states away. It was not a quick run home. I would go home in the holidays, but not every weekend or anything like that. So all signs pointed to go. I thought this was as good as an escape as it was a place to go to university.

CB: When you became a Mormon do you think it was in part a reaction to what you had had at home? Here was a community that could close around you.

NL: Yes, in a way I was searching for something and there it was whether, ultimately, I wanted it or not. It was also the most pervasive thing around. I was completely inundated with it, surrounded by it at school, and in that context it made complete sense. I still have relatively few difficulties with it. I think the desire for something outweighed the scrutiny of it. It was more about the people. It was more about the need to belong to something.

CB: And you married somebody who was a Mormon.

NL: Yes.

CB: The impression I get is that she was more of a Mormon than you were and, that being so, did she have difficulty with some of your work?

NL: Yes, sure. That only grew along the way. And my kids have real difficulties with it. They are not proud of a lot of the work. They wish a lot of it didn't exist. That makes it strange because, whether children follow you into that work or not, you want to believe that they are going to support or love it, even if it is not written for them. You do not want to believe they are going to hate it outright because there are swear words in it, or that sort of thing. So it has been a strange atmosphere that I have had to live with at the same time that I was creating. I am always keenly aware that this will at some point get back to them and so am I going to censor myself or what am I going to do? Am I just going to write, and live with what happens? That is usually the case as the spirit and the desire to write usually takes over most other sensible thoughts and you do what you are, I guess, meant to do, and you live with the results. I am no longer in the family.

CB: Your most recent play to be staged as we speak is *Wrecks*. It is a monologue, though there is another character, is there not?

NL: There is. The wife. At one point I wondered if I should write a monologue for her, if I should stretch the evening out. It has never been anything other than a thought, but she was personified in production. She literally hung over the proceedings in a really powerful way. The image that the designer came up with was, strangely, from Ed Harris. She reminded him of his own mother and he wanted a picture so he could stay connected to this woman who was meant to be his wife. The designer placed a huge image literally at the back of the stage so you couldn't help but feel the power of that over the proceedings. And since the picture is on stage he refers to it literally a couple of times.

CB: I think some people are baffled by the idea of monologue in drama. It is as though you are throwing away what you are taught is its essence, which is conflict. You have a single voice.

NL: It is a strange technique and yet highly theatrical. It is one we often only get away with on stage. You rarely see it in cinema and when you do it often strikes you as false or strange. I tried to do one of the longer monologues I could find in films when Jason Patric did a long unbroken take in *Your Friends & Neighbors*. I think we have since found a couple of longer ones, if only because they are from Shakespeare. I don't know if we set a record but we certainly made a long one.

CB: But in *Your Friends & Neighbors* there are other people present during that monologue.

NL: Yes, but in conversation it is strange how often friends just sit and listen to someone talking without any kind of interjection. In *Your Friends & Neighbors* we get around that by just keeping the camera on Jason and pushing in, which excludes our memory of them until we want them, for reactions. It is a little bit cheap, really, but it is part of the nature of creating that conflict which lies in their reactions to what he is saying. The conflict is also there within the person. This is really a kind of confession. In that sense I was extending an approach I had used in *bash*. But in *Wrecks* there is also a conceit within a conceit. It is a monologue but the character also exists in the next room. The conceit is that he is in that other room, dealing with everyone at the funeral, but simultaneously has stepped into this room for a moment to get away from that and that you, the audience, are there with him. Strange as that notion is people seem to get it and go with it. If you talk to people about it occasionally they will say 'Who is he supposed to be?' And I say, 'You are who you are. You are the audience. Are you the audience in his mind? I don't worry about it too much.' What I do know is that there is a confessional quality to it. He has a need to talk, to confess to what he has done. Does he at the end find that he is confessing to a crime? He seems not to think so. He gets to a place where he says, 'I dare you to tell me that I have been wrong. I dare you tell me that you could love more than I have. I don't think you can.'

CB: But in his case he takes a kind of pleasure from this. The essence of his power lies in withheld knowledge. He has a secret that he keeps to the end. But that, surely, is exactly what you do as a playwright?

NL: That is probably because I get pleasure from it as well. I probably get pleasure from it when it is done to me as an audience member. We don't just write our Sam Shepard play or our Noël Coward play. There are models, and I am very curious about the way they did it, and how successfully they did it, but we find our own voice along the way. The things that have worked best on me as an audience member are the times that I have been surprised, taken to a new place, shocked. There are certain things that have made me stand up and take notice and therefore I want to do that same kind of thing. I think that one can get stuck in that and so I have been careful to hold back in some cases, to make sure it isn't always the same trick because you don't want it to be just a trick. You have to work it into the fabric of what you are doing. But the idea of a secret is a provocative tool to use in the theatre, the idea of someone who willingly withholds information, that or a strong reversal of plot.

CB: The withholding of information, the guarding of a secret, is also surely associated with power, and power seems to be a concern of yours, the power of an individual over another individual.

NL: That is true. But I am not only interested in individual men and women. I am fascinated by small groups of people who are related through friendship, work, marriage. I like taking that group and trying to find some way to turn it on its ear, and that is often based on power. 'I want the job that you have. I want the man or the woman that you are with. I want something different than what we have now.' It is a shift in the power dynamics and certainly in one of the traditional power dynamics of a relationship. That is definitely an interest to me.

CB: Often that sense of power derives from the fact that a character refuses to enter the ethical world, refuses to recognise the values that we assume everyone subscribes to. The moment you do that you accrete power as a result. You don't care what you do. You do something because you can do it.

NL: I hope that they recognise it. I think you have to recognise it to know how you are using it, that you are subverting it.

CB: Chad, in *in the company of men*, never seems to acknowledge a moral world.

NL: To acknowledge that it exists doesn't mean that you are ever going to apply it to yourself. He may be as close to a sociopath as I have created because I think he is a constant and vigorous liar, in the sense that he actively knows that he is lying and uses it to his advantage in relation to the audience. He keeps us in the dark to the same degree that he keeps Howard, until the moment of revelation, as he does his girlfriend. Everyone is played by him so I think he has a conscious sense that 'I am above the actual moral fabric of the way life is lived and in fact I will use that against people.' Others, though, I think, are less aware of their manipulative power. I think that is so with Jason, in *Your Friends & Neighbors*. For the most part, he is very truthful, but he is unrelentingly brutal. He professes not to be someone who lies. He absolutely has a kind of Old Testament eye-for-an-eye justice – if you hurt me I will hurt you even worse – but he doesn't do it for pleasure. So I think he is the opposite. Yet the results are similar in that people get wounded by them.

CB: How far do you project these personal relationships onto a social and political level? I am thinking of *The Distance from Here*, in which two of the male characters have served in the Gulf War and evidence exactly that kind of callous indifference that you find elsewhere in your work. Here you seem to be nudging beyond the personal into the political. Is there a part of you that sets out to offer a portrait of society as well as a portrait of alienated individuals within it?

NL: I suppose if you paint enough portraits, and they are from seemingly different walks of life – although they are often in a vague world of my making, the Midwest, or a city, or wherever it is – it begins to become a glimpse of a larger world, a larger society. I think 9/11 provoked the same sort of thing, though the other way around. We started with a highly nationalistic reaction. CNN responded with headlines that said, 'America attacked. America responds. America rebuilds. We are one.' I felt there could be no way that everybody had reacted in the same way. A moment of catastrophe like that often breeds both true heroism and true deceit. The people who wouldn't believe they had it in themselves to grab someone and carry them down the stairs do that but another person tries to save himself and discovers his true nature. I felt that to focus on this real individual, struggling to survive and manipulate the situation, was more interesting than just saying here is a portrait of that next morning. I think that that speaks to a larger degree to a world that is in fact made up of individual portraits. So, yes, I think there is some notion of an outside world.

CB: The other writer who hovers over *The Distance From Here* is Edward Bond but he has a clear politics. His alienated individuals are not evidence of a corrupt nature, they are the product of capitalism and he clearly believes that there is a need to address that fact. Is there anything in you that shares that kind of feeling because, taken together, your work seems to picture an empty, uncommunal society. Is there underlying this a politics to your work?

NL: I suppose there is, although as a person, certainly, and no doubt as a writer, I have found myself less drawn to the overt politics of the world around me than to gender politics, the politics of friendship, the politics of the workspace. I tend to make those the microcosms. It is hard to go through my works without finding some reference to how I feel about a certain kind of materialism. But I don't think it is particularly American or, I should say, only American.

CB: No, but when I read your work I see somebody who looks as though they grew up in the seventies and eighties, the 'me decade', the 'greed decade', a time of self-interest, self-concern, when politicians declared that there was no such thing as society.

NL: There is no doubt about that. Even into the nineties, it became more important to get ahead than to care about people. In particular, I would go back to the world of business, having worked around that world and been fascinated with how people go about daily life within that world. In business you are asked to become part of a machine that works for the good of the company. It is not about you. It is about this thing so that it becomes difficult to switch gears and go back to being a person who cares and can have the give and take that a relationship requires. I think you systematically strip that from a person. It becomes very difficult to then deal with people. I suppose it hearkens back to German expressionism, I like that school very much. I think someone like Mamet does that. His *Edmond* is a direct reflection of it. People become labels. They become just the doctor and the journalist and the wife. Even things that are meant to bring us together, like the Internet, have a great capacity for pushing us into our own little dark corner so that we feel as though we are all sitting alone in our houses by ourselves, not connected in any way other than by a few symbols. If we tire of someone a click will get rid of them. Compare that with the work it takes when you are in a relationship with someone. I am fascinated now by my kids who go to MySpace. I never knew how needy my community was, how much people wanted to say, 'Look at me,' reach out and say 'Take a look at my pictures. Listen to what I have to say.' I had no idea that I was surrounded by quite such a needy, narcissistic society until the advent of that.

CB: Is that narcissism or is that people having a chance to say, 'I am an individual, I am not just part of this bland society out there. I do things.'

NL: One can look at it either way, I suppose.

CB: There is nearly always a tincture of possibility in your plays. It would be true, for example, even of such an apparently bleak play as *The Distance From Here*, in which there is a very Bond-like minimalist gesture which nonetheless works against what seems to be the force of the play.

NL: Hugely important, I think, in the same way that humour is. It leavens the experience and allows one to have a greater sense of doubt in the sense that it is not just like someone rolling a rock uphill. There is a ray of hope because, unless characters die, there is always hope. If you kill the character it is pretty much final. You shouldn't bring them back as a ghost. In *The Distance From Here* there are some younger people and for all the things Darrell does in that piece I think the audience is still willing to go with him because he is so young. They feel he is as much damaged goods or as much a victim as he is a victimiser. He is railing against the way he has been raised. He did say a lot of horrible things and do awful things but all it takes is for them to hear his mother say that she did not remember that much about him growing up for them to gasp. It is uniform across the theatre. They gasp. You don't say that to a kid. You see his little face melt because he is trying to be so tough but, when he hears that, there is no going back. So I think youth helps him in that case. But who knows what will happen to him? A kid like Tim, in that play, is very susceptible to the charms and dangers that he provides. You sense there is a good kid in there somewhere, as you do with his girlfriend Jen, who has obviously had her own difficulties. Here is someone who is not afraid of the idea of changing her life and doing something different.

People have asked me why the ending of *Fat Pig* is so sad, when it was really a lot of fun for so long, and I thought 'What is the worst thing that could happen now to these people? What is the most real thing that could happen to them? Where does this look like it is headed to me?' For me, the ray of hope is that Tom finally learns to tell the truth. He has been asked by his ex-girlfriend, he has been asked by his new girlfriend, 'just tell me what is going on. Tell me the truth,' but when he finally tells the truth nobody wants to hear it. For ninety pages they have asked for the truth and now here it is. 'The truth is I am not a strong person,' and we leave them there. But who knows what will happen next? They still have to get back home. We don't know what tomorrow will bring them. There is a conversation that has got to take place somewhere along the way. They might reconcile. In a way, that is none of my business. What I have done is done. That is the end of it.

CB: For all its humour, though, that is one of the more painful of your plays because until that moment it is basically a love story. He wants to continue their relationship but lacks the courage to face what people think. Whatever it takes for him to stand up against received opinion he doesn't have.

NL: I think that in itself is a political statement without being one. We are a country that talks about the moral majority. We ask what is the value of one vote against the many, but my concern is not about that. In the end, what matters to me is the story. I think that it is most important to be true to those characters, to what I think would happen to them, rather than give the audience what they want.

CB: To be honest, you rather like not giving them what they want.

NL: I don't know that I get off on it. I could make it worse, if that is what they are asking for. I could do that, but I am most worried about being true to where I found myself in the telling of the story.

CB: You must have had another kind of worry when you wrote *The Mercy Seat* and were preparing to put it on stage. You must have asked yourself two questions. One is, why am I writing this? The second is, why am I putting in on in New York so soon after 9/11? You must have been in doubt as to how this was going to be received.

NL: You are right about the second part, that I was in doubt about how it would be received, and I think I became more acutely aware of that when the people who were working with me began saying, 'I don't know how this is going to go.' For myself, I would have put it on six months earlier if I could. I just didn't have the idea until six months after it happened. It was about March, 2002, that I had the notion and started writing the play. I don't think it is ever too early to talk about something, to ask why and look at some experience or some idea or some institution through the eyes of a person, whether it is fictive or not. I instinctively said to myself, 'We really need to put this on in New York.' A number of my plays have been put on in England but I said 'I am going to do this first in New York because how the audience respond to what is being said will be a test.' Along the way, though, as we were getting close to opening, I became more doubtful.

CB: There must have been an accusation waiting for you, namely that you had written a play about people exploiting 9/11 while as a playwright you were doing essentially the same thing.

NL: That was thrown in my face a number of times, by the critics or just people from the audience who said, 'Here you are making money from 9/11.' And there is no denying that fact, not a lot of money, but, yes, the fact of it is I was not doing it just out of the goodness of my heart, saying, 'I am going to put this play on and come and see it for free.'

CB: But that is the nature of the writer isn't it? The writer can get immense pleasure out of getting something absolutely right however painful that thing is. There is a detachment which goes with the job. The writer gets a different kind of pleasure from the person receiving it.

NL: There is a queer sort of duality when you know you have got it right and people respond, to whatever degree, in the way in which you imagined they would. There is a pleasure in a job well done. You know that you have done dramatically what you were supposed to do, what you set out to do, and yet you are aware that people are responding to it. I saw this production of *bash* and I asked how it had been going. They said it had been a good run and that the reviews had been very good for the most part and that it had had nice audiences. But then one of the actors, a very good young actor who played the character of John in the piece that takes place in New York, in which he beats a gay man in Central Park, said that in a matinee he had just reached the point at which he describes the incident when there was an explosion in the audience. A guy just started weeping openly and loudly. And the actor asked himself, 'Holy shit, what do I do? Knowing that the beating is about to get more horrific, do I stop or do I keep going?' And at the same time he was thinking, 'Fuck, yea, I am just standing here talking and I have made this guy feel this thing, so that is what I am supposed to be doing, so on

I go. I don't have any other choice.' And he said that this guy just wept throughout the play and that he had a strange perverse feeling that, 'This is what I was supposed to do. This is me getting the job done right and yet I am making this guy go through this and he is obviously making some connection to the material.' Yes, as a writer you stand in more than one place and it is a Faustian bargain because you can never get that innocence back as a writer.

I would never go to the movies now without trying to experience it while at the same time wondering how do they do that, the curiosity of how that shot was created, why did that work. It is the same thing in the theatre. You have this sense that I have to detach, in a way, suspend my disbelief, but at the same time you know it is a theatrical exercise and you always want to know how this has been done. Your mind cannot completely give over to the experience any more. And so you feel as though you have given up something too.

CB: You mention films. Unusually, for a playwright, you first established your public reputation through movies, even though you imported theatre aesthetics into your film making. Then there came a moment when you began to make more mainstream movies. Once a film is made it is inert. It doesn't respond to an audience. It doesn't change the next time you see it. You are sacrificing many of the satisfactions that you get from theatre in turning to film so, apart from a truck load of cash, what do you get instead of all those things that theatre offers?

NL: One thing you get is visibility. Any success or failure in the theatre was in Seattle, in Washington, in Chicago. The reviews were great or they were lousy but it was all very ephemeral and filtered through somebody else's hands. I would get a few things sent to me and that was it. So in film there was a certain desire to say, 'Here is a testament of what I am doing. This is the work and it will stay this way, in a kind of pristine fashion, so that people twenty years from now can experience it in much the same way.' That was especially true of pieces like *Your Friends & Neighbors* and *in the company of men*. I want to be able to look at them down the road and have them, hopefully, have the same kind of impact. I had always been a film lover but really had no designs on making films but at the same time I saw that as a way to testify to where I was as a writer or as a director. In the case of *the shape of things*, I literally wanted to put the play on screen. There is no extra material. There is no broadening of the scope of it. Taking the exact same cast and doing it that way came out of a desire to say 'Here is what I was doing on stage at that time.' So I think there is that testimonial element to it.

CB: As we record this, you are in England to see a production of *bash*. Why, under pressure from the Church, did you agree to cut the Mormon references? Surely they are basic to the play.

NL: The Mormon references still exist because those texts exist and people do it that way or they don't do it. This group chose to do it that way, so it is out there being done. When I agreed to it I was still a member of the Church and unsure as to where I was going to go so I said that I would not write any further Mormon characters. I really didn't have any interest in them. I only used the Church in that particular play because I felt I knew the religion and I could use it, but I realised that there was a certain assurance for the audience in watching that play because it was so pervasively Mormon, in the sense that these characters all had some attachment to Mormonism. That allowed the audience off the hook, in a way, in that they could say, 'That's not me. Mormons must really be touchy. Push the wrong button and these guys start killing kids.' I didn't want that to be the experience. For me, it was not a harangue about the Church. It was a look at a person who felt as if he were under the umbrella of a religion, that being a member of that church and being essentially what we think of as a good person, was no assurance for a life well lived or for not making a mistake.

CB: So it could have been Jewish, Catholic . . .

NL: The professor that I had at one time said, 'Why couldn't you have made them Catholics?' I probably could have but I would be palming that off on somebody else when I firmly believe they could be Mormon, too, and so that is what I made them. It is not really speaking to the Church as a whole other than here is a person who fancies himself as what we would say is a good person and it is often those kinds of basic generalities that I am comfortable looking at. That question is often asked of people in movies, plays that I work on, are you a good person, is that a good guy? It is such a simple thing but sometimes the big questions are not asked because we forget about them. But that idea of what is good and bad remains fascinating to me. So the idea that someone who we think of as good could do a bad thing, and then have to live with that for a certain amount of time because they want to remain within the frame of goodness, was something that I thought worked well within that context. But I decided to change that because I thought this could still work as just a generalised Christian idea rather than a very specific Mormon one.

CB: Your first films had modest budgets, were quickly shot, and were directly related to your work in the theatre. Then came *Nurse Betty* and a budget of $24 million. Did that project give you pause?

NL: There was certainly a pause, but a brief one. In retrospect, I am thankful I wasn't given a lot of time to think about it because it was certainly a moment when I could have spent a lot of time thinking. 'Gosh, should I write everything that I direct? Am I an auteur?' All those questions that you are better not asking yourself. I had a producer put the thing in front of me who I had just worked with on *Your Friends & Neighbors*, and say 'I am making this movie. I like this. What do you think of it? It is yours if you want it, but I am going to give it to somebody else if you don't take it.' He said, 'Let me know by Monday.' So I had a couple of days of thinking, 'What do I want to do?' In the end I said, 'I certainly don't want to give it up. I like it. It is different.' I believe that, as a director, I am interested in trying my hand at a number of different genres, but, as a writer, I have been fairly consistent in terms of the work I have been doing.

CB: Being British, the biggest question I have in terms of movies is *The Wicker Man*. The original was not a great film. It was an idiosyncratic film, but it slowly became a cult classic. So why on earth did you want to bugger around with it?

NL: For a lot of the reasons that you just mentioned. I, too, saw it when I was younger and was impressed by how strange it was, how different. I appreciate that I can't in one sentence tell you what it was about or liken it to another picture. I didn't think it was particularly well made and while I am a fan of it I was not the kind of fan that I have run into since then who are quite vicious and very territorial about the material.

CB: Do you have to be British to appreciate that part of its appeal is that it is not very well made and yet oddly compelling?

NL: Oh, yes. I still found it compelling. I found it good storytelling. I think what Shaffer wrote worked very well as a procedural. I kept a lot of it and the ending offered is what really everybody remembers. The only way in which it should ever be considered a horror film, since the author himself often called it an anti-horror film, is the fact that the ending is so horrific.

CB: And you make it a touch more horrific.

NL: I probably do. It wasn't my idea initially to do it but when they approached me about it I thought there was something I could do with it, especially since they were looking for a legitimately different approach to it. They said, 'We don't just want to translate it to the States. So how can we make that work if we want to do that?' I said, 'Well, here is one way. I would, for the most part, strip out all the religious discussion, because they did it quite well in the first one and I am actually tired of religious discussion. I have been talking about it ever since people became aware of who I was. I am much more interested in this even deeper-rooted male/female theme. It is almost like the white American male nightmare.' I said, 'I'll create something like that for you, that is the idea of women ruling the world. Let me give you a taste of what that is.' They seemed intrigued in including that and so I said, 'I will write it up.' It came through many different hands and voices but I felt that we were going to get to the same place in the end. We all wanted it to end in the same way but I was going to take people on a very different journey. It was a blast to do. We had a great time doing it but it was rather savagely greeted when it was released. But this is the thing you do. You put yourself out there and then you go on to the next piece.

CB: Which is more of a blow, a poorly received film or play?

NL: I am very straightforward about the critics. I try to treat them as good, bad or indifferent. One voice telling me something is no more important than the person who stops me in the lobby and has something to say. Granted, a couple of those voices might have the ability to close the show, but I am generally not working on Broadway or in a situation where it is make-or-break with one review. It may colour how some people see it but it is usually not that kind of situation. I am sure it is much worse in film because of the sphere of influence that film has today. From when I grew up, even until now, every Monday the box office is in the news and it has become a competition, just like most other things in the States. We love the idea of competing and so now it is the Oscar race. You have just got nominated and now you are in a race with somebody for the next few weeks. The question is who won at the box office and unfortunately that is equated with what is good. My mother will say, 'Oh, so-and-so is number one. I should go and see that. It must be very good.' Sometimes that is true and sometimes it is not. Sometimes it is just purely marketing, but because of the amount of money that is at play, and because of the exposure that comes from being in thirty-five hundred theatres around the country instead of one theatre in one city it has a significant impact. The magic of the theatre is that a new play opens in one place. *Wrecks*, which had this amazing actor, Ed Harris, opened in Cork. You could read about it anywhere in the world but you had to go to Cork to see it and you had better be there because it was going to be over and there would be no record of it other than when it was published. That is an amazing feeling. If I was drawn to film because I wanted to have a record of a performance, the most magical thing in the world is the idea that, in the theatre, you are in the here and now of it and that this world exists every night, newly formed for you and that two hours from now it will be gone. It is a pleasure that happily can repeat itself but only in some slightly varied form.

CB: In *The Wicker Man* Aaron Eckhart makes a momentary appearance. It is as though he is your talisman. When he appeared in your film version of Antonia Byatt's *Possession*, however, he appeared in a principal role as a character who, in the novel, is English. Why make him American?

NL: Again you wouldn't be alone in that concern. There are several people who have said that same thing. I am waiting for the article that says, 'He says he likes England so much he took *Possession* and he took *The Wicker Man*. What is he going to do next?' The idea that the figure of Roland should be an American really came from Byatt herself. It was sparked for me by some notes she had written. The piece had been around for ten years or more but for all the various drafts and various writers and directors, no one had got the right formula as far as Warner Bros was concerned. So I got involved and I read some notes that she had passed on from one of her earlier drafts saying that Roland is a fictional creation but he is not a movie character yet and has to become one. I thought that there were only so many ways in which to spark the conflict between these two pretty reticent people at the heart of the story and so I thought it would be interesting to make Roland an American, someone with a different approach, who is a bit more of an outsider, who has the brashness to steal the letters, which are central to the plot, without even thinking about it. I thought that that way I might create a friction between these two characters that takes dozens and dozens of pages in the novel. I had to compress that into an immediate friction on screen. So the American came first. It wasn't a case of, 'OK. God, how am I going to get Aaron into this movie.' I have no doubt that having called upon Gwyneth Paltrow to play English I could have called upon Aaron to play English. He would have studiously gone off and come back with a perfect accent. But it was my desire to create some other source of friction in the work that led to Americanising that character.

CB: Are you ever going to make a film without Aaron?

NL: It is getting harder and harder to get him in. Certainly his appearance in *the shape of things* was his most tenuous. He appears on magazine covers in Rachel's hands. That took some doing. For a moment I thought 'should I replace one actor and put Aaron in the movie?' Then I realised that, 'I can't do that. I need to keep this same cast.' So I thought, well, what if I start in the museum, just looking at a painting or whatever, and simply move past him. We would never see him again. He would be just one of several people in the museum. But I wasn't sure it would work. Then he became unavailable so I thought, 'Now what do I do?'

CB: So he is a talisman.

NL: Yes, by now he is a good luck charm but he is doing well enough on his own and it is hard to get him there all the time. I have a couple of people that I have worked with a number of times and when they are great agents of the language, and understand the mindset, and you like them in what is a very vagabond existence, a familiar face every so often helps. It is harder to find a reason not to work with them than it is to find reasons to work with them.

CB: That sounds a little like Woody Allen.

NL: That's right. He worked with a number of people, more than I have I think. There are certain faces that you are just happy to see show up again and you can just work with them quite easily.

CB: We have talked about the films and plays but you have also written short stories. It seems to me that a number of the short stories could be plays and there are plays that could be short stories. What would you lose, for example, if *Wrecks* had been a story?

NL: I think you would lose the personification. There is something about seeing someone physically on stage while another version of him is in the next room. I don't know how that would translate if you just read it. In the theatre you are so in the moment while as a reader you are at a certain distance. And, frankly, you just lose out on the performance. But there are certain pieces that are simply a dialogue between characters. You could stage those things.

CB: The obvious logical question is why does it emerge as a story rather than a play?

NL: It is ultimately pure instinct, I think. This feels like a story to me so therefore I don't write any stage directions with it. I am rare in my descriptions of people anyway because I just want to ensure that any number of people could play them. I can't be as specific as Shaw or O'Neill, and go into detail about what a person looks like. Actors are going to bring their own particular charms to a part so it is not important for me to describe their physical appearance. I am more interested in what is inside them.

CB: Is the choice between play and story in part a matter of time? Some of your stories are very short. Were they written on the run, in the gaps between doing other things.

NL: I started writing a lot of them on aeroplanes, and there was a certain satisfaction with finishing them in the course of a flight, or in the course of a couple of days. Here was something that was finished as opposed to writing the first few pages of something. There was a satisfaction in that. But there was also a satisfaction in the writing of the prose, because most of them feature a healthy section of prose writing which I had not done a lot of and therefore found intriguing. It was difficult but it was interesting and it wasn't until I did a reading, with Sam Shepard, for the *New Yorker* magazine, that someone approached me about doing a book. So it was only then that I started to give shape to the idea of a collection of these things in any formal way and that is where the idea of keeping them short came from, the idea of seconds of pleasure [the book's title]. There is, though, a thread that runs through them. None of the men are named. There is a reference to redheads throughout. There is a thematic connection, a unity to them. They are often about someone who is straying from one relationship into another. A conceit started to form once it was going to be formalised as a book. I felt the need to create a structure to it in a way that I didn't necessarily as I was writing a few of them.

CB: Some of them are quite extreme. You seem to want to go right to the edge.

NL: I don't know if I believe there is an edge.

CB: Is there a door through which you can't walk? Is there any subject do you think which is closed to a writer?

NL: No. It just depends on the writer. There are probably doors that I would close. They would open if I only put my hand on them and went through but there are ones that I would probably stay away from. I know there are certain things that are triggers for me, but relatively few. I don't think there is anything that can't be talked about or examined. It just depends on whether it is worth it for you to do it. I have never felt that there should be some boundary that I must keep to this side of. There are times when you look at material and say, 'Is it right for what you are doing?' A case in point in that book, which could probably be seen as one of the more extreme pieces, is a snuff film piece ['Ravishing']. That was the one that I kept talking to the editor about saying, 'I think this one is so outside most people's experience, almost everyone's experience, that maybe we should take out.'

CB: Where did that one come from in you?

NL: That is an unanswerable question. I don't have a process that allows me to answer that, not because I don't want to but because I often go where the wind blows me as a writer. I have seen something. I feel I saw an image. I get titles. I always follow in pursuit of a story and, for me, that has also yielded the greatest results because I do work, I do finally sit down and put pen to paper, or my fingers to the keyboard, though that doesn't say that I do it every day. I sit down and do that when I am compelled to write. When there is nothing in my way, I need to write. I don't like to just sit there and stare at the screen. I feel as though I am writing all the time but it is often in my head. I walk around thinking, 'How is this going to work?' or, 'What haven't I done on that story yet?' I feel that the process is always happening. Getting it down is just the last stage of the process.

CB: You write short. Can you see yourself writing long? Can you see yourself writing a novel?

NL: A novel or a television show? I have been talking to people about that. I don't know. A novel would probably be the most out of the ordinary for me. I tend not to think of stories in that size, or in a number of episodes of a television series. I tend to think in ninety-minute, two-hour bits. But the idea of writing something with so much prose would be pretty extreme for me as opposed to the idea of saying, 'I am going to write ten episodes of something' after I have just written what is the equivalent of two episodes by writing a film script or a play script. I can see it without necessarily saying it is going to happen.

CB: What can you tell me about what is currently scheduled to be your next play, *In a Dark Dark House*, formerly *Swallowing Bicycles*?

NL: The play is in three scenes and primarily focuses on two brothers who are in their thirties. One of them is in a rehab facility. He has been in a couple of them previously but he has been court-ordered to this one and is facing charges on a couple of levels in terms of possession of narcotics and a car accident that took place. He is also on the brink of losing his family. The play opens in the grounds of the hospital, a private hospital that houses this rehab unit. His older brother has been asked to come by doctors because the brother has been experiencing suppressed memories from their past and is insinuating that he was abused when he was younger, abused by a family friend, a person who was active in the family, who happened to be the mentor of the older brother. The older brother comes and basically says, 'Look, we are very estranged. You are a fucking liar all the time.' They are very much at odds. It is the classic clash between brothers which interests me. I always loved those plays, like Arthur Miller's *The Price*. So while I have written about conflict between friends or within a marriage, I had not written about a blood relationship.

The first scene raises the question of whether this brother, now that he has heard this information, will believe it. Will he go to the doctors and corroborate it, explaining that this was possible, and that the abusive man had existed? He was someone who was hitchhiking his way across the country and ended up in our part of the world and became a big friend to me, but this is possible. And through a lot of recrimination between the two of them they come to an understanding. The brother does believe him and 'Yes,' he says, 'I will talk to these doctors for you.' The younger brother says, 'I would love to find that guy. I would love to kill him.' The other brother quickly says, 'I don't believe that. You never stood up for yourself. I always did the dirty work for you. I took all the punches from our father. I stood up to all the bullies at school. I am the one who always protected you. You never took any punches.' The younger one says, 'You can do it. You do it for us, because he has hurt you as much as he has hurt me. You thought he was your friend and he did this.'

The second scene is between the older brother and a young woman. It is a seduction scene between this man, who is in his late thirties, and this sixteen-year-old girl. He has met and talked to her and only as you listen closely to what is going on between these people, and only by the third scene, really, when you see the two brothers together again, do you realise that this girl is the daughter of the abusive man, grown up. The older brother has hunted down the man and found his way from the man to the daughter and you see him slowly seducing her to the point at which they are going to go off together in a car.

The last scene is a party for the brother's release from rehab. He is home with his family. This takes place out of doors. They are removed from the rest of the world, in a forest. The brothers come back together and the older brother is getting ready to leave. He is uncomfortable being around all these people and he sees his brother standing around with a glass of champagne and he lets him know, 'I have found this guy, by the way. I have looked him in the face again and he didn't know who I was. He had no idea who I was. I met his daughter.' The brother is very surprised and asks what he has done. He says, 'I just talked to them briefly and he didn't know who I was. I didn't say who I was. I met the daughter and then came back. But it was worth getting that out, seeing that guy again.'

258

We are finally given the bigger picture of what has happened here and, whether you have sensed it or not, you realise that the reason that the older brother has believed his younger brother is that he had had the same experience with the guy and is trying to tell his brother that the same thing happened to him. That is the culminating conflict between the two of them because we ultimately realise that the younger brother had not, in fact, gone through that experience. He simply believed that this was what happened to his older brother and has used it to bring his brother here to corroborate his story because that is his way of getting out of the court-ordered confinement. So that older brother has been forced to face the thing that has been hanging over him but was manipulated into doing this by his brother who has simply used him to get to safety.

I don't know if it will ever be as good as those moments at the end of Caryl Churchill's *Top Girls* when the two sisters realise that they will never be friends, but that is what I am shooting for, that moment where two people who are so closely related realise that they don't really like each other, that their only connection is that they are not tied together by anything but this strange connection that we have to our siblings.

Notes

Chapter 1   Introduction

1. 'Neil LaBute; Rules Are Far Breaking', www.iofilm.co.uk/io/mit/001/ uiff_neil_labute20051026.php
2. Quoted in James E. Miller, *Words, Self, Reality: The Rhetoric of Imagination* (New York, 1972), p. 156.
3. Robert Birnbaum, 'Interview with Richard Ford', *Identity Theory: The Narrative Thread*. www.identitytheory.com/people/birnbaum37.html
4. Neil LaBute, *The Distance From Here* (New York, 2003), p. 8.
5. *The South Bank Show*, London Weekend Television, 2002. Abbreviated to 'SBS' in subsequent notes in text.
6. 'This Cultural Life: Neil LaBute', *The Independent*, 22 May 2005.
7. John Lahr, 'A Touch of Bad: Why Is the Director Neil LaBute So Interested in Jerks?' *The New Yorker*, 5 July 1999.
8. www.geraldpeary.com/interviews/jkl/labute.html
9. Lahr, 'A Touch of Bad'.
10. Email to author, 16 December 2006.
11. David Amsden, 'Up with People', *New York*, 29 November 2004, http:// nymag.com/nymetro/arts/theater/10464
12. http.weeklywire.com/xx/09-21-98/slc_story.html
13. http.newyorkmetro.com/nymetro/arts/theatre/10464/
14. Mary Dickson, 'Who's Afraid of Neil LaBute?' *Salt Lake City Weekly*, 21 September 1998, http://weeklywire.com/ww/09-21-98/slc_story.html
15. Peter Brook, *The Empty Space* (London, 1968), p. 9.
16. Alan Morrison, 'Neil Labute', *Guardian Unlimited*, 2 November 2003, http://film.guardian.co.uk/interview/interviewpages/0,1080365,00.html
17. Neil LaBute, 'Heaps of Money? No Thanks', *Guardian Unlimited*, 14 June 2004. http://arts.guardian.co.uk/features/story/0,11710,1238171,00.html
18. Brook, *The Empty Space*, p. 141.
19. Neil LaBute, 'Preface: The Weight of the World', *Fat Pig* (New York, 2005), p. xi.

20. Lahr, 'A Touch of Bad'.
21. Neil LaBute, 'Preface', *This is How It Goes* (New York, 2003), p. x.
22. 'This Cultural Life: Neil LaBute', *The Independent Online*, 22 May 2005, http://enjoyment.independent.co.uk/theatre/features/article222708.ece
23. Lahr, 'A Touch of Bad'.
24. Neil LaBute, "Introduction: Neil Labute," *in the company of men* (London, 1997), p. i.
25. Commentary on DVD of *Your Friends & Neighbors*, Universal Studios, 1998.
26. Neil LaBute, 'Preface', *The Mercy Seat* (New York, 2003), p. x.
27. Dickson, 'Who's Afraid of Neil LaBute?'
28. Amsden, 'Up with People'.
29. Dickson, 'Who's Afraid of Neil LaBute?'
30. *in the company of men*, p. 8.
31. David Mamet, *Oleanna* (London, 1993), p. 79.
32. Neil LaBute, *the shape of things* (New York, 2000), p. 127.
33. David Hare, 'Battle in the Bedroom', *The Guardian*, 5 July 2006, G2, pp. 18–20.
34. Wendy Mitchell, 'A Kinder, Gentler Neil LaBute?', http://www.indiewire.com/people/int_LaBute_Neil_020814.html
35. 'Neil LaBute: Rules Are for Breaking'.
36. Email to the author dated 15 June 2006 and timed at 07.02 a.m.

Chapter 2   *bash: latterday plays*

1. Neil LaBute, *bash: latterday plays* (New York, 1999), p. 55.
2. Dickson, 'Who's Afraid of Neil LaBute?'
3. Rosalynde Welch, 'An Interview with Neil LaBute', *Times and Seasons*, 19 January 2005, www.timesandseasons.org/index.php?=1873
4. Ibid.
5. John Simon, 'LaBrute', *New York Magazine*, 12 July 1999. http://nymag.com/nymetro/arts/theater/reviews/96/

Chapter 3   *in the company of men*

1. J. M. Morrell, ed., *Four English Comedies* (Harmondsworth, 1950), p. 134.
2. Christopher Hampton, *Dangerous Liaisons: The Film* (London, 1989), p. 8.
3. Stephanie Sheh, 'Director Works in Company of Controversy', *Daily Bruin*, 24 August 1998, http://dailybruin.ucla.edu/archives/id/13196

4. *The Way of the World*, p. 21.
5. David Mamet, *Some Freaks* (New York, 1989), p. 86.
6. Jenny Labroff, 'Playing the Game', *Salon*, 1 August 1997, www.salon. com/aug97/entertainment/labute970801.html
7. Neil LaBute, *in the company of men* (London, 1997), p. 15.
8. Neil LaBute, 'Introduction: Interview with Neil LaBute', *in the company of men*, p. xi.
9. Ibid., p. xii.
10. Glenn Myrent, 'Neil LaBute on *in the company of men*', *Film Scouts Interviews*, 15 May 1997, www.filmscouts.com/scripts/ interview.cfm?File=nei-lab
11. Ibid.
12. Ibid.
13. www.salon.com
14. http://www.filmscouts.com/scripts/interview.cfm?File=nei-lab
15. Betty Jo Tucker, 'In the Company of Aaron Eckhart', *Reel Talk Movie Reviews*, www.reeltalkreviews.com/browse/viewitem.asp?type= feature&id=132
16. J. M. Morrell, ed., *Four English Comedies* (Harmondsworth, 1950).
17. Lucinda Rosenfeld, 'Interview with Motion Picture Director Neil LaBute', *Interview*, February 1999, www.findarticles.com/p/articles/ mi_m1285/is_2_29/ai_53747373
18. Myrent, 'Neil LaBute on *in the company of men*'.
19. Stephen Dalton, 'Misanthropist, Misogynist, Blasphemer', *Sunday Herald*, 23 November 2003.
20. Ibid.
21. Warren Curry, 'Art in the Flesh: An Interview with *the shape of things* Writer/Director Neil LaBute', 7 May 2003. www.cinemaspeak.com/ Interviews/labute.html
22. Jennie Yabroff, 'Playing the Game', *Salon*, 1 August 1997, www. salon.com/aug97/entertainment/labute970801.html
23. Ibid.
24. Dalton, 'Misanthropist, Misogynist, Blasphemer'.
25. Kate Sullivan, 'Love to Loathe Ya Baby', *City Pages*, 6 September 2000, http://citypages.com/dtabank/21/1031/articles8957.asp
26. Rosenfeld, 'Interview with Motion Picture Director Neil LaBute'.

Chapter 4 *Your Friends & Neighbors*

1. Jules Feiffer's *Carnal Knowledge*, directed by Mike Nichols.
2. Neil LaBute, Director's Commentary, *Your Friends & Neighbors* DVD Universal Studios, 1998.

3. Stig Bjorkman, ed., *Woody Allen on Woody Allen* (London, 1995), p. 154.
4. Neil LaBute, 'Introduction: Some Thoughts on Creation', *Your Friends & Neighbors* (London, 1998), p. vii.
5. *Your Friends & Neighbors*, p. 65.
6. Stephanie Sheh, 'Director Works in Company of Controversy', *Daily Bruin*, 24 August 1998, www.dailybruin.ucla.edu/archives/id/13196/
7. Ibid.
8. Josh Morowitz, 'The Shape of Things According to Neil LaBute', www.moviepoopshoot.com/interviews/20.html
9. John Lahr, 'A Touch of Bad: Why Is the Director Neil LaBute So Interested in Jerks?' *The New Yorker*, 5 July 1999.
10. Laura Miller, 'Two New Movies Take a Look at Why, When It Comes to Romance, People Treat Each Other So Badly, Salon, 21 August 1998, www.salon.com/ent/movies/feature/1998/08/21feature.html
11. Peter Cowie, *Annie Hall* (London, 1996), p. 23.
12. Ray Pride, '*Your Friends & Neighbors*', *New City Net* www.filmvault.com/filmvault/chicago/y/yourfriendsandnei1.html
13. Ibid.
14. Lahr, 'A Touch of Bad'.
15. *Woody Allen on Woody Allen*, p. 156.
16. Mick LaSalle, 'Not Your Typical "Friends and Neighbors"', *San Francisco Chronicle*, 21 August 1998. www.sfgate.com/cgi-bin/article.cgi?f=/c/a/1998/08/21/DD55657.DTL
17. Stephen Hunter, 'No "Friends" of Ours', *The Washington Post*, 21 August 1998, www.washingtonpost.com/wp-srv/style/movies/reviews/yourfriendsandneighborshunter.htm
18. J. Hoberman, 'Slippery Creatures', *The Village Voice*, 19–25 August 1998. www.villagevoice.com/film/9834,hoberman,3383,20.html
19. Barbara Shulgasser, 'LaBute's Creepy Bunch of "Neighbors"', *San Francisco Examiner* 21 August 1998. www.sfgate.com/cgi-bin/article.cgi?f=/e/a/1998/08/21/WEEKEND15614.dtl

Chapter 5 *the shape of things*

1. www.painterskeys.com/auth_search.asp?name=Herbert%20Read
2. John Dewey, *Art as Experience* (New York, 1934), p. 3.
3. Christopher Bigsby, ed., *Writers in Conversation*, vol. II (Norwich, 2001), p. 73.
4. Warren Curry, 'Art in the Flesh: An Interview with *the shape of things* Writer/Director Neil LaBute', 7 May 2003. http:www/cinemaspeak.com/Interviews/labute.html
5. Ibid.

6. Ibid.
7. Dalton, 'Misanthropist, Misogynist, Blasphemer'.
8. William Wycherley, *The Country Wife*, ed. John Dixon Hunt (London, 1973), p. 41.
9. Henrik Ibsen, 'Preface to *Hedda Gabler*' in *Last Plays of Henrik Ibsen* (New York, 1962), p. 107.
10. Jack Foley, '*the shape of things* – Neil LaBute Q&A', *Indie London*, www.indielondon.co.uk/film/shape_of_things_labuteQ&A.html
11. *Writers in Conversation*, p. 153.
12. Foley, '*the shape of things* – Neil LaBute Q&A'.
13. *Writers in Conversation*, pp. 146–7.
14. Christopher Bigsby, *Writers in Conversation*, vol II (Norwich, 2001), pp. 153–4.
15. Foley, '*the shape of things* – Neil LaBute Q&A'.
16. Alan Morrison, 'Neil LaBute', *Guardian Unlimited*, 2 November 2003, http://film.guardian.co.uk/interview/interviewpages/06737,1080365,00.html
17. Ibid.
18. Jonathan Romney, 'Neil LaBute: A Darker Shade of Male', *The Independent*, 29 October 2004. http:enjoyment.independent.co.uk/books/features/article30884.ece
19. James A. Miller, *Word, Self, Reality: The Rhetoric of Imagination* (New York, 1972), p. 7.
20. Foley, '*the shape of things* – Neil LaBute Q&A'.
21. Erving Goffman, *The Presentation of the Self in Everyday Life* (Harmondsworth, 1971), pp. 28–9.
22. Warren Curry, 'Art in the Flesh: An Interview with *the shape of things* Writer/Director Neil LaBute', *Cinema Speak*, 7 May 2003, http://www.cinemaspeak.com/Interviews/labute.html
23. D. Spence, 'An Interview with Rachel Weisz', http://ukmovies.ign.com/articles/394/394625pl.html
24. Stig Bjorkman, ed., *Woody Allen on Woody Allen* (London, 1995), pp. 107–8.
25. Ibid.

Chapter 6   *The Mercy Seat*: a crucible of conscience

1. Andrew Sparrow, 'Sept. 11: "A Good Day to Bury Bad News"', *Daily Telegraph*, 10 October 2001, www.telegraph.co.uk/news/main.html?xml=/news/2001/10/10/nmoor10.xml
2. Jonathan Franzen, *The Discomfort Zone: A Personal History* (London, 2006), p. 16.

3. Julie Salomon, 'Neil LaBute and an Unheroically Human Thought', *New York Times*, 15 December 2002, www.lievschreiber.org/ mercyseatreviews.shtml
4. Neil LaBute, 'Preface', *The Mercy Seat* (London, 2003), p. ix.
5. Dalton, 'Misanthropist, Misogynist, Blasphemer'.
6. www.dukecityfix.com/interview.php/nucleus/www.cabq.gov/crs/intervi
7. Edward Albee, *Who's Afraid of Virginia Woolf?* (New York, 1962), p. 157.
8. Albert Camus, *The Fall*, trans. Stuart Gilbert (Harmondsworth, 1963), p. 37.
9. Arthur Miller, *After the Fall* (London, 1965), p. 119.
10. Kevin Hylton, 'In *The Mercy Seat*', *Playbill*, 4 December 2002, www.playbill.com/features/article/76879.html
11. Rosalynde Welch, 'An Interview with Neil LaBute', *Times and Seasons*, 19 January 2005, www.timesandseasons.org/index.php?p=1873

Chapter 7 *The Distance From Here*

1. Neil LaBute, 'Preface', *The Distance From Here* (New York, 2003), p. 7.
2. *The Distance From Here*, p. 7.
3. Edward Bond, 'Introduction: The Rational Theatre', *Bond: Plays Two* (London, 1978), p. xvii.
4. Edward Albee, *The Zoo Story* (New York, 1961), p. 40.
5. Edward Bond, *Bond: Plays One* (London, 1977), p. 11.
6. Ian Stuart, *Selections from the Notebooks of Edward Bond, vol. I, 1959 to 1980* (London, 2000), p. 87.
7. Edward Bond, 'Author's Note', *Saved* (London, 1966), p. 6.
8. Jonathan Franzen, *The Discomfort Zone: A Personal History* (London, 2006), p. 113.

Chapter 8 *Seconds of Pleasure*

1. Neil LaBute, *Seconds of Pleasure* (New York, 2004), p. 33.

Chapter 9 *autobahn*

1. Neil LaBute, 'Introduction: The Pleasures of Limitation', *autobahn: a short-play cycle* (New York, 2005), p. xi.

Chapter 10 *Fat Pig* and *This Is How It Goes*

1. 'Neil LaBute's *Fat Pig*', www.npr.org/templates/story/story.php? storyId=5163405
2. Neil LaBute, 'Preface: The Weight of the World', *Fat Pig* (New York, 2005), p. ix.

3. Eugene O'Neill, *A Moon for the Misbegotten* (London, 1953), p. 111.
4. *Fat Pig*, p. 5.
5. 'NY Play *Fat Pig* Tackles the Last Taboo', www.chinadaily.com.cn/english/doc/2004-12/28/content_403864.htm
6. 'Neil LaBute Interview', *Talk Theatre in Chicago*, 16 October 2006, www.theatreinchicago.com/talk/interior.php?podshowID=77
7. Ibid.
8. Walter Starkey, *Luigi Pirandello 1867–1936* (Berkeley, 1967), p. 217.
9. Neil LaBute, 'Preface', *This Is How It Goes* (London, 2002), p. ix.
10. *This is How it Goes*, p. 87.
11. Iris Murdoch, *The Sea, the Sea* (London, 1978), p. 33.
12. Robert Corrigan and James L. Rosenberg, eds., *The Context and Craft of Drama* (San Francisco, 1964), pp. 233–4.
13. Edward Albee, *The Play About the Baby* (New York, 2002), p. 8.
14. Ibid.
15. Thornton Wilder, 'Preface', *Three Plays* (London, 1958), pp. xii–xiii.

Chapter 11 *Nurse Betty, Possession* and *The Wicker Man*

1. Arthur Miller, 'On Screenwriting and Language', *Everybody Wins* (London, 1990), p. v.
2. David Mamet, *Some Freaks* (New York, 1989), p. 134.
3. Neil LaBute, 'Introduction', *Nurse Betty: The Shooting Script*, (New York, 2000) p. ix.
4. John C. Richards and James Flamberg, 'The Genesis', *Nurse Betty: The Shooting Script*, p. xiii.
5. Neil LaBute, 'Director's Commentary', *Nurse Betty* DVD, IMF (Internationale Medien und Film) GmbH & Co., 1999.
6. John C. Richards and James Flamberg, *Nurse Betty: The Shooting Script*, p. 95.
7. Joanne Latimer, 'Soft Soaping Neil LaBute', *Montreal Mirror*, 2000, www.montrealmirror.com/ARCHIVES/2000/083100/cover.html
8. Ibid.
9. Neil LaBute, 'Director's Commentary', *Possession* DVD, Warner Brothers, 2002.
10. Martin A. Grove, 'Women Dominate in 'Wicker Man' remake', *Backstage.com*, 29 August 2006, www.backstage.com/bso/news_reviews/film/article_display.jsp?unu_content_id=1003054306
11. Devin Faraci, 'Exclusive Interview: Neil LaBute (*Wicker Man*)', 26 July 2006, http://www.chud.com/index,php?type=interview8id=7227
12. *Hollywoodreporter.com*

Chapter 12   *Some Girl(s)*, *Wrecks* and *In a Dark Dark House*

1. Neil LaBute, 'Preface(s)', *Some Girl(s)* (New York, 2005), p. xi.
2. Sara Wilkomerson, 'Nanny Shows Fanny: Foghorn-Muted Fran to Un-Drescher Onstage in LaBute Play', *New York Observer*, 8 May 2006. www.observer.com/20060508/20060508-Sara-wilkomerson_page one_featurebox-2.asp
3. Jonathan Franzen, *The Discomfort Zone: A Personal History* (London, 2006), p. 114.
4. Christopher Bigsby, ed., *Arthur Miller and Company* (London, 1990), p. 139.
5. Boris Kachka, 'Man, Oh, Man: Ed Harris is Not a Control Freak', *New York*, nymag.com/arts/theatre/profiles/21970
6. Typescript of *Wrecks*, October 2006.
7. Kachka, 'Man, Oh, Man'.
8. Jon Robin Baitz, 'Neil LaBute', *Bomb Magazine* 83, Spring 2003. http://bombsite.com/labute/labute2.html
9. Daniel Zalewski, 'Can Bookish Be Sexy? Yeah, Says Neil LaBute', *New York Times*, 18 August 2002. AR10.22.
10. Edward Bond, 'Author's Note', *Saved* (London, 1966), p. 5.
11. *Conversations with Richard Ford*, pp. 119–20.
12. Quoted in Richard Ford, 'Where Does Writing Come From?' www.granta.com/extracts/683
13. Quoted in Milan Kundera, 'What is a Novelist: How Great Writers are Made', *The New Yorker*, 9 October 2006, p. 43.
14. www.theatreinchicago.com/talk/interior.php?podshowID=77
15. Baitz, op. cit.

Index

All films are indexed by title. Stage plays by writers other than NL appear as subheadings under the author's name.

Works by NL to have had a life on both stage and screen have two separate headings. General references to content/ethos/characterisation etc. appear under the stage version.

Index